The Word of Truth
and
Disputes about Words

The Word of Truth
and
Disputes about Words

by

Douglas Farrow

CARPENTER BOOKS
WINONA LAKE, INDIANA
1987

Published 1987 by Carpenter Books,
a division of Eisenbrauns
PO Box 275
Winona Lake, IN 46590 USA

Library of Congress Cataloging in Publication Data

Farrow, Douglas B.
The word of truth and disputes about words.

Includes index.
1. Bible—Evidences, authority, etc. 2. Bible—
Hermeneutics. I. Title.
BS480.F33 1987   220.1′3   87-17656
ISBN 0-931464-36-6

Table of Contents

Foreword

Ideas, like cars, must be steered; otherwise, sound notions can run off the road and do damage. Rogue theological ideas, in particular, can be very disruptive. Douglas Farrow, a younger scholar of whom much more will be heard, has written this essay in order to stop the sound notion of biblical inerrancy running amok. He wants to shield it from the rationalisms that too often corrupt it, and to lock it into a thought-out theological concept of Scripture as coming from Christ, being about Christ, and leading to Christ. As he defines Christ from data supplied by Scripture, so he seeks a bottom-line account of Scripture that shows it to be, and responds to it as, the word of Christ. Hermeneutically, he reaches for a way of understanding Scripture that, by imposing nothing on the text, allows it to function fully and freely as the instrument of Christ's authority. He looks in what is surely the right direction, and I am delighted to commend his endeavor as a right-minded and significant contribution to current debate.

Farrow believes that today's talk about inerrancy has reached something of an impasse. I think he is right. He holds that the discussion can only become fruitful again when exegetical, hermeneutical, and epistemological interests intersect and coalesce. Once more I think he is right. His own opening up of such discussion is impressive. He shows himself an excellent exegete, one who understands how language works; he shows himself also a learned and discerning theologian who appreciates equally the absoluteness of God's written Word and the relativities of its verbal form. He does not lose sight of the forest among the trees, nor does he allow zeal to generalize about the forest to divert his gaze from the particular trees that make it up. He takes note of what God has joined—his Word with his Spirit; his own speaking, the Christ through whom he speaks, and the message about Christ that he sends us; the ontological and functional aspects of biblical inerrancy—and he takes care not to put them asunder. By disentangling crossed wires and connecting loose ones he builds a theological circuit through which the power of the biblical message can flow with a good deal less internal resistance than before. His achievement is to my mind quite spectacular.

To be sure, there are places in the argument where I would speak a little differently, or wish for a little more. Some passages leaving me feeling that I have been given a cookbook on a plate and told that this was my meal. And the concept of inconsequential error seems strange, for it applies only where exegesis shows that no substantive assertion is being made (that is why it is called inconsequential), and where no assertion is attempted no error can be committed: Q.E.D. But the book as a whole seems to me an outstanding piece of theological steersmanship. It merits the most serious attention of all who see the importance of the inerrancy discussion for the church today and tomorrow, for it is fundamental theology in the best and truest sense.

J. I. PACKER

Preface

The Word of Truth, heard in Holy Scripture, is a gift that ought to bring great joy into every reflection it inspires and every study it demands. But of late a long shadow has been cast over the confidence and comfort the community of faith has always had in the Scriptures. Disputes have arisen about their reliability, growing to such proportions that books and articles on problems associated with the authority of Scripture are found everywhere. In evangelical Christianity, many recent works attest the fact that the inerrancy issue has been catapulted into the forefront of rather heated discussions on the purity of the Church's confession, a fact which many consider regrettable but necessary, others just regrettable. Perhaps, then, it should be asked whether any more books on this subject are needed. I would like to answer "no," but cannot for one simple reason: we are still short of a satisfying solution, one that marks out firm ground on which to stand without fencing off the pathway ahead.

The difficulty to which the inerrancy problem belongs requires the spelling out of a solution that is as viable for believing scholarship as for the person in the pew, as viable for the future concerns of theology as for the present concerns of scientific biblical research, and as viable for hermeneutics as for doctrine. This is not an easy task, and most of what I have to say here is built on what others have said, often much more capably. Yet perhaps it is put together and supported in a way that will open for some a new doorway through which such a solution can be found. I suspect, at any rate, that in the final analysis I am only articulating what is implicit in the faith and good sense of more than a few. It is my hope that these thoughts will prove to be a constructive contribution to the Church's effort to return—considerably wiser, no doubt—to concentration on the compelling power and beauty of Scripture in its sacred service to Christ. And as this is achieved, it is my prayer that we may discover a new sense of the Presence of God, and a new overflow of gratitude, through a greater penetration of our hearts and lives by the divine Word himself.

Two approaches to Scripture which have surfaced in the evangelical inerrancy debate concern me a great deal. The one reflects a mode of thought I would liken (not innovatively) to a ship that has lost its anchor, and the other to a ship that has got its anchor stuck on the bottom. The first is in a sort of libertarian mode, championing the responsibility of the free-thinking and free-acting individual to come to the authors of Scripture as one adult comes to another, listening, interacting, and deciding: "Come, let us reason together. . . ." Unhappily, it is so concerned with man's intellectual "integrity"—used more or less as a synonym for freedom—that it loses track of the awesome Voice of God and no longer trembles at his word (Isa 66:2). It forgets to be concerned with the fact that derivative intellect, let alone the derivative intellect of a fallen creature, cannot lay claim to genuine integrity or meaningful freedom apart from worshipful, faithful dependence on the one Intellect that is truly *integra* in the full sense of the word. I speak, of course, of Jesus Christ, the incarnate and self-revealing Word of God, to whom we must be subject in mind, as in heart and soul and strength. This mode, given the radical right of judgment with which it approaches Scripture, threatens recognition of the divine authority wielded in the Word of Truth. In so doing, it also threatens the ultimate coherence of human thought and speech.

The second suggests a sort of authoritarian or "conservationist" mode which is concerned with the maintenance of a sacred preserve of words wherein the Church may be assured of seeing nothing other, and nothing less, than each one stamped with "Thus saith the Lord." When the Bible is approached in this way it is frequently handled like a defensive weapon, rather than respected as the two-edged sword it is. This approach all too often comes down to tangential "disputes about words" (though perhaps of a different sort than those in mind in 2 Tim 2:14) and threatens serious dialogue of any sort.

While both of these approaches have obvious merits not to be gainsaid, neither of them does justice to the character of Scripture, which was not given for *our* inspection except that it might inspect *us*, rather like a talking mirror (Jas 1:23–25). Each also engenders a faulty hermeneutic, the first tending toward certain forms of modern philosophical relativism incompatible with the Judeo-Christian outlook, and the second toward a static and rationalistic grasp of the text. Either way, the talking mirror is inflicted with a case of laryngitis. But these are things we may hope to overcome in continuing to work toward a solution to the controversy over biblical authority and the debate about inerrancy.

Sometime after the temporary peak in the inerrancy debate reached upon issuance of the Chicago Statement, the editors of *Christianity Today* asked evangelicals the question: "Where do we go from here?" (Sept. 4, 1981; p. 18). The defense and progress of the faith in the present day require both *sure foundations* and *freedom to mature*; our doctrine of Scripture is vital to both. It is encouraging to see that the International Council on Biblical Inerrancy, with its more recent statement on hermeneutics, has now concerned itself with the latter as well as the former. On the other hand, the epistemologically eclectic band of scholars that has gathered under the inerrancy banner (despite common sorties against the likes of Kant) has been unable to dispose of some very basic tensions underlying its own definitions, and hence, its actual handling of the biblical materials. There is a need to face up to the telltale effects of epistemological commitments. There is a need also to undertake new exegesis of the pillar passages of the inerrancy edifice. There is a need to allow biblical expressions and compositions their proper freedom and flexibility as message-bearers. To these endeavors I would like to lend a helping hand, or at least a voice of approval, for through them the Church may clearly establish her commitment to the Word of Truth and her discomfort with unnecessary disputes about words.

The tide of the inerrancy debate continues its ebb and flow, and it remains a risky proposition to set sail in plain view, particularly when one is interested in avoiding quarrels (the only spirit in which we should ever proceed!). Avoiding quarrels, however, is a matter of attitude and demeanor, not of wishy-washy thinking. Cautiously, then, but with conviction, I come to the debate appealing both to conservative and fundamentalist circles and to those who do not embrace any inerrancy doctrine at all to reexamine their concepts of inerrancy, listening once again for the leading of Scripture in the entire matter. It is a time for rethinking—though I say without embarrassment that the present work is committed to maintaining genuine continuity with the traditional confidence in the veracity of the Scriptures, even while striving for revisions in current statements of the doctrine.

Too much has been published on the inerrancy issue to allow for a comprehensive analysis in a project of this size. Consequently, I have chosen to pursue my own course, making reference to other works primarily where they may aid my own purposes or serve as a resource for the reader. If I seem to stray from a strict consideration of infallibility and inerrancy it is because perspective at times demands a consideration of the broader foundation, even where the endeavor is more exploratory surgery than incisive analysis. The unusually heavy use of footnotes, often for brief excursuses, is intended to facilitate a lighter reading of the text as well as to serve the more studious. I should perhaps add that the main themes of this work were set down in early 1980 as part of my own formal studies under the title "The Inerrancy Issue in Methodological and Linguistic Perspective." What follows bears the marks of a sometimes difficult redaction process (I can only add yet another echo to Augustine: "I count myself one of the number of those who write as they learn and learn as they write"), but having kept my ear to the ground I am more convinced than ever that these things need to be heard.

I would like to express my gratitude to just a few of those to whom I have become indebted for personal and scholarly support, though the views expressed here are my own, of course: James E. Eisenbraun, Weston W. Fields, James M. Grier, and David E. Lewycky. A particular word of appreciation is in order to Dr. J. I. Packer for his kind assistance by way of a foreword, and to the patient staff at Carpenter Books. Special thanks to my parents and to dear friends in the Lord who have encouraged me constantly throughout my studies.

Part 1
The Word of Truth

1 | The Inerrancy Debate in Focus

A Common Quest

To speak appropriately about the nature of biblical revelation is a quest in which modern scholarship and the modern Church are showing unprecedented interest. It might not be too much to say that this quest has always been associated with the epicenters of Protestant thought; Catholic scholarship has more lately taken up the challenge, to the extent that distinctive new concepts were achieved in the discussions of Vatican II.[1] The knowledge of God in the Judeo-Christian tradition is intimately connected with the Scriptures, and the Christian faith cannot be looked at anew in any age without giving the most careful attention to the doctrine of Scripture. The increased pluralism in the Church (both theologically and culturally), the progress in scientific thinking, and the challenge of secularism have all contributed to the high profile this subject now carries.

It is helpful to see the evangelical's concern with biblical inerrancy in the light of, indeed, as part of this quest. This is so for a number of reasons. To begin with, we must understand that the inerrancy debate in its broader terms is not entirely a new concern for evangelicals; rather it is fundamental to evangelicalism itself. As J. I. Packer responds to those who think otherwise, it is no

> trivial domestic squabble among those quarrelsome evangelicals of the U.S.A. On the contrary, you should see the inerrancy debate as the latest chapter in a great controversy about the Bible which has been going on continuously in the Church for the best

[1] The brief, but very significant, "Dogmatic Constitution on Divine Revelation" (Vatican II, *Dei Verbum*, 18 Nov. 1965), which may be found in *Documents of Vatican II*, ed. Austin P. Flannery (Grand Rapids: Eerdmans, 1975), deserves and rewards the closest attention of Catholics and Protestants alike. See also David F. Wells, *Revolution in Rome* (Downers Grove: InterVarsity, 1972).

3

part of the last 500 years: a controversy centering in the last analysis on the question, whether there ought to be any such thing as evangelicalism at all.[2]

That is, beginning with the Reformers or even with Wycliffe, it is the question of the authority of the Bible—or rather, of God speaking through the Bible—to rule the Church.[3]

To this question that of inerrancy ultimately belongs when properly put. Modern developments in epistemology and a number of other areas, together with approaches to biblical criticism springing from the soil of thought alien to the Bible itself, have led to the undermining of the authority on which the Reformers rested and renewed emphasis in the Church. The evangelical inerrancy debate reflects a lively concern to help reassert and make plain in the modern context the unique and fully authoritative function of Scripture in God's self-revelation and churchly rule. Of course, the inerrancy debate itself must be held responsible to the implications of modern biblical insights and the knowledge gained in all matters pertaining to revelation, a fact not always sufficiently appreciated.[4]

Second, then, and with a view to constructive criticism, it is important to understand that despite the evangelical engagement in this quest its contribution has not always been impressive. One of the most noteworthy reasons for this can be seen in a further observation made by Packer as he introduces an article entitled "Hermeneutics and Biblical Authority":

> The importance of my theme is obvious from the single considera-
> tion that biblical authority is an empty notion unless we know
> how to determine what the Bible means. This being so, I have
> been surprised to find how rare evangelical treatments of the
> relation between hermeneutics and biblical authority seem to be.[5]

---

[2] *Beyond the Battle for the Bible* (Westchester, IL: Cornerstone, 1980) 37.
[3] Ibid., 38.
[4] Here many evangelicals could benefit from books with a much wider purview than the present one, such as John Baillie's *The Idea of Revelation in Recent Thought* (New York: Columbia University, 1956), or even a book with the integrative aspirations of Charles A. M. Hall's *The Common Quest* (Philadelphia: Westminster, 1965). Unfortunately, the situation among evangelicals is such that the very idea of revelation—"by definition, God's disclosure of his Word to man" (Hall, *Common Quest*, 134)—is often naively held, in a confused sort of way, as if it simply referred to the Bible *per se*.
[5] *Themelios* 1 (1975) 3.

Toleration of such poverty is surely a significant failing which often cripples the inerrancy discussion and drives it off on a tangent from the central issue of any sincere quest concerning biblical revelation. It offers no encouragement to speak adequately to the hermeneutical question of "how the real and essential message of the Bible may be grasped by the man of today,"[6] the only context in which biblical authority can be meaningfully contemplated. An evangelical integration of these issues is paramount for a realistic confession of the authority of Scripture. Fortunately, more and more this call is being felt and heeded.[7]

Finally, it is important continually to recognize and respect the fact that only as we allow the very literature belonging to revelation to speak to us again and again, and to speak about its own service to God, can we properly address the inerrancy question or any other aspect of the doctrine of Scripture and its authority. Otherwise—whatever the appearances—there is in fact no quest, no genuine hermeneutic, and no context which may justifiably be called Christian. These observations, then, ought to establish, orient, and direct the debate.

The Task at Hand

Quite obviously, to acknowledge the importance of the inerrancy issue is not necessarily to accept the terms in which it is commonly set out. As a small contribution to continuing reflections on the character and role of the Scriptures, it is my aim here to test the focus of the inerrancy issue by means of observations and conclusions arising out of the three concerns above. I am convinced that no adequate response to the problem can be achieved apart from the intersection of epistemological, hermeneutical, and exegetical interests. There must be a three-way discussion, addressing questions of the intellectual authority belonging to revelation, of the function of written texts in the service of that authority, and of Scripture's own express thoughts on the matter in question. This discussion must be three-dimensional in another sense as well: that is, no approach can

---

[6] Ibid.
[7] See, e.g.—the title says it all—Robert K. Johnston, *Evangelicals at an Impasse: Biblical Authority in Practice* (Atlanta: John Knox, 1979).

be valid for the Church which does not move within the depth dimension provided by the activity of the living God in relation to both author and reader of Holy Scripture. In such a context, I believe, the authority of Scripture can be clearly recognized and articulated with respect to the inerrancy issue in terms of reliability in the full range of Scripture's communicative purpose and function.

To be sure, the questions to be addressed run broader and deeper than the channels in which my arguments will flow in this one little book, but I can still hope that the juxtaposition of these considerations, despite many deficiencies, may carry the discussion a little further in the direction of a healthy unity. It is true that I will be drawing from some who have resisted very commonly held opinions and ways of thinking, but if we are to be true to the Lord who addresses us in Scripture we are required to have with such men the courage to address boldly any challenge to his Lordship, whether from within the Church or from without. We must brook no dishonest truce, not even with ourselves.

With that in mind, let me also make clear from the outset my concurrence with the view that any modern confession of the Word of Truth must continue to come to grips with the humanity of sacred literature, and may not merely withdraw the biblical texts forthwith and altogether to the artificial citadel of perfect (or as I shall call it, "exhaustive") inerrancy. Faithfulness to the Spirit of Christ includes rejection of both the skeptic's posture and that of the idolater of texts. More positively, such faithfulness means with respect to Scripture—*all* Scripture—a wakened and open ear in order to listen "like one being taught."[8] Then Scripture does indeed confront us as address and summons and application and claim, as Karl Barth put it.[9] And in thus recognizing its sacred character as Christ's own self-witness, are we not immediately inclined to confess that "it is to be believed, as God's instruction, in all that it affirms; obeyed, as God's command, in all that it requires; embraced, as God's pledge, in all that it promises"?[10]

---

[8] Isa 50:4; 2 Tim 3:16.

[9] Karl Barth, *Church Dogmatics* (trans. G. W. Bromiley, Edinburgh: T. & T. Clark, 1961) 4/2. 303f.

[10] Quoted from "The Chicago Statement on Biblical Inerrancy," released by the International Council on Biblical Inerrancy in connection with their confer-

Of course, the question arises as to how we ought to understand "affirms," "requires," and even "promises." It is here that opinions differ within the Church's commitment to the Word of Truth and disputes about words sometimes develop. When I say "disputes about words" I am thinking not only of divergent definitions of terms within doctrinal constructs, but of strongly-held views on the biblical materials themselves. We shall have to concern ourselves with the bearing of a commitment to Scripture as the canonical embodiment of the Word of Truth on disputes about the trustworthiness of information and instruction carried in the actual linguistic units employed there. For the purposes of this introduction I need only say the obvious about this relationship, namely, that the nature and dynamic of the whole is reflected in the parts and provides the criteria relevant to the parts. If this fact were more consistently attended to, many unnecessary disputes and tensions would be avoided and the issues of genuine significance kept plainly in view. But let us begin our pursuit of a solution by looking at the inerrancy question in the actual asking of it, for it is there that the most basic determination will be made.

ence in October, 1978. This document can be found in *Inerrancy*, ed. Norman L. Geisler (Grand Rapids: Zondervan, 1979) 493f.; see the second point of the Short Statement.

2 | Working Under the Word

No one can approach the inerrancy discussion without soon becoming aware that it is not simply biblical interpretations and conclusions about historical or scientific realities which differ from scholar to scholar, but more importantly, that approaches to the question itself differ profoundly. We can hardly expect to get off the ground, then, without serious attention to methodology, and to methodology of the most basic sort. We should recognize that we are immediately engaged by matters of genuine gravity in connection with the doctrine of canonical Scripture—a very special doctrine in that it necessarily regards not simply the development of our knowledge in relation to a given biblical concern, but also the special relationship of the Bible to the rest of our knowledge. If we are thoughtful here, we will come face to face with crucial epistemological commitments having a powerful bearing on our conclusions about inerrancy. It seems clear to me that both the broader terms of the inerrancy question (basic and consistent biblical authority) and the narrower focus of the debate in some circles (the errorless purity of the texts) can and should be clarified by an analysis of the essential function of Scripture in Christian thinking. In fact, it is only in that manner that the inerrancy question can be properly asked or answered.

Embarking on this task we can only begin by acknowledging our present situation. When the Church professes to hear the Shepherd's voice through careful attention to the biblical texts, and takes seriously both those texts and the objective creaturely reality within which and of which they speak, it is natural enough that questions of consistency in knowledge should appear, leading to the question of biblical (in)errancy. That at least is the situation in which we find ourselves in the concreteness of our interaction with the texts themselves and with the world around us. Compelled, however, by our commitment to the

Bible as canon to ask the inerrancy question epistemologically—
that is, while facing directly the matter of the relationship
between the intellectual authority belonging to revelation and
that which we attribute to our own discovery of reality in
common creaturely experience—we are required to pause long
enough to indicate concerning Christian thinking both "whence
it cometh and whither it goeth," to clarify its source and
direction. In doing this the role of Scripture becomes plainly
visible, and we will find in consequence that we have already
come a great distance in responding to the inerrancy issue.

It would be an entirely mistaken notion to suppose that
there is any neutral, *a priori* forum in which to assess the basis
and obligation of Christian thought and life, for such a reflective
task always remains one of concrete review within a known
reality.[1] It includes, then, the full obligation to keep before us
even as we proceed the very fact of canonical Scripture, the
unavoidable fact that the faith and world view of the Christian
Church have always been bound up with Holy Scripture. This is
not to compromise the analysis, but to legitimate it. To acknowledge our present situation, to begin where we are as part of a
community of faith within the Life of a living Head, is already
to have received the witness of Scripture in the proclamation of
that community and to be standing under the authority of that
Head. Though it is within this reality that the believer and the
Church actually confront the inerrancy question (as indeed all
other questions), the frequent failure to recognize this and to
operate by and within its methodological implications has led
to unhappy excesses at both poles of the inerrancy debate.

This should become clear in what follows. It will be useful
to take stock first of common procedures in handling the inerrancy question, which will lead not only to a recognition of
the demand for mature methods here, but also to the real issue
on which a stable and successful employment of appropriate
methods ultimately depends: a genuine commitment to working
under the Word.

---

[1] Thomas F. Torrance makes this very plain in *Theological Science*
(London: Oxford University, 1969). "In the nature of the case," he says, "a true
and adequate account of theological epistemology cannot be gained apart from
substantial exposition of the content of the knowledge of God, and of the
knowledge of man and the world as creatures of God" (p. 10). Cf. Karl Barth,
Church Dogmatics 1/1. 45f.

Methodology: The Debate

Inerrancy, of course, is not a biblical term and no assertion of errorlessness per se can be found in Scripture. The direct statement closest in appearance to anything like "The Bible is inerrant" is found in John 10:35: "The Scripture cannot be broken." After exegesis most do not consider this sufficient to make inerrancy a biblical doctrine of direct statement. Thus Dewey Beegle, for example, considers those who hold to inerrancy to do so on the basis of a methodology that is ultimately deductive, given that no incontrovertible statement directly corresponding to inerrancy can be produced. He maintains that a methodology allowing priority to the inductive process (which he himself advocates) will not lead to a conclusion of biblical inerrancy.[2]

R. C. Sproul, on the other hand, distinguishes the methodology of inerrantists according to three divisions: (1) the confessional method, that is, a method correlated with a personal faith-response to Scripture; (2) the presuppositional method, wherein *a priori* the Scriptures speak with the self-attesting authority of the triune God; (3) the classical method (approved by Sproul), which follows the probability of inductive logic to a Christological foundation, from which it produces inerrancy by deduction.[3]

Paul D. Feinberg, drawing primarily on an exchange of articles by Arthur F. Holmes and Norman L. Geisler and a paper by John Warwick Montgomery, supports an inerrancy doctrine built by handling the scriptural data in a manner that has been called "retroduction," involving a two-way relationship between induction and deduction in the creative process of discovering a paradigm to fit what is actually the case.[4] This he

---

[2] Dewey M. Beegle, *Scripture, Tradition, and Infallibility* (Grand Rapids: Eerdmans, 1973) 16f., 213f.

[3] R. C. Sproul, "The Case for Inerrancy: A Methodological Analysis," in *God's Inerrant Word*, ed. John Warwick Montgomery (Minneapolis: Bethany Fellowship, 1974) 242f.

[4] Or "abduction," or "imaginative retroduction" (following C. S. Peirce); Feinberg's association of Montgomery's "retroduction" with Holmes' "adduction" is not satisfactory, though there are similarities here. See Feinberg, "The Meaning of Inerrancy," in Geisler, *Inerrancy*, 269f. Cf. Holmes, "Ordinary Language Analysis and Theological Method," *Bulletin of the Evangelical Theological Society* 11 (1968) 131–38, and "Reply to N. L. Geisler," 194–95;

believes to be an improvement on the classical method by maintaining a greater continuity with general methodology, a broader base of support in the text, and a more resilient relationship between theory and data. An inerrancy theory built along these lines, says Feinberg, carries greater weight and better sustains itself, despite anomalies, against opposing ideas.

Holmes himself, however, appears to leave room for a position between that to which Beegle subscribes and the inerrancy position of the others (in the formation of which deductive extrapolation always figures prominently). His methodology in the article mentioned above deserves further attention as he argues for what he calls "adduction":

> Theology seems to me to involve hermeneutical assumptions and pre-understandings, the selection of materials, the choice of some preferred materials in interpreting others, the adoption of guiding hypotheses, the use of models, the gradual hesitating construction of conceptual maps.

> This is neither deduction nor induction. The logic of theological language is different from that of mathematics or early modern science. . . . Recent philosophy of science is increasingly explicit that concept-formation means *adducing* models and developing constructs. . . .

The evangelical, says Holmes, will employ scriptural models insofar as possible, but forming theological constructs is a complex process in view of the multiplicity of models found in different contexts. Still, the theologian is not to dispense with biblical models or reduce Scripture's pregnant cognitive devices to strictly literal or univocal language, but to explore them in the total context of Scripture. He is to remember also that the statements of Scripture are frequently found in model-contexts and in varying language-games. In this process diversity is not hard to account for:

> If theology is neither rigorously deductive nor the result of a complete and pure induction, but is sometimes conducted by less

---

Geisler, "Theological Method and Inerrancy: A Reply to Professor Holmes," ibid., 139–46. Cf. also Montgomery, "The Theologian's Craft: A Discussion of Theory Formation and Theory Testing in Theology," in his book *The Suicide of Christian Theology* (Minneapolis: Bethany Fellowship, 1970) 267–313. The literature referred to in the present discussions should not be assumed to have been programmatic for the debate itself.

formal and conclusive means, then its systematic structure and to a certain extent its concept-formation will vary with the selection and creative interrelation of models. After all, Protestant theology is an open-ended and somewhat pluralistic venture.

Though theology cannot be verified by direct empirical verification or by formal consistency, however, doctrinal constructs must be required to respond to truth criteria of some sort. They should embrace the entire scope of relevant data without distortion, yet still " 'fit' closely enough to avoid being the sort of generality that fits any conceivable facts at all." Insofar as a theological construct is an attempt to interrelate and unify, it must fit some appropriate coherence criterion as well; its broader relations, then, may influence the particular form in which a construct is adduced. At all events, in view of the sufficiency of both inductive and deductive principles and the less formal nature of the adductive method, Holmes finds helpful a distinction between first- and second-order doctrines (first-order doctrines being those that Scripture "plainly teaches"). In this he wishes carefully to maintain the consciousness that all theologizing is fallible.[5]

Now Holmes believes that inerrancy is a second-order doctrine, and that "in its usual extension to all historical details, scientific allusions and literary references" it cannot be inductively demonstrated or deduced from Scripture without a fallacy of equivocation. It has been adduced as a second-order doctrine because of the high level of expectation created by the first-order biblical doctrines of revelation and inspiration. But a strict form of the inerrancy doctrine does not "fit," he says, and even the term itself may be a hindrance by evoking a malfitting model based on twentieth-century standards. In view of all this he wonders whether the intramural evangelical debate really involves substantive differences.[6]

Holmes thus criticizes methods being used on both sides of the debate, and his note of caution with respect to inerrancy constructs is well-taken. Among inerrantists Feinberg, for one, has benefited from his discussion of method, though he seems somehow less concerned than Holmes when it comes to awkward questions of fit (or shall we say "anomalies"?). But it must be

---

[5] "Theological Method," 134–37.
[6] Ibid., 137. On the question of equivocation, see below, p. 116.

said in response to Holmes—though his article discussed inerrancy only as an illustration—that he appears to take a rather
light view of the entire matter as a result of a somewhat facile
distinction between first- and second-order doctrine and an
unguarded stress on the informality of theological thinking. All
exegesis, all theologizing, and all doctrines are in fact fallible,
but to confess that must not be to alleviate the scientific rigor of
theology or the force of its claims upon us in the face of
conflicting views. If any distinction is to be made between orders
of doctrine, then it is the distinction between doctrines (whatever
refinement or revision may yet be demanded) whose correspondence with Scripture in the service of the Object of theology is
objectively forced upon us in a way that compels the abandonment of contrary ideas, and those that have yet (if ever) to pass
that test in the ongoing theological response of the Church to
the divine Word in Christ.[7] Some such distinction will indeed
prove useful in responding to the fact that the inerrancy debate
has both broader and narrower terms.

   With these correctives, Holmes's article is helpful as a
pointer toward what particularly needs to be noted about method
in the inerrancy issue, namely, that no single-minded approach
or single-track method will suffice to address satisfactorily what
is actually a complex matter involving the intersection of inqui-
ries directed to a number of different aspects of the nature and
function of Scripture. This fact renders naïve and inappropriate
the more direct procedures, governed either by induction or
deduction in their pursuit of a simple answer to the question of
errors in the Bible: "Yes, Scripture may sometimes err and
apparently does so, despite the contrary implications you think
you find in biblical teachings and in other doctrines." "No,
Scripture cannot err, despite the fact that it does not exactly say
so itself and despite the mistakes you think you find in the text."
The respective contexts in which the question is asked and

---

[7] The early ecumenical creeds indicate the roots of the former category
(without by any means exhausting it), and reflection on the difficulties with
which they were formulated make evident the insufficiency of Holmes' distinction, or at least of the manner in which he presents it. On the scientific rigor of
theology, see Torrance's *Theological Science*, 116f., 337ff. I am heavily indebted
to this work (though perhaps not always consistent with it) for insights
pertaining to much of the substance of the present chapter, and to his more
recent works as well.

answered (perhaps legitimately in both cases) are simply too narrow to allow either answer to stand alone. But to let them stand together would not be to answer the question either, unless it can be asked in such a way as to interrelate these contexts, making room for an answer that satisfies every concern and proves to be both stable and functional.

Now we might ask right away why thoughtful scholars, who do not even need to be reminded of such things and who always have a cartload of qualifications ready at hand, have had so much difficulty in bringing these contexts together or holding them together. The answer to this may be surprising to some.

Methodology: The Problem

At this point our discussion of methodology must move downstairs to begin facing a very fundamental difficulty. The surprising reason why there remains such a polar opposition between so many inerrantists and those who cannot whole-heartedly confess the errorless purity of the Bible's original texts is that both groups are operating with the *same* epistemological shortcoming, while caught up on opposite horns of the dilemma it creates for them. The shortcoming, which we will consider in a moment, is just that failure already mentioned. It is the failure to think deliberately within the reality of the faith, to operate intellectually within the demands and implications of the grace of God's self-disclosure. It is a dualistic acceptance of the independence of the human mind in its approach to reality, even the Reality of the God who speaks as Lord in addressing us through the Scriptures.[8]

What really matters, as I have indicated, is not so much how the inerrancy question is *answered*, but how it is *asked*. If

---

[8] A helpful series of articles touching on this matter is that by Walter R. Thorson in the *Journal of the American Scientific Affiliation* 33 (1981). Drawing heavily on the thought of Michael Polanyi, Thorson—after commending the evangelical emphasis on personal commitment and practice as the context in which the power of Christian truth is properly known—criticizes the fact that "in the main, evangelicalism still works within a medieval rationalism as the *epistemological* framework for its doctrinal beliefs" ("Reflections on the Practice of Outworn Creeds," 4f., 11). The most thorough elaboration of this multifaceted problem and its solution is to be found in Torrance's many works; see esp. *Reality and Evangelical Theology* (Philadelphia: Westminster, 1982).

implicitly or explicitly the question is to be taken up by believers as if they were standing over against the knowledge of God, or sitting in judgment of the Word of God addressing them, in this autonomous posture they face an immediate dilemma and a parting of ways. For some, a commitment to consistency in their procedure, to honesty and intellectual integrity in their investigation, demands that certain difficulties or "anomalies" in the biblical text be admitted for what they appear to be and for what they would be called in any other text, namely, errors. These same people would also be compelled to admit that the entire biblical witness stands open to such criticism, and potentially and hypothetically—though many are convinced both intellectually and in the certitude of their spiritual experience that it is otherwise—error might be shown to extend beyond those incidental errors that have been recognized. For the rest, it is their very consent to the principle at work here, and the insecurity it generates with respect to a gradual dismantling of biblical authority and Christian faith, that makes absolute inerrancy such an important doctrine. The hope of maintaining a hedge for Scripture against the progressive inroads of what might appear as contrary evidence or conflicting data predisposes them toward a deductive approach leading to a conclusion of comprehensive scope and marked rigidity. They are bound under their deductive topsail for the port Inerrancy, as the only perceived safe harbor for biblical authority.[9]

It is this tension between integrity and authority that is largely responsible for the polarization and lack of harmony within the evangelical debate, and for the inability to produce a solution that not only fits and coheres, but functions within the community in a supportive manner. Even those who attempt to bring together into one working principle both full confidence in the veracity of Scripture and due regard for problems in the text have difficulty articulating any basis for stability in their procedure. This situation, existing side by side with that of a secular scholarship knowing no loyalty to the moral and intellectual authority of Scripture, is indeed capable of posing a serious problem—as if the tensions of the debate itself were not damag-

---

[9] "I have already demonstrated that once inerrancy goes, it leads, however slowly, to a further denial of other biblical truths" (Harold Lindsell, *The Battle for the Bible* [Grand Rapids: Zondervan, 1976] 203).

ing enough! But the problem, being self-imposed, is certainly not without solution if we are willing to rethink the way in which we ask the inerrancy question. To do this means to correct the epistemological anomaly of the posture adopted, and to learn to think theologically (i.e., according to the demands of the divine Lordship engaging us in Christ) at *every* level of our task.

Interestingly enough, a recent volume examining the philosophical roots of so-called errantists begins with the comment that "a number of contemporary evangelical writers have pointed to the epistemological roots of the current denial of the inerrancy of Scripture, but few have attempted to identify and elaborate them." Chapter one concludes with this assessment:

> In summation, the denial of the inerrancy of Scripture is not primarily a factual problem, though it has factual dimensions, to be sure. The root problem of modern errancy is philosophical. . . . [I]t seems to me that the best *refutation* of biblical errancy is a clear *exposition* of the premises on which it is built, whether these presuppositions be grounded in inductivism, materialism, rationalism, or naturalism.[10]

While there is something of value in these remarks, there is an ironic ring to them when the inerrantist's own position is so often made to rest on the very foundation that produces such "isms" as those being criticized.

The popular classical method, with its two-tier approach, illustrates the problem here.[11] Confidence in the Scriptures is tied, as it must be, to Christ the Lord, but only after Christ and

---

[10] Norman L. Geisler, "Inductivism, Materialism, and Rationalism: Bacon, Hobbes, and Spinoza," in *Biblical Errancy: An Analysis of its Philosophical Roots*, ed. N. L. Geisler (Grand Rapids: Zondervan, 1981) 22.

[11] R. C. Sproul ("The Case for Inerrancy," 248–49) sets out the argument as follows:

Premise A—The Bible is a basically reliable and trustworthy document.

Premise B—On the basis of this reliable document we have sufficient evidence to believe confidently that Jesus Christ is the Son of God.

Premise C—Jesus Christ being the Son of God is an infallible authority.

Premise D—Jesus Christ teaches that the Bible is more than generally trustworthy: it is the very Word of God.

Premise E—That the word, in that it comes from God, is utterly trustworthy because God is utterly trustworthy.

Conclusion—On the basis of the infallible authority of Jesus Christ, the Church believes the Bible to be utterly trustworthy, i.e., infallible.

the Scriptures are first secured by independent human judgment, a judgment hypothetically free from the actual personal knowledge of (and unconditional commitment to) the divine Lordship. This reflects an *a priori* epistemology linked with the "isms" and implicitly at odds with the true nature of the Reality encountered in Christ, an infinite personal Reality who does not cease to transcend and relativize the creaturely while embracing and affirming it. Confidence in Scripture, which should be rested on the Reality of God himself in the grace of his self-communication in connection with Scripture, is instead transferred to *man* in his attempt to corroborate that which is said by "objective" inductive and deductive means.[12]

The scholar affirming this method thinks he must stand shoulder-to-shoulder in the starting gate with any and all opponents, armed only with what is essentially an empiricist commitment, hoping on these imagined neutral terms to present a persuasive inductive argument for the "general reliability" of the Scriptures.[13] The unique divine person and authority of Christ recounted therein are to be accepted on that basis, he contends, then acclaimed as grounds for ascribing a completely infallible authority to Scripture (a characteristic which can be deduced, so it is thought, from teachings of Christ regarding Scripture as the word of God). Thus he proposes to defend himself, and God as well. But this approach completely ignores the reality that Christ is, and always has been, known to the Church as her present and articulate *Lord*. It is therefore not properly objective, nor is it properly personal. Unlike the biblical witness, it is willing to treat God himself as a hypothesis, thus reducing him to the sphere of human management.[14]

---

[12] I.e., from a detached standpoint. Michael Polanyi has done more than anyone to correct the inadequate understanding of objectivity which implies that true knowledge is attained from a detached and impersonal point of view; see esp. *Personal Knowledge* (University of Chicago, 1962). Such "objectivity" is actually a most unfortunate kind of subjectivity, for the knowing subject is not properly submitting himself to the full impact of the object(s) of his attention. Karl Barth comments on the "objective" ideal, as applied to biblical exegesis, that it is "merely comical" (*Church Dogmatics* 1/2. 469).

[13] I.e., his commitment entails an exclusive reliance on mutually manageable courtroom exhibits, as it were, on the outwardly observable and on acceptable generalizations from same. Of course, it is just such an approach to knowledge which makes much of Scripture seem so obviously fanciful, whatever its general qualities.

[14] Is this sort of thing not confronted and roundly rejected by Christ's last great word? His commission—"All authority in heaven and on earth has been

These are deep waters. Christ, or the transcendent God disclosing himself in Christ, is not known as the conclusion of an argument. Nor is his word received on that basis despite its clear and genuine bearing on reality. He is known and believed because he makes himself known and believed. In the triumph of his very personal love for the Church he reveals *himself* as Lord, and this knowledge cannot be made to rest upon human determinations, for all the legitimacy and value man's study of the documents and events belonging to his revelation may have.[15] The folly of attempting to make it do so involves, among many other destructive elements and ramifications, the introduction of an implicit reserve clause into the relationship with God—reducing the license for the desired union between intellectual integrity and an authoritative word to the status of a temporary permit, even for the inerrantist. This in turn may result in the eventual breakdown of the marriage, or else suggest an unfortunate overprotectiveness in the form of a rigid inerrancy commitment.

Excessive rigidity, in fact, is one of the problems to which a two-tier approach like the classical method is inherently prone. The underlying folly of self-reliance is exposed here through inconsistency or fear, for inerrancy becomes an embarrassing servant or a demanding master. What I mean is this: If the inerrancy doctrine is used simply to close the books on contrary data, it represents advance closure on empirical procedure, a deductive abortion which fails to take into account that some form of inductivist/empiricist commitment preceded the Christ-commitment and maintains methodological primacy. If, on the

---

given to me. Therefore go . . . *and surely I will be with you always,* to the very end of the age"—turns on the fact of his present, personal Lordship in the face of the apostles' doubt (see Matt 28:17ff.).

[15] For a renewed awareness of this fact in modern dogmatics and biblical theology we are indebted (in God's grace) to Karl Barth in particular, and to John Calvin before him. "As if the eternal and inviolable truth of God depended upon the decision of men!", says Calvin in his *Institutes of the Christian Religion,* I/vii/1 (ed. John T. McNeill, trans. Ford Lewis Battles [Philadelphia: Westminster, 1960]). R. C. Sproul and others show considerable confusion in their handling of Calvin on this matter. Sproul ("The Case for Inerrancy," 250–51) has the case for Christ and for the infallibility of Scripture resting "on a premise that can only be established on the inductive basis of historical-empirical evidence," while quoting Calvin on the next page as saying "that Scripture, carrying its own evidence along with it, deigns not to submit to proofs and arguments, but owes the full conviction with which we ought to receive it to the testimony of the Spirit"!

other hand, it is allowed that inerrancy is dependent on constant defense against apparently contrary data, then it remains conceivable that at some point this defense should fail. That would make it necessary to find an alternative view of Scripture's accuracy and value in speaking for Christ, perhaps even an alternative view of Christ himself. Because there really is no release from the reserve clause contributed by the autonomous intellect, and therefore no escape from the fear that the whole process might slip into reverse (posing an uncontrollable threat to the Christ-commitment), this is a characteristically defensive posture. In the presence of such fears and the accompanying suspicion that to accept any error in Scripture, however trivial, triggers an inevitable slide through erosion of confidence, it is not difficult to understand why the defense of inerrancy is often so volatile, while the definitions proposed are not infrequently rigid and difficult to uphold in the text.

The problems of the inerrancy debate cannot be dealt with in mere cross-fire with the "isms." What really requires to be brought out into the open, if tensions are to be relieved for a united affirmation of Scripture as the earthen, but unbroken, vessel of the Word of Truth, is the futility of attempting to set the testimony to Christ and his Scriptures on a lesser foundation, or under any other dictation, than the God who speaks *in persona* out of his own unqualified Lordship.[16] The confessional nature of the affirmation of Scripture must be made clear. This involves recognition of perhaps the most basic epistemological requirement which all reality, divine and creaturely, imposes upon us, namely, that the object or reality with which we are concerned must always govern our approach to it according to the terms of its own real being.[17] This is of special importance

---

[16] "The highest proof of Scripture derives in general from the fact that God in person speaks in it," says Calvin; " . . . they who strive to build up firm faith in Scripture through disputation are doing things backwards" (*Institutes* I/vii/4, 78-79).

[17] See Torrance, *Theological Science*, v-viii: "Scientific theology is active engagement in that [direct] cognitive relation to God in obedience to the demands of His reality and self-giving. . . . Scientific knowledge is that in which we bring the inherent rationality of things to light and expression, as we let the realities we investigate disclose themselves to us under our questioning and we on our part submit our minds to their intrinsic connections and order. . . . It is always the nature of things that must prescribe for us the specific mode of rationality that we must adopt toward them, and prescribe also the form of verification apposite to them . . ." (etc.; see also p. 37).

(and clarity) in confrontation with the uniquely self-evidencing Being of God, who does not simply give himself over, as the incarnate Christ of the Scriptures, to human mastery and to the stewardship of human resources for inquiry, but who rather takes that stewardship to himself and expresses it in sovereign self-revelation and self-communication.[18]

The Christological fact of God's own lordly Presence exposes to the Church the error of any partnership in what amounts to a specifically secular and lordless epistemological principle: the pre-commitment to think out reality from the standpoint of one's own resources, to conduct an independent examination, even of the divine Word, according to the self-sufficient determinations of an autonomous mind. This is a characteristically formal and dualistic approach that frequently loses touch with reality and has led naturally enough to a perverted view of rational knowledge which focuses exclusively on the demonstrable and has no room for God.[19] The seeds of this sort of thinking, with its inadequacy to both God and creation, were treacherously sown in the Garden as man was encouraged to move out of subjection to the Lordship of the living Word (already well known to him), and out of his bond with the cosmos as ruled by God, in order to establish an imaginary independence from God and correlatively with him.[20]

[18] See Matt 11:27, 16:15-17; John 14:15-24.

[19] For a helpful discussion of this matter in terms of the divorce between faith and reason, see Torrance, "The Framework of Belief," in *Belief in Science and in Christian Life: The Relevance of Michael Polanyi's Thought for Christian Faith and Life*, ed. T. F. Torrance (Edinburgh: Handsel Press, 1980) 7f. Note also the definitions of dualism, empiricism, rationalism, etc., found on pp. 133ff. Torrance (*Theological Science*, 26) describes autonomous reason as "the reason turned in upon itself, and claiming as inherent in itself the forms which it can derive only in relation to the objective world upon which it reasons."

[20] The problem, in other words, may be methodological, but it has moral roots, as Paul makes clear in Romans 1. Man was well aware of the derivative, *re*-sponsive nature of his own person and knowledge and speech, and similarly of his authority to interpret and rule creation *under and in relation to* the living God—nothing could be plainer from the account of his origin and early days in Genesis 1-2. Man was created a *sponsus*, we might say, betrothed from the beginning to the Word of God. Even to enter the preposterous debate on God's reliability proposed by the Enemy necessitated both an epistemological dualism, a divorcing of the theoretical aspect of his knowledge from the empirical aspect, and an ontological dualism, in differentiating between the revelation of God and the Being of God himself. (On the modern theological ramifications of such distinctions, see the preface to Torrance's *Reality and Evangelical Theology*.)

Any partnership here epistemologically, whether in empiricist or rationalist versions, falls under the ban of Col 2:8-10.[21] Within such a partnership, which distorts and aggravates the inerrancy question at its very roots, one is permanently trammeled by the hypothetical nature of the dualist program and by the company of the undesirable "isms." This indicates a failure to recognize the epistemological impact of grace and the true relationship between Christ and the Scriptures.

The best way, indeed the only way, to correct this problem is by an exposition of the *a posteriori* context of the knowledge belonging to revelation. In short, we must call for an approach to the inerrancy problem that immediately insists on a return to methodology appropriate to the God who reveals himself as Lord.[22] In this can be found firm ground on which to stand, and along with it the freedom to study openly the biblical testimony and its character without fear or inhibition. This matter (which I shall take up first under the rubric "Christian Confessionalism") is a very large one indeed, and can be accommodated in little more than outline form, in order that we may get on as quickly as possible with the rest of the task.[23] The space allotted to it, however, reflects its importance.

All this could only serve the newly-arising will to establish a sort of parallel cosmos to the one in which man actually existed, with its center so clearly in God. In one sense, this anthropocentric cosmos was indeed brought into being; in fact, there was one for everybody, as the new self-consciousness of personal nakedness indicated (Gen 3:7).

[21] As Torrance points out on several occasions, there is a natural tendency within the dualist framework for one extreme position to pass over into its opposite. In any event, I will simply make reference from here on to "empirical/rationalism," while meaning to include all the various guises under which the human mind attempts to assert itself falsely in the knowing process and closes off to full determination by reality itself, and particularly to the sovereignty of the divine Word.

[22] Reflection on the broad methodological implications of this fact (belabored by Barth) must certainly not be neglected by reason of the more recent focus on the power of God in terms of the triumphant *weakness* of self-humiliating Love, for these are not incompatible, but rather mutually intrinsic and qualifying, despite impressions sometimes left in the modern discussion (cf. Ps 62:11-12, Phil 2:5-11, 2 Cor 13:4).

[23] In this discussion we will touch on the so-called presuppositional method as well. Certainly the pitfalls of partnerships like those I have been criticizing have long been the concern of Cornelius Van Til in his many works, though he himself does not shake loose altogether from the rationalist tendencies of the dualist heritage that has developed even in Reformed circles.

Christian Confessionalism

There is one foundation, and only one, for the Christian testimony and all that belongs to it, including the doctrine of Scripture: the speaking God *himself,* who speaks sovereignly to man in the Spirit. He does so in connection with the biblical messengers, of course, but ultimately and only "in the Son," who is the Word of God.[24] The faith of the Christian Church is her embrace of the living Jesus as God the Son come in the flesh, simply and powerfully expressed in the age-long affirmation prompted afresh by the Spirit in every believer: "Jesus is Lord."[25] To think christianly is to think under the compulsion of the lordly Reality of God in Christ, thinking about worldly realities in terms of their actual center in him; it is by Christ and for him that all things exist, we read in Colossians, and in him all things hold together.[26]

This thinking makes no partnership for its supposed justification with secular empirical/rationalism, for its well-spring is God in his self-revelation, a Reality in which those outside the Church do not participate. Naturally, Christian thinking employs inductive, deductive, and adductive procedures and is scientifically committed to the testing of its thought, for it has a thoroughly *a posteriori* footing. But this footing is in the self-disclosure of the eternal I AM to the community of faith,[27] and it is against this grace in Christ that Christian thought is ultimately tested. Because revelation takes place in and through the incarnate Son, and does so precisely without compromising its nature as sovereign grace, Christian thinking is therefore both *objective*

---

[24] Heb 1:1-3, John 1:1-18 (note v 17).

[25] Rom 10:9, 1 Cor 12:3, 1 John 4:2-4. "If in the fourth century the Christian church clarified the fact that, in making himself accessible to us in the incarnation once and for all through the Son and in the Spirit, God himself is the real content of his revelation, the church in the sixteenth century clarified the fact that, in his continuous self-revealing and self-giving through the Son and in the Spirit, God himself *remains* the real content of his revelation . . ." (Torrance, *Reality and Evangelical Theology,* 15; emphasis mine).

[26] τὰ πάντα ἐν αὐτῷ συνέστηκεν (Col 1:17; cf. Eph 1:9-10).

[27] Note Walter C. Kaiser's discussion of the divine name in *Toward an Old Testament Theology* (Grand Rapids: Zondervan, 1978) 107: "His name was 'I am the God who will be there' (Exod 3:14). It was not so much an ontological designation or a static notion of being (e.g., 'I am that I am'); it was rather a promise of a dynamic, active *presence.*"

and *uniquely confessional*. It is a corporate, objective activity because it is bound to the living Jesus as its true Object, and it is singularly confessional because this binding is not self-secured, but a given of revealing and recreating grace in the Spirit.[28]

Christian thinking ought always to recognize itself, therefore, as response, and not simply in the sense that all true thinking is part of the human steward's response as he inhabits and explores creation.[29] Christian thinking is first and foremost an answer, however stumbling, *to direct address*, to the triune God who brings men, however haltingly in the wraps of their spiritual grave clothes, into the majestic Light and Sound of his very Presence. This he truly grants to us in and through his humanity and articulates in the words of his messengers, without in the least compromising the divine, self-evidencing Lordship of his own Speech. For God, whose Act and Being cannot be abstracted from his Word (as Barth labored to make clear again in the modern confusion), discovers his very Self to us in the Christ-Word calling us forth from the tomb, as the Spirit of Life makes the Father known to us in the Son. His articulate Presence thus becomes the foundation of our faith-response.[30]

---

[28] See Torrance, *Theological Science*, 32–33, 190f.: "Therefore there can be no talk of verification except, as Barth has expressed it, in a readiness to have our knowledge or our statements tested and revised with reference to the criterion whether they take place under the claims of our own majesty or under the claims of the Majesty of God, whether they are put forward as our own work or with the humility of those who are ready to receive justification from Him who alone is capable of justifying them" (pp. 196–97). It should not be necessary, by the way, to stoop to the redundancy of saying *objective* confessionalism, for "subjective confessionalism" is a nonsensical idea. All knowledge is subjectively held, but true knowledge is determined in both form and content by its object. As such, it is also always "confessional" after a fashion, but the knowledge of God uniquely so, for only with respect to the knowledge of God is the human subject up against an Object which is also pure Subject, and against which it can lay no claim.

[29] Cf. Gen 1:28, 2:19, Isa 45:18, etc.; on Gen 2:19 see Walter Thorson, "Science as the Natural Philosophy of a Christian," *JASA* 33 (1981) 65f. See also Michael Polanyi (*Personal Knowledge*, p. 5), who describes knowing as a participatory skill and the discovery of objective truth as "the apprehension of a rationality which commands our respect and arouses our contemplative admiration." Even the later Heidegger (*Poetry, Language, Thought*, trans. Albert Hofstadter [Colophon Books; New York: Harper and Row, 1975] 181) speaks of genuine thinking as a co-responding, as "the thinking that responds and recalls"—though his radical ontology hardly fits with that of the other sources mentioned!

[30] Cf. Matt 11:27, John 14:6ff., Rom 10:6–8, 20. See Karl Barth, *Church Dogmatics* 1/1. 150f.; also Torrance, *Theological Science*, 25–54, 141f., who

When we examine the epistle mentioned above, for example, we see the Christian confession clearly set forth in terms of thinking that flows, not up to or into, but *out of* just such a genuine knowledge of God given in connection with the apostolic word. The gospel is represented in Colossians, as in many other places, as active agent; the Word of Truth comes to us and produces its fruit among us, reconciling alien minds to God and enabling them to focus on things above.[31] It comes to us, in fact, as Someone to meet: a Man given to us in space and time in whom "all the fullness of the Deity" dwells and acts. It effects in us personal knowledge of God securely attached to the living Jesus, a knowledge disclosed among the gentiles to the saints at God's own initiative as nothing less than "Christ in you, the hope of glory!"[32] Here, then, is a truly indwelling Word, a oneness of word and Reality which overflows into our own speech as wisdom and worship and witness.[33] Only in this personal intimacy of divine self-disclosure (served by the public apostolic witness and the corporate spiritual context of Christian proclamation) do we come to know "the mystery of God, namely, Christ, in whom are hidden all the treasures of wisdom and knowledge" comprising the potential of Christian thought and life.[34]

The matter is put to us in this way, we are told, precisely so that no one may deceive us with fine-sounding arguments or "through hollow and deceptive philosophy, which depends on human tradition and the basic principles of this world *rather than on Christ.*"[35] The Christ we know, and whose message we acknowledge, we do not know by speculative reason or by virtue

---

writes that "the given fact with which theology operates is God uttering His Word and uttering Himself in His Word, the speaking and acting and redeeming God, who approaches us and so communicates Himself to us that our knowing of Him is coordinated to His revealing of Himself, even though this does not happen to us except in a complex situation involving our cognition of the world around us and of ourselves along with it" (p. 32).

[31] 1:3ff.: . . . ἐν τῷ λόγῳ τῆς ἀληθείας τοῦ εὐαγγελίου τοῦ παρόντος εἰς ὑμᾶς, καθὼς καὶ ἐν παντὶ τῷ κόσμῳ ἐστὶν καρποφορούμενον καὶ αὐξανόμενον καθὼς καὶ ἐν ὑμῖν, αφ᾽ ἧς ἡμέρας ἠκούσατε καὶ ἐπέγνωτε τὴν χάριν τοῦ θεοῦ ἐν ἀληθείᾳ (cf. 1:21, 3:1f.); similarly throughout Acts, and see 1 Thess 1:4–5.

[32] 1:25–27.

[33] 3:15–17.

[34] 1:28–2:3.

[35] 2:4, 8: . . . διὰ τῆς φιλοσοφίας καὶ κενῆς ἀπάτης κατὰ τὴν παράδοσιν τῶν ἀνθρώπων, κατὰ τὰ στοιχεῖα τοῦ κόσμου καὶ οὐ κατὰ Χριστόν.

of any self-sufficiency or independent initiative. We do not
ascend to heaven, as it were, to bring Christ down; we are
graciously rooted by God in Christ, transplanted into his fullness, included in his New Reality, reconstituted as new creatures
in conscious fellowship with our Creator, Redeemer and Lord.
To us Christ is made known by the Spirit in his centrality as
Head over all, and it is only in connection with that Head that
one is able to think christianly or to be truly determined by the
Object of Christian thought.[36] From start to finish, in fact,
Christian thinking derives its life from Christ and has the
character of confession and response. Was this not clearly pic-
tured for us on the road to Emmaus and on the road to
Damascus?

Nor does the fact that we (like the Colossians) now meet
Christ in and through a carefully-preserved witness to such
historical events mean that we proclaim a knowledge enshrined
in history and captive to historical science.[37] Our proclamation,
though assisted by historical science, is not merely the product
of historical science. It is the product of encounter through the
gospel with the living Lordship of one who is his own proof
and for whom no detached evidence can properly answer. We do
not proclaim a Lord whom our research has shown once *was*,
but the Lord of Pentecost, a Lord "who *is*, and who was, and
who is to come, the Almighty."[38] The Church bears witness to a
compelling Reality here and now, who makes himself known in
continuity with a canonical witness to the there and then of
biblical testimony.

T. F. Torrance begins his very helpful book *Theological
Science* by recognizing "the impossibility of separating out the

---

[36] 2:6f., 19.

[37] The exact nature and circumstances of the Emmaus and Damascus
experiences were uniquely apostolic, to be sure, but the essential principle of
confrontation with the risen Christ himself as the basis of faith's confession is
pointed to nonetheless—especially in Acts, where Paul's story is recounted for
us, not once, but three times. And it may be noted that on the road to Emmaus it
was Christ "opening" the Scriptures to them and breaking the bread for them
which led to recognition of his actual physical presence (Luke 24:16, 27–32), not
the reverse. The grace of unlooked-for revelation stands as the NT pattern (cf.
Rom 10:20) quite apart from the *bodily* presence of our Lord; an exclusive focus
on the latter, it will be recalled, landed Thomas a gentle rebuke.

[38] Rev 1:8; see Acts 2:33–39: "Exalted to the right hand of God, he has
received from the Father the promised Holy Spirit and has poured out *what you
now see and hear.* . . . The promise is for you and your children and for all who
are far off—*for all whom the Lord our God will call.*" Cf. n. 27 above.

way in which knowledge arises from the actual knowledge that it attains."[39] It is scientifically false in any sphere to begin with epistemology, he points out in the company of several other scholars; for "genuine critical questions as to the *possibility* of knowledge cannot be raised *in abstracto* but only *in concreto*, not *a priori* but only *a posteriori*.[40] Theological epistemology, if genuine, must be distinctly Christian, a reflection within the Church's confession of the triumphant grace by which it has been captured. It shares in common with other realist epistemology the fact that human knowledge is gained and held in the commitment of the personal subject to the object of knowledge according to the claims of its own being in space and time—that primacy, in this sense, always belongs to the object of knowledge. But in view of the unique lordliness of the Object of theological knowledge, theological epistemology is determined by the fact that here alone the knowing subject is truly *taken in hand* by the Object of his knowledge in order that he may know. It is cognizant of the fact that every legitimate theological pursuit has this context: "Speak, Lord, for thy servant heareth." It recognizes that the Church knows Jesus as Lord, not because it has established that he is so, but because it has been established by the fact that he is so. It is determined by the triumphal procession of Christ in which the Church is constantly led.[41] Christian knowledge of God arises out of the present exercise of his Lordship and the compelling nature of his Speech.

Naturally, then, the Church articulates the essence of its knowledge of God as creed and invitation, cast in the simple mold of the "We believe." "We argue that . . ." or "It has been demonstrated to our satisfaction that . . ." would never do. That would suggest something less than genuine confrontation with the Lord; it would imply a contradictory condition of distance and self-determination.[42] On the contrary, the more clearly and distinctly God is heard in the progress of the believer's

[39] P. 10.

[40] Ibid., 1. We might say that genuine *epistemo*logical thinking can only be done while "standing on" reality itself.

[41] 2 Cor 2:14. It is in view of this taking in hand that Isaiah prophesies: "In that day the deaf will hear the words of the scroll, and out of gloom and darkness the eyes of the blind will see" (29:18).

[42] Whether expressed with the personal touch of the singular, as in the Apostle's Creed, or with the corporate consciousness of the plural, as in the Nicene Creed, the Christian confession indicates nothing more or less than

knowledge of him, the more evident it becomes that the penetration of his majestic Voice has initiated and guided every true step from the beginning. It also becomes clear that this Voice (while its vibrations in the testimony of creation and history and Holy Scripture and the Church embrace every kind of evidence) transcends all evidence that one might present, for it is the very approach and self-presentation of God. God persuades us, not from afar by the clamoring of all that clearly points us toward him—which is sufficient, to be sure, for condemnation of our deliberately contrary and irrational self-worship—but by giving himself to us in *fulfillment* of all pointing, sounding through to us ultimately in the testimony of Christ himself.[43]

Of course, it is very important to underline the fact that this compelling impingement of the divine Glory on our human situation is not an impingement from without, but from within, gathered up once and for all in the face of Christ, where the intersection of the divine and the creaturely is grounded in actual ontological unity.[44] Otherwise we are again at risk of substituting some idolatrous *a priori* for the actual revelation of God via the grace of the Incarnation. What is not statically "enshrined" in history is nonetheless revealed through history; what speaks to man's deepest existential requirements is not subjectively grounded in man himself, but must be contemplated in and through external realities as they meet and are summed up in the life, death, and resurrection of Jesus Christ. It is only thus that the Christian confession has any substance or achieves the credibility which Christ himself gives it.[45]

---

straightforward first-person attention to God the Father, Son, and Holy Spirit—whose living Word in Christ, in being thus heard and received, constitutes the Church as such (Barth, *Church Dogmatics* 1/2. 588).

[43] 1 John 5:6–12, Rev 1:1–2, 9; cf. Rom 1:18–23. Creaturely evidence can and does point to God, but only God himself can answer to this pointing and so confirm himself. In any case, I am put in mind here of Eberhard Jungel's statement (*God as the Mystery of the World*, trans. Darrell L. Guder [Grand Rapids: Eerdmans, 1983] xiv) that "too much, not too little(!), speaks for the reasonableness of God's revelation and of faith in him for it to be rational to provide a rational foundation for that reasonableness."

[44] 2 Cor 4:6, Heb 1:3.

[45] Perhaps the great Catholic theologian of this century, Hans Urs von Balthasar, to whom I am also indebted here, has done as much as anyone from that side to try to hold together nature and grace without badly blurring the distinction between the two, and to unite the empirical and the contemplative aspects of Christianity. For an overview of his work, see *International Catholic Review: Communio* II:3 (1975); the entire issue is dedicated to his accomplish-

Quite obviously, then, this testimony to the knowledge of God, though it has the character of pure witness, does not leave Christian evidences without place or value; on the contrary, it involves a constant encouragement to behold Christ's glory on the stage of creation and history, and to behold the glory of God in *all* creation as it is lit up by Christ. But all that has been said does highlight the absurdity of using Christian "apologetics"— and/or an inerrant Bible—*to justify and protect God in the very grace of his glorious Presence,* thus reversing the relationship between the Truth of God and the truths of creation and history in and through which his revelation takes place. This is the basic flaw in classical apologetics, which seeks to show proof of God in Christ from a detached, uninvolved perspective. Not content to display the fact that personal knowledge of God intersects with (and takes the way of) every lower level of knowledge, a vain attempt is made to contain its actual justification in these lower levels. Not content to let the authority of the faith rest on God himself in the personal fellowship of his self-disclosure, there is a willingness to set aside the fact of his Presence (so engagingly described in John 14:15ff. and Rev 3:20, for example) for a footing "on the inductive basis of historical-empirical evidence"![46] But it must be asked: Is God known to be present among us or is he not? If he is, we do not rest on an *argument,* but on the Reality.[47] If he is not, of what real consequence is the argumentation?

---

ments. He concerns himself with "the visibility of God's revelation precisely in its Lord-liness and sublimity" (ibid., 212) as we behold it in the face of Christ, remaining conscious of the fact that "we can encounter the deep mystery of God nowhere else but in the context of the world it informs" (*Word and Revelation,* trans. A. V. Littledale [Montreal: Palm, 1964] 156; on this cf. Karl Barth's important little book, *The Humanity of God* [Atlanta: John Knox, 1960] 44f.). I note in passing that a fruitful comparison might be made between von Balthasar and Polanyi with regard to the symphonic nature of truth, the inarticulate component of beauty as the basis of credibility, faith as contemplation and the concepts of "indwelling," perception and rapture, and a number of other central motifs.

[46] R. C. Sproul, "The Case for Inerrancy," 250. As I have already made plain, I am not arguing against having one's feet firmly planted in objective history, but only against a form/content dualism that attempts to consider the historical mediation of God's self-revelation independently of the revelation it continues to mediate and the vision of Christ thus disclosed. Mere historical examination cannot produce this spiritual depth-perception, nor unveil the splendor of Christ, nor serve as a foundation for the Church.

[47] "Blessed are those who have learned to acclaim you, who walk in the light of your presence, O Lord" (Ps 89:15; note that this is not merely an "infused"

And if we say that this sort of argumentation (as an attempt to present "proof" on the terms of empirical/rationalism) is necessary not for self-assurance, but in order to convince unbelievers, are we not still attempting to justify him who can only justify himself, thus leaving room for the unbelief of our listeners rather than simply allowing the visible evidence of Christ's Lordship to stand forth as a context for direct confrontation with Christ through the gospel, in expectation of which the Church bears its witness? And must we not also then criticize, rather than extol, the faith of a little child or of an uneducated tribesman, in his naïve response to the gospel invitation? Perhaps some portions of the Church, both liberal and evangelical, need to be reminded that the Christian faith and its Scriptures must not be treated as if they were the special charge of a well-educated elite (a "papacy of the professors," in Kähler's expression). That is because the Christian faith as such is not a hypothesis suggested by a complex body of data, nor is personal faith a commitment to the path recommended by that hypothesis or a reaching out toward the Christ-figure of such a hypothesis. Christian faith is born in and as response to Christ himself. It is not a cerebral affair involving a single party—a meeting of ideas in the mind, so to speak, "without the fuss and bother of meeting" (as the advertisement goes). Faith is conceived and sustained in personal confrontation with Christ, a meeting which the Church holds forth in its attestation of the gospel and in the life of its communities.[48]

It is the unhappy disjunction between faith and reason that allows one to get caught up in the serious error of suspending basic Christian belief within the vacuous realm of the hypothetical and conditional, losing sight of its true relational footing. Constructive criticism here among both Catholics and Protestants has been slow to sink in. Implicitly accepting "what Michael Polanyi called the 'massive modern absurdity,' the limitation of rational knowledge entirely to what can be tested by reference to observations or logically deduced from them"—a view, as Torrance goes on to explain, in which belief necessarily falls short of knowledge and objectivity instead of being recog-

---

light distinct from that cast by God himself; cf. Torrance, "The Framework of Belief," 6f.).
   [48] Cf. John 17:20–26.

nized as the mode by which knowledge is actually grounded in reality[49] —defenders of the faith are tempted to rescue the gospel from the derision of the skeptical by seeking its justification on lesser grounds than its own. That move, however, depersonalizes (in fact, "unfaiths") the faith by cutting it off from its actual ground in the Holy Spirit, whose Sound is heard and whose Voice is recognized, but whose comings and goings cannot be told.[50] Thus arises the hypothetical and conditional character of the Word of Truth expressed in Scripture, as subject to revision—not, as should be, simply in terms of our comprehension as we are drawn into the growing dawn of the Reality there disclosing himself,[51] but in view of contrary possibilities on the level of phenomenalist observation and rationalist reconstruction. Of course, the whole attempt to treat revelation in this manner, as the handing over of truths (or alleged truths) rather than as the approach of God in Christ, remains within a dualist frame of reference and gives up the transcendence-in-immanence that is the essence of revelation. In distilling out revelation from personal confrontation with God himself, in substituting a static for a personal and dynamic view of the Truth of God, all is lost, just as surely as it is when revelation is isolated in existentialist fashion from the historical and worldly way God has chosen in encountering man.[52]

When it is recognized, on the other hand, that faith and reason are everywhere inseparably intertwined, and that rational thought, as Polanyi says, "can live only on grounds which we adopt in the service of a reality to which we submit" (i.e., commit ourselves),[53] then it is seen that the real question of

[49] Ibid., 7f.; see Polanyi, *Personal Knowledge*, 9.

[50] See John 3:8.

[51] 2 Pet 1:19.

[52] Revelation is neither the doling out of truths nor of the goods of salvation; Christ *himself* is the Truth and the Life, and as such, the Way (John 14:6). Barth, von Balthasar, and Torrance, among others, have all labored in their own fashion to make various aspects of this clear as it bears on Christian faith and the doctrine of Scripture, though their works have not received the attention they deserve from most evangelicals in North America, many of whom see only an imaginary threat to their own concern over the verbal truthfulness of Scripture. But see *Church Dogmatics* 1/1. 155-58; *Word and Revelation*, 9ff.; *Reality and Evangelical Theology*, 15-19.

[53] *The Tacit Dimension* (Routledge and Kegan Paul, 1967) xi; quoted by Torrance, "The Framework of Belief," 11. Basic convictions and beliefs, whether religious or otherwise, are thus unprovable; they arise "as a kind of listening

Christian faith is not the faith element itself, but the question we have been dealing with, namely, the bearing of Christianity's unique Object on the *manner* in which Christian knowledge is grounded through faith. The heart of the answer to this question can be found, or at least anticipated, in the "call and response" motif which runs throughout Scripture (to which I shall have occasion to make reference again). Christian knowledge is not rooted in the mastery and measurement of a mute reality, but in *being* measured by the incarnate Word in a manner that both invites and elicits response, through the catching up of the creaturely into the conversation and communion of the Father and the Son. Faith in God as a mode of response to Christ corresponds to this *conversation-creating* Word, which comes from the Father and proceeds back to the Father.[54]

So far as our immediate concern here goes, we may simply summarize all this by saying that Christian faith is determined at once by both the transcendence and the immanence of the incarnate Truth of God, and is therefore engendered by a uniquely compelling and self-verifying Word, which is nonetheless freely embraced in its own earthiness and in no other way.

Now this entails both an affirmation of human stewardship in the knowledge of God as well as a radical relativization of it. In the process of human knowledge (following the pattern of Gen 2:19-20) we are aware of the openness of reality to rational perception and of a certain freedom and adequacy for the task. The human steward is, in a manner of speaking, both servant and master of his charge in the ordinary knowledge context. On the one hand, he is accountable to the rationality inherent in the

---

obedience of the mind to reality, without which the human reason cannot begin to operate" (ibid.). In man's encounter with the splendor of God, says von Balthasar ("In Retrospect," *Communio* 2 [1975] 213): "The first desideratum for seeing objectively is the 'letting-be' of God's self-revelation. . . . This first step is not the mastery of the materials of perception by the categories of the subject, but an attitude of service to the object."

[54] The Word of God is invariably creative, and invariably a *response* to the Father as well as his own Word (the Word is glorified precisely in returning to the Father, as von Balthasar notes in *Word and Revelation*, 191). Thus the faith of the believer is in fact the faith of Christ in him; thus also the word of Christ "dwells among us richly," overflowing in praise to the Father (Col 3:16). It is the grace which comes to man in the revelation of the Word of God that he is included by the Holy Spirit in the very fellowship of the divine Trinity!

reality he encounters (and he encounters much that he did not seek out), yet he is also free to disregard or disbelieve, or to pursue and to devise means of extracting answers to questions legitimately asked. But theological epistemology cannot avoid recognition of the unique knowledge situation created when the Master himself confronts the human subject within his world. Despite all that is similar here in terms of responsibility and freedom, this is an unparalleled situation well-symbolized by Moses' startling encounter at the burning bush. Here there is a disclosure from out of ineffable hiddenness, a sovereign unveiling and an unveiling of sovereignty, an answering of what was not asked and a giving that cannot be coerced.[55] Here we must speak of a stewardship without mastery, a pursuit that is pure response, a freedom and "adequacy" that depend on the active grace of self-revelation. Here alone we must speak of knowledge as *worship*;[56] and to approach this Object truly, according to the terms of his own Being, we must approach without sandals, as one who is judged rather than one who judges.

Though the pathway of theological knowledge, as of other knowledge, is certainly traveled with many tentative steps, the basic conviction of the present Reality of God in Christ is neither hypothetical nor conditional where it is truly known, nor is it thought to be so as it properly penetrates the murkiness of human consciousness. The magnetism of the Goal, and the authority with which his Voice invites us forward, refuse to admit of valid reservation.[57] It has been opened to us to share in the genuine confidence of Christ, formed in us on the pattern of the responsiveness that belongs to the Father-Son relationship in the Spirit. When we ask how it is that we are so taken in hand by the Object of our faith, the answer lies before us precisely

[55] Cf. Job 38:1; Isa 45:15, 19; 55:6-11; 57:15; 65:1. There is a partial analogy here on the strictly human level, of course, where the object of our knowledge is another person who chooses to open up to us.

[56] Cf. Torrance, "The Framework of Belief," 12-13.

[57] I.e., we are called to rise above the many reservations which nonetheless suggest themselves to us; cf. Hos 6:3. Torrance (ibid., 13) is worth quoting here: "Belief is not something that is freely chosen or arbitrary, that is, without evidential grounds, for that would be highly subjective, a mere fancy. Nor is it something hypothetical or conditional, for then it would not be genuine, since we would entertain it, as it were, with our fingers crossed. Rather does belief arise in us . . . because it is thrust upon us by the nature of the reality with which we are in experiential contact."

here. Theological *epistemology* is trinitarian just as theological *knowledge* is trinitarian. Does the creed not testify to the Lordship of Jesus by recognizing that in him the Father Almighty has really made himself known to us *by drawing us into the fellowship of his Spirit?* In his threeness the one God sustains his sovereignty over our very knowing, as over our entire being. His objectification for us in Christ does not preclude his encountering us as "absolute Subject" by way of the Spirit of revelation. We know God as Christ, but also through Christ and in the Spirit of Christ, and no other way. We know him in the grace of his unique ability to give himself to us: "For God, who said, 'Let light shine out of darkness,' made his light shine in our hearts to give us the light of the knowledge of the glory of God in the face of Christ."[58] To know him in any other way is to know him, not according to the terms of his own divine Being and grace, but only κατὰ σάρκα. Insofar as we proclaim the Lord, we proclaim one of whom anything less than personal knowledge, that is, genuine recognition (ἐπίγνωσις) determined by his triune nature, is inadequate.[59]

When, therefore, as members of the community of faith we inquire as to the whence and whither of our thinking, as to its

[58] 2 Cor 4:6; cf. Eph 1:17, 3:14–19. "He does not give Himself to us as a mere object subjected to our knowing, but . . . as the one Lordly Subject who approaches us and assumes us into personal relation with Him as subjects over against His own divine majestic Subjectivity," says Torrance (*Theological Science*, 38–39). One need not attach a great deal of philosophical baggage to the idea of absolute Subject. What I am saying here hinges quite directly on the person and work of the Holy Spirit, and is implied in the threefold creed, where testimony to the Father and to the Son who descended to reveal him is completed this way: "And we believe in the Holy Spirit, the Lord and Giver of Life, who proceedeth from the Father and the Son . . ."—whence follows immediately, "and we believe one holy catholic and apostolic Church," namely, that fellowship in the knowledge of God (John 17:3) which owes its existence to the divine Breath that catches us up and involves us in the Word which comes from the Father and returns to him, i.e., in the dialogue between the Father and the incarnate Son. (See Rom 8:15, Gal 4:6; Barth's discussion of the Holy Spirit in *Church Dogmatics* 1/1. 516ff., is also helpful, though his views require some restatement, in response to certain criticisms made by Jürgen Moltmann, von Balthasar, and others.)

[59] Cf. 2 Cor 5:16, Eph 1:17. Note the instructive passage in Calvin's *Institutes*, III.ii.14, revealing his own realist epistemology: "For very good reason, then, faith is frequently called "recognition" [*agnitio*] . . . , but by John, "knowledge" [*scientia*]. For he declares that believers know themselves to be God's children . . . and obviously they surely know this. But they are more strengthened *by the persuasion of divine truth than instructed by rational proof.*"

origin and impetus, its direction and control, we can give but one answer: the knowledge of God in Christ according to the Spirit. This actual (not hypothetical) knowledge of the triune God reconciles alienated minds to such an extent that Paul is able to insist on a uniquely divine power whereby "we demolish arguments and every pretension that sets itself up against the knowledge of God, and we take captive every thought to make it obedient to Christ."[60] Under the compulsion of his majestic Voice, in the Light that enables us to see, every form of contrary rationalization is exposed in its pretense and failure to meet its obligation to reality and to God himself. Among the consequences of encounter with his divine Lordship is the eradication of all fancied ontological or epistemological independence, not to mention a natural confidence that creation and history will not sustain any interpretation contrary to that which is heard from the Creator.[61] And when the uniquely confessional nature of Christian thinking is comprehended in the trinitarian content of the Church's faith, the divine work of establishing the believer in the treasures of wisdom and knowledge is unhindered by the tensions that dualistic, often deliberately skeptical, thinking would introduce.[62]

It is just this basic Christian truth, applied with renewed vigor, that is capable of setting the inerrancy issue back on track. There is no room here for any commitment to self-sufficiency in the knowledge of God or his Scriptures, and no provision for any implicit reserve in our commitment. It is the very principle of such thinking that we are compelled to reject when confronted by Christ in the hearing of the gospel. For in this redemptive event (however it may have appeared to us formerly) we recognize

[60] "For though we live in the world, we do not wage war as the world does. The weapons we fight with are not the weapons of this world. On the contrary, they have divine power to demolish strongholds . . ." (2 Cor 10:3–5).

[61] But one Word creates, sustains, *and* authoritatively interprets the sphere of our existence, namely, the Word who is heard in Scripture. Faith in God means to have ears for this sovereign Word, with the result that one's ultimate beliefs—those rational but non-demonstrable foundations of thought rooting our intellectual activity in reality itself (Torrance, "The Framework of Belief," 10)—are now biblically shaped.

[62] Such thinking, whatever its motivation, is typified by Descartes' dictum, *Cogito ergo sum*, though it assumes a variety of contrary forms in manifesting its autonomous, anthropocentric starting-point (even Hume's empiricism, e.g., or Heidegger's existentialism, by which he thought to oppose Descartes radically).

ourselves to be operating no longer in the isolation of our own resources, but to be already standing under the Word.[63] Partnership in the resolutely autonomous secular thought-principle is negated, not because we dwell in a different world, but because in hearing we indwell the world differently, as those also seated in the heavenlies with Christ. In our involvement with reality as rational creatures our thinking is lifted to reach as far as the obligation to God himself, for we have heard the Word who creates and sustains and redeems reality. Thus fulfilled, our thinking does not fall back on itself in a reversal that renders reality susceptible in the end to the woefully inadequate interpretive frameworks finite and sinful minds are prone to devise for themselves.

The real character of the secular epistemological *a priori* cannot remain hidden when viewed from this heavenly vantage-point. Its common determination to know only that which can be *compelled* to come before the bar of human reason for the presentation of its claims does not sit well in the company of Christ, for God cannot be compelled. Neither, of course, does the corresponding difficulty, the reduction of the subjective pole of human knowledge to the isolation of the individual in his own (necessarily) self-centered acts of judgment, which is a denial of the Light that enlightens every man.[64] Bound up in all this is simply the refusal to know Christ as Lord, the echo of the "Yea, hath God said . . . ?" on which man allowed himself to be carried out of Eden. The intellectual ground of natural man is a fictitious cosmos in which all truth is first responsible to him, that is, to the sanctity of his private judgment, before he is responsible to it. Any god which might exist, therefore, by virtue of his "might-ness" must subject himself to man for verification. But the Almighty cannot be known in such fiction. Nor is man actually seeking him, for though his Presence presses upon men still in their creaturely existence, and more particularly in the Good News, the Truth of God is continually exchanged for a lie and suppressed in word and deed. This is man's Genesis dominion gone wild. Christian proclamation must continue to insist in the face of this that mankind began, and remains, under

---

[63] Barth, *Church Dogmatics* 4/2.1 303f.
[64] John 1:4–5, 9; cf. A. F. Holmes, *All Truth is God's Truth* (Grand Rapids: Eerdmans, 1977) 43f., 79.

obligation to the Light of the World in whom we live and move and have our being.[65]

The right of verification from a stance outside, and therefore over, the Word, of verification from the standpoint of one's own resources, is not common ground but fallen ground. It belongs to man's fanciful independence and futile attempt to serve as his own reference point. When shared by the Christian apologist, even the biblical inerrantist, it is at the very least an unfortunate attempt to accommodate an approach to verification completely inapposite to the nature of the Object with whom Scripture is concerned. God remains the self-attesting divine Subject even in the accommodation of his Incarnation, and rational knowledge of him is not adaptable to the deliberate isolationism and self-imprisonment of the human mind. The autonomous mindset is just what needs to be abandoned in order to cope with the living and present Truth of God in which every man has his existence.[66]

Perhaps a further brief excursus is permissible here, or even necessary, in order to underline more specifically the fruitlessness of partnership in the faulty methodology I have been criticizing. The believer, of course, shares with the unbeliever in exploring creation, and ought to dialogue respectfully in the pursuit and declaration of temporal truth. In so doing he is able to point to the ultimate Reality of God in Christ, who has shaped worldly realities and to whose hand they bear silent

---

[65] Cf. Acts 17:16ff., Rom 1:18ff.

[66] Cornelius Van Til (see esp. *A Christian Theory of Knowledge* [Nutley, NJ: Presbyterian and Reformed, 1969]) has contributed something of value here by recognizing in his own way that the final justification of human thought, with respect to its most fundamental interpretive frameworks, must repose on the unique self-sufficiency of the Creator's own knowledge as revealed by Christ, and by pointing out that no other comprehensive validation of thought exists. He also points very boldly to the spiritual isolationism and will to self-determination belonging to the natural mindset of fallen man, and to the distorting impact this has on interpretation of the cosmos and its history. However, his approach appears to lack the vitality of some of the thinkers he criticizes, for his constant occupation with the "in principle" aspects of Christian vs. non-Christian thought betrays a certain dualist inspiration of its own and leaves little room for recognition or encouragement of that dynamic openness to the call of reality which commends and justifies all profitable thought, whatever its failures or restraints. Christian doctrine and Christian certitude too easily gravitate here toward a disguised rationalism built systematically around a canonized interpretation of Scripture, rather than subsisting in continued response to the Word himself in and through Scripture, within the context of the mutual indwelling of his creation.

witness. But he must keep in mind the fact that only as God speaks his own Name in answer to the testimony offered are prisoners set free, and either Creator or creation authoritatively disclosed for what they actually are in Christ.[67] For otherwise a man's knowledge, even of worldly things, does indeed remain bound up with his own finitude and with his very process of knowing, as modern philosophy and modern science have clearly recognized. While man continues in hiding, shunning because of his nakedness the dialogical relationship with God once enjoyed in Eden, he can find no *pou sto* for a holistic interpretation of worldly realities and no grip on the divine Reality, despite the attraction these may yet hold for him.[68]

Man is unable to transcend the isolation of his own anthropological starting-point, which he nonetheless insists on in opposition to the truth out of the culpable egocentricity of his thinking. He cannot do so in independent examination of creation, even in order to discover God, for God is not in creation but creation in the grace of God. The eloquence of creation in its utter dependence on the eternal power and divine nature of its Lord is the eloquence of the silent rebuke. It is the frolicking-ground of faith but the frustration of unbelief, its witness the obvious antithesis to the premise on which this alien, man-centered approach is made. Thus it is that when man turns from natural science (however formal or informal) to attempt on his own terms a natural theology apart from the pure theology of God's grace in revelation, and apart from the *torah* of the Lord that revives the soul, he claims to be wise but becomes the fool, exchanging "the glory of the immortal God for images made to look like mortal man." He cannot break out of his own subjectivity.[69]

---

[67] 2 Cor 4:3f.

[68] Torrance (*Theological Science*, vi) comments on the situation when the truth has been stifled at the very roots of human knowledge: "All a man may be able to do then in his sense of the presence of God is to give it oblique, or symbolic, meaning only to discover that he has thrust himself into its content, or he may try to straighten out the connections of his thought and make them point beyond him, only to find that they break off and point into emptiness and nothing, even though he remains haunted, as it were, by the ultimate rationality of God all round him." Cf. Job 37:19ff.

[69] I.e., he cannot cross the twofold chasm fixed by his finiteness and his sinfulness. Calvin (*Institutes* I.vi.4) had this to say: "For, since the human mind because of its feebleness can in no way attain to God unless it be aided and

He cannot do so in his examination of history either, despite the fact that the infinite and eternal God has stooped to enter history and meet mankind within creaturely reality. Even if he does not succumb altogether to a positivist or determinist view of history or withdraw to a strictly subjectivist philosophy, from the standpoint of his own control over knowledge he cannot suppose that he knows the actuality or the nature of past events with certainty, for he cannot deal with these as simply given, but as requiring reconstruction from a distance. Further, such reconstruction will depend a great deal on his ability to penetrate the actual coherence of these events and to do so from within the realm of the world that he himself is able to know. But then with respect to Christ he is up against two problems. First, his primary resource materials (the substantial documents reconstructing events from close at hand) represent an openly committed interpretation of events and he has nothing against which to test them. Of much greater significance is the problem in the explanation for their total commitment—the rationality to which they are pointing in their accounts of Christ involves the intersection of the divine with the human! This is without genuine analogy and certainly incapable of assessment on any ground other than its own, and this ground transcends the world of the human knower. It is entirely necessary that Christ be self-interpreting, then, and self-verifying.[70] But in this he bursts the bonds of historical science, for he cannot be known as he is and for who he is on its terms alone.[71]

---

assisted by his Sacred Word, all mortals . . . because they were seeking God without the Word, had of necessity to stagger about in vanity and error." See also Torrance, *Theological Science*, 102ff., who points out that we should be concerned here only with a methodological, not a metaphysical, rejection of natural theology; cf. Psalm 19 and Romans 1.

[70] "You are from below, I am from above," said Christ to the Pharisees who were rejecting his claims. "You judge by human standards." Verification in his case was to be unique: "I am one who testifies for myself; my other witness is the one who sent me. . . . If you knew me, you would know my Father also." This single, but twofold, divine witness—made from within the sphere of the creaturely, but on its own special terms—is what leads to faith. The Reformation taught us (and Barth reminded us) that God can only be known and recognized by God. See John 8:12–30.

[71] "Ordinary historical science," writes Torrance (ibid., 325), "has to do with events that do indeed have continuing effects for longer and shorter periods but which themselves die away into the past. In this event, however, in the life of Jesus Christ, we have to do with something more than a passing historical

This is not to say, it must be added, that historical science is not responsible to the Christian documents, or that any satisfactory alternative interpretation of Jesus can be found within its resources; nor is it to deny that the literary, moral, and logical force of these documents plays a genuine role in the conviction of their readers and in the recognition of their credibility. Nor yet is it to say that the New Testament writers were not concerned to establish the orderly facticity of the Christ-event, if I may use that terminology, and particularly of the resurrection.[72] But that concern does not justify the radical demand of the uninvolved, "impartial" skeptic for *independent* proof of God's marvelous actions in history. The primary interest of the New Testament witnesses was to show that the promised redemption and time of renewal had arrived, and that it must be interpreted in all its implications for tangible as well as spiritual realities, and for the reformation of worship and witness. They wrote within the context of the existing historical community of faith and demonstrated the new course of God's action. The spectacular signs which God performed in this New Reality were also directed at the establishment of that new course;[73] they were not given (nor did they linger) to serve incredulity. When signs

---

episode: with a word-act of the eternal and living God that did not pass away and that has reached out . . . into the present. Insofar as that act has entered into our creaturely existence and has in that way become a fact of this world it may be 'observed' like the other facts of nature, and insofar as it has assumed form and process within our space and time in a whole complex of historical events it can be investigated as a historical happening within the context of general history, but the word-act of God itself cannot be observed or investigated merely in these ways for it cannot be treated as if it were only a dead fact of history—treated in that way it could only prove illusory, for historical inquiry could not get to grips with it in its real actuality. It requires an act of discernment beyond common historical observation and a mode of rationality on our part appropriate not only to its character as enduring historical event but also to the personal and articulate nature of the divine activity intrinsic to it. . . . The object to which the reason is directed in faith is not the bare act of God as such, nor the mere historical event as such, but the word-act of God in and with the historical event through which He encounters people in every age in the present, and calls for their rational acknowledgment of faith. . . ."

[72] See Luke 1:1-4, Acts 1:3.

[73] Luke writes about "the things that have been fulfilled among us" (1:1), recorded "that you may believe that Jesus is the Christ," says John (20:31); for the apostles were contending that the crucial event in salvation-history had taken place. Paul too, even when speaking to the Pagans on Mars Hill (Acts 17:31), put forth the resurrection in theological rather than apologetical terms, noting that God had thus "provided a pledge" (πίστιν παρασχών) of the nearness of judgment by establishing one who is fit to carry it out (cf. BAGD, 662).

were demanded from Christ himself, they were refused to that "adulterous generation." And when the resurrection took place the risen Lord showed himself not to Jerusalem, not to the Roman procurator, not on Mars Hill, but to those who were to be servants of the Word.[74] The interest of the New Testament is to secure history for Christ rather than the reverse, by which one can at best know Christ "from a worldly point of view," as did his unbelieving contemporaries. Christ remains self-revealing and self-verifying in the presence of his most qualified witnesses to men, for it is inclusion in the self-witness of the Father and the Son that convinces men of the truth.[75] What does Paul say?

> Since in the wisdom of God the world through its wisdom did not know him, God was pleased through the foolishness of what was preached to save those who believe. Jews demand miraculous signs and Greeks look for wisdom, but we preach Christ crucified: a stumbling block to Jews and foolishness to Gentiles. . . .[76]

Now if man is unable to speak meaningfully of God through his own endeavors and out of his own resources apart from actual personal fellowship with God, then he remains cut off from him who is the meaning-giving Center of the universe. In that case it must also be admitted that there is serious fragmentation taking place in all of man's knowing. Not that natural man has no true knowledge or familiarity with beauty and truth, but that even such knowledge as he has is twisted out of proper or natural relation of its parts.[77] His participation in creation is not consciously or willfully conformed to the coherence of reality in

[74] Matt 16:1-4; Luke 1:1-2. To be sure, Paul claimed that all this "was not done in a corner" (Acts 26:26), but the immediate context of his statement, not to mention the character of all the argumentation in his trials as recounted in Acts 24-26, was clearly oriented to the question of fulfillment of Scripture within the community of faith: "The king is familiar with these things, and I can speak freely to him. . . . King Agrippa, do you believe the prophets? I know that you do" (26:26-27). Cf. Luke 16:31!

[75] Cf. John 5:37, 2 Cor 5:16; this is why we ourselves can stand with Christ's appointed witnesses and say of each one: "we know that his witness is true" (John 21:24).

[76] 1 Cor 1:21-23. Note that Paul's message in the face of skepticism remained "Christ crucified," not the resurrection.

[77] This is how *The American Heritage Dictionary of the English Language*, ed. William Morris (New York: American Heritage/Houghton Mifflin, 1970), defines "distort." Distortion is exactly what is taking place whenever the Ground and Teacher of wisdom is ignored by the knowing subject.

Christ, and his interpretation of what he may discover is not aided by any dialogue with the Truth concerning the order and purpose of the vast relational nexus in which every part of reality exists and apart from which it will not properly disclose itself. Human judgment consequently suffers frequent setbacks in the pursuit of its proper knowledge of the human nature and function, habitat, culture and history (though some areas are far less susceptible to distortion than others), for it is trying, as it were, to wrench truth away from reality. To add insult to injury, in such a condition man must ultimately fall silent when it comes to asking or answering the most basic ontological and epistemological questions, for his knowledge cannot possibly reach a sufficient level of involvement with reality as long as it remains uninvolved with Christ.[78]

In summary, then, what must we say of the epistemological partnership which occasioned these discussions? Certainly that it is unsound, that it is futile, and that rather than lending itself to intellectual integrity or to a serious apologetic, it actually frustrates same. It does so by a failure at the very heart of the matter, generating trauma for the entire body of man's knowledge by perverting its dependent creaturely context. A genuine agreement (if such were possible) to think within the isolation of natural man would be to abandon the Christian gospel at the outset, and to abandon it irretrievably. It would be a denial of the Christian testimony to Immanuel, "God with us!" The *a priori* commitment that is the operating principle of this partnership is an aspect of man's rejection of God and opposition to him, resulting in many self-imposed problems like that characterizing much of the inerrancy debate. At root it is the imposition of self in the process of knowing to the exclusion of God. The mistaken notion of common ground, indeed of any ground at all, for independent judgment of the truth or truthfulness of him who is himself the Truth must be abandoned as an absurdity.

What must be substituted in its place is the *a posteriori* principle that works under an unconditional obligation to the God whose grace has found us in Christ, overturning our previous independence. It belongs to his Lordship to entirely

---

[78] Torrance (*Theological Science*, 278) speaks of "the flight from reality" that affects everything man thinks and does from below.

recast human epistemology along with human existence—how could it be otherwise? When God makes himself known, nothing becomes more apparent than that every human crown must be cast down before his throne, including the ruling rights of reservation and doubt.[79] No one can truly abide in the Presence of God apart from unconditional surrender of the whole person, a surrender that, as it is perfected, denies in retrospect every form of reservation and every sovereign use of the human faculties. We should note that it is nothing more or less than what is already known of the Presence of the unimpeachable God that quietly guards the commitment of the faithful, whatever challenges they may face in the unnatural knowledge relations rampant in the present age. This is the fact of the matter, and it ought to be recognized without equivocation. The Church of God consists of sheep who hear and know their Shepherd's Voice.[80]

[79] Not that doubts immediately disappear or that God refuses to address them (remember Thomas!), and not that perplexity, even reservations, cannot serve a greater revelation (remember Job!), but they must be prepared to submit to the rebuke: "Brace yourself like a man; I will question *you*. Were you there when I . . . ?" "Stop doubting, and believe."

[80] And that on the very pattern of the knowledge the Son has of the Father—see John 10:1-5, 14-16, 22-30. In view of all this it must be said that even what we are inclined to present to call "honest doubt," meaning that no conscious duplicity of motivation is apparent in one's basically skeptical stance, cannot be considered a morally neutral or intellectually sound position (Romans 1 again; Heb 11:6). Of course, it cannot on that account simply be turned aside, but I am not entirely comfortable with the apologetic approach advocated by evangelicals such as E. J. Carnell, Gordon R. Lewis, David L. Wolfe and many others in recent years, despite the serious contributions made. It fails to escape an anthropocentric evaluation of faith and Scripture. Lewis (*Testing Christianity's Truth Claims* [Chicago: Moody, 1976] 287) thinks that Carnell "provides the interpretive principle necessary to test evangelical Christianity" without presupposing the point in question: "He considers the biblical viewpoint a tentative conclusion to be checked out by its adequacy to the entirety of experience." Wolfe takes a very similar approach in *The Justification of Belief* (Downers Grove: InterVarsity, 1982), while correctly stressing that the necessity of remaining open to criticism is not at all incompatible with a deep conviction of one's ultimate beliefs (cf. Torrance, *Reality and Evangelical Theology*, 57-58). Like the others, unfortunately, he never seems to come to grips with the absolute qualitative difference between *God* as the Object of belief and the objects (even other persons) in view in the epistemological analogies he employs. In all the talk of testing Christianity against our own criteria, there is simply too little account taken of the actual lordly Presence of God in the Church, which requires and effects that everything, ourselves included, should be tested against *him*. A. F. Holmes does a little better in *All Truth is God's Truth*, it seems to me, and one might turn to Donald G. Bloesch, *The Ground of*

We ignore the epistemological and procedural implications of Christ's Lordship at our own peril. Man was not created to function in intellectual isolation from God in any sphere. Rather, all objects of his knowledge are to be known in the context of a dialogical relationship with the one Lord in whom both subject and objects have their being and stand together. Thus is every thought taken captive to Christ and liberated to the truth of its worldly object at the same time. But to speak of a dialogical context in which Christ's Lordship is realized is certainly to speak of hearing him in the biblical Word of Truth. In being given ears to hear we find ourselves in an altogether new situation, in which verbal authority and intellectual integrity can and do exist for man in inalienable unity in connection with our incarnate Lord. And now there is a need to explicate the assumption I have been making all along, namely, that to listen to Scripture is to listen to Christ, that to stand under Christ the Word and to stand under the biblical word of Christ are indistinguishable postures.

Confession and Canon

When we acknowledge the Lord himself as the one foundation of our faith, and admit that in the very nature of the case we cannot trace our knowledge of him back behind his meeting us in Christ in active self-communication (a given which is therefore ours, not out of our own resources, but in the Holy Spirit), we recognize our entire indebtedness to Christ. If we are to operate truthfully within this obligation, in setting forth our confession we will have to resist being drawn into the vacuum of unbelief, where the Truth of God has not been received and can hardly be verified. We will not be content to work within the partnership (with its fears and tensions) in which the classical method is willing to remain, and in dialogue with those outside the Church we will find ourselves unable to speak within the pretense and constraints of what is not the case. We will fulfill our responsibility instead simply in pointing to him whom we

---

Certainty (Grand Rapids: Eerdmans, 1971), for some solid help in this area. What is required is a humanly relevant, but nonetheless *theocentric*, apologetic— and not theocentric in theory only, after the rationalist fashion, but in dynamic *a posteriori* fashion.

know and have received. But not for a moment do we lost sight of the fact that the One we know, we know precisely in the concrete objectivity of the incarnate Son. And to proceed in any direction from this statement we are obligated to speak a clear word in affirmation of Holy Scripture, which was given and sanctioned by the Spirit to serve as the articulate channel of God's living revelation in Christ, and has in fact done so again and again.

We are so obligated because in the Incarnation the Truth and Life entered personally and decisively into the human realm. The Word of God spoke with human words from within his own humanity and himself was made truly amenable to the witness of human words, and received such witness. Moreover, and more specifically, we are so obligated because it is precisely in the Scriptures and through the witness of the apostles and prophets that we ourselves are pointed to Christ and brought before his Lordship. It is only in their company that we come to know him. The Church is being built on the foundation of the apostles and prophets; they are the servants of the Word, and their witness was and is (in Christian proclamation) the chief instrument for the furtherance of "all that Jesus began to do and to teach." In professing to know Christ as the Λόγος which God speaks, we are *already* confessing the λαλία by which we are directed to him and through which our hearing him comes about.[81] We stand under the Scriptures as under the Word himself because it is in and through Scripture that the Word comes to meet us. In the Scriptures the objectivity of the one revelation of God in the living Jesus is articulated and maintained as the context for the objectivity of his personal Lordship in present self-giving to the Church.[82] It is through the Scriptures as his κανών, as the staff by which he rules the boundaries of Christian thought and life on every side and points the way forward, that the Lord directs and speaks to the Church. In so doing he now establishes and guards it *as* the Church in the organic mode

---

[81] See Torrance, *Theological Science*, 197; cf. John 1:18, 8:43 (Greek text).

[82] "It follows that all the preaching of the Church, as indeed the entire Christian religion, should be nourished and ruled by sacred Scripture. In the sacred books the Father who is in heaven comes lovingly to meet his children, and talks with them"—Dogmatic Constitution on Divine Revelation, 21 (*Documents of Vatican II*, 762).

proper to the age of the Spirit, transcending previous dependence on the formal channels and structures that once served and
housed the community of faith prior to the fullness of time and
the appearing of our Lord Jesus Christ, to which and to whom
all Scripture testifies in one way or another.[83]

That confession of the triune Lord and confession of full
submission to Scripture are inseparably linked is a fact that rises
above the disputations so undeservedly surrounding it, if Holy
Scripture is where we hear the speaking God speak and thus
know ourselves to be the Church and the subjects of his Kingdom.
Throughout the long history of God's revelation to his people
the developing canon has imposed itself as a witness and objective functionary of revelation, and of the Lordship of Christ
which refuses to leave the community of faith to its own devices
in the ordering of its life, worship, and proclamation.[84] Thus it
can be said of the inspired Scriptures, as the Second Vatican
Council has it, that they "present God's own Word in an
unalterable form, and they make the voice of the Holy Spirit
sound again and again in the words of the prophets and
apostles."[85] The Church, says Barth, if it would see Christ, is
directed and bound to Scripture: "it can distinguish between
seeing Jesus Christ, hearing his prophets and apostles and
reading their Scriptures, and yet it cannot separate these things,
it cannot try to have the one without the other."[86]

We ought to agree, then, that it is the Scriptures themselves
which put us in the position to make our confession—this very
confession in which they are included—*as Christ speaks in and*

---

[83] Calvin speaks of Scripture as "God's scepter" (*Institutes*, "Prefatory
Address to King Francis I of France," 2). In this sense, Scripture stands over
against the Church, as Barth says, as a concrete expression of the distinction
between Head and body. Κανών, he remarks, "means rod, then ruler, standard,
model, assigned district" (*Church Dogmatics* 1/1. 101). And where the word of
God is truly spoken and heard, this canon becomes "the movable canon, the
publisher of revelation" (p. 115). "When the Canon, the staff which commands
and sets moving and points the way, is moved by a living, stretched-out hand,
just as the water was moved in the Pool of Bethesda. . . , then it bears witness,
and by this act of witness it establishes the relation of the Church to revelation,
and therewith establishes the Church itself as the true Church . . ." (p. 111).

[84] Cf. ibid., 113f.

[85] Dogmatic Constitution on Divine Revelation, 21 (*Documents of Vatican
II*, 762).

[86] *Church Dogmatics* 1/2. 583. "It is thus a Bible-related revelation of God,"
as Torrance says (*Reality and Evangelical Theology*, 84), "that we must have in

through them. Because of this "as" we do not enter into debate to prove Scripture, as if this were another and separate matter preceding our confession or following after it. Rather its proof, as Calvin says,

> derives in general from the fact that God in person speaks in it. . . . Let this point therefore stand; that those whom the Holy Spirit has inwardly taught truly rest upon Scripture, and that Scripture indeed is self-authenticated.[87]

When the Bible has spoken as a witness to divine revelation and been recognized as such, insists Barth, the confession of Scripture that is called forth remains an affirmation and a clarification, not a justification, of our attitude of obedience to Scripture. It springs from no other place than our actual exegesis of Scripture and is clearly stated for the purpose of ordering ourselves by it in the face of contrary inclinations and the temptation to step out from under the authority and direction of God.[88]

To set forth our commitment to the Word of God with a view to displaying its integral role in the soundness and vitality of our entire confession of Christ's Lordship, we need to make very plain the bond between Christ and the Scriptures. The Scriptures, it must be said, can only be properly characterized and confessed in terms of their actual content and their service to God's revelation in Christ. Likewise, Christ can only be properly confessed according to the Scriptures which he employs in that revelation. G. C. Berkouwer, in his volume on Holy Scripture, is particularly helpful in his consistent rejection of any abstract or formal approach to acknowledgement of the Bible, whereby on one basis or another "Scripture is received as writing, as a book of divine quality, while its content and message as such are not taken into account from the outset." That would be already to drive a wedge between Christ and Scripture. Proper reflection on Scripture, he says, can only proceed from a subjection to the

---

view and seek to interpret, for it is in that articulate form of human word, spoken and written, which divine revelation has taken in space and time, that God continues to make himself known to us as we meditate upon the Holy Scriptures and hear his Word addressing us."

[87] *Institutes* I.vii.4, 5.
[88] *Church Dogmatics* 1/2. 461–62.

gospel and to the Christ of the Scriptures.[89] And here we must say "subjection to," and not merely "consideration of" as we would with other books, because in this unique book Christ is revealed as the Lord. His Lordship is the aim and purpose and possibility of its contents. Thus Christ has bound Scripture to himself in that he comes to us as Lord in this concrete form. We recognize therefore, as Berkouwer does, that there can be no separation between faith in Christ and faith in Scripture.[90] This recognition is on the one hand an essential element in remaining true to Christ, and on the other it is the key to the doctrine of Scripture, for the Bible's contents and character, its function and authority and reliability, are not many subjects but one, and that subject is the canonical service of Scripture to the God who reveals himself in Christ. The doctrine of Scripture is not therefore an indication of faith in Scripture in and of itself, but of Scripture as the servant of the Lord.

Some, however, still contrive a separation between Christ and Scripture by mistaking the meaning of statements like that quoted from Calvin a moment ago, and attempting to distinguish the inward witness of the Spirit of Christ from the outward witness of his word. This too must be rejected promptly, lest it ruin the entire doctrine of Scripture. Calvin, of course, intended no such division in the *testimonium Spiritus Sancti*, for it is precisely in and through the Scriptures that Christ makes himself known and that the Spirit testifies to our sonship in unity with him. That is, the Spirit does not testify *to* the Scriptures, as some carelessly maintain, but *through* them to Christ; it is as and because he does testify through Scripture that he causes us to rest upon Scripture.[91] The indivisibility of word and Spirit in our communion with Christ was a fundamental pillar of Reformation thinking, for the Church was reminded at that time that it is only in conjunction with Scripture and its

[89] G. C. Berkouwer, *Holy Scripture*, trans. and ed. Jack B. Rogers (Grand Rapids: Eerdmans, 1975) 33, 42–43; he leans especially on H. Bavinck.

[90] Ibid., 54–55. Barth, however, makes clearer yet the fact that the latter must be understood as a subordinate principle with respect to the former, which has in view the superior principle of revelation as actual event; Torrance also develops this important distinction.

[91] Cf. John 15:26, 16:14–15, 1 John 5:6–10; cf. also Rom 8:15–16, Gal 4:6. Note Barth's brief discussion (*Church Dogmatics* 1/2. 536f.) of the gradual historical reversal of Calvin's teaching.

proclamation that the Spirit shows forth Christ and commits men to his Lordship. It is in the biblical word that the Church recognizes Christ and the Spirit of Christ, and thus tests its own purity and faithfulness as the Church of Christ. Likewise, it is only in the Spirit that believers recognize the biblical word for what it is and are persuaded of its essential relation to Christ, as he opens it to us like a treasure house or wields it like a sword. Calvin maintained the necessary unity between Spirit and Scripture, and therefore between Christ and Scripture, a unity which both exalts Scripture and at the same time rejects any false attention to it, whether in judgment or adoration. He did not suggest or model a focus on Scripture, but a focus through Scripture, as if through spectacles, on the God who wills in this manner to be seen as he shows himself to us in Christ.[92]

From every approach it becomes obvious that the unity and integrity of our Christian confession require the full acknowledgement of Scripture, but in such a way that all our consideration of its qualities and characteristics should be tied to our actual contemplation therein of the glory of God in the face of Christ. No merely formal endorsement, one in any way isolated from Scripture's content and its service to the basic confession, "Jesus is Lord," will do. Negatively, there are two major reasons for this. First, to separate the acknowledgment of biblical authority from the knowledge of Christ belonging to the Lordship he has already exercised through Scripture constitutes, as I have been arguing, a serious error whereby a foundation in human subjectivity is substituted for the objectivity determined by the sovereign Word. This is so whether this formal endorsement is put forward rationalistically as a precondition of faith, or extra-rationally as a prerogative of faith. In either case there is a major element of self-direction involved, and the latter is only another

---

[92] *Institutes* I.vi.1, xiv.1; note I.ix.3: "The letter, therefore, is dead. . . . But if through the Spirit it is really branded upon hearts, if it shows forth Christ, it is the word of life. . . ." Calvin then argues the dignity and necessity of the word as the avenue of the Spirit's power, adding this comment: "And what has lately been said—that the Word itself it not quite certain for us unless it be confirmed by the testimony of the Spirit—is not out of accord with these things. For by a kind of mutual bond the Lord has joined together the certainty of his Word and of his Spirit so that the perfect religion of the Word may abide in our minds when the Spirit, who causes us to contemplate God's face, shines; and that we in turn may embrace the Spirit with no fear of being deceived when we recognize him in his own image, namely, in the Word."

form of the self-reliance already criticized with regard to the former. Certainly we cannot wish now to set mere faith itself— that is, *our* responsiveness rather than the Reality confronting us, even a responsiveness arising like some private γνῶσις out of an inexpressible and indeterminate inner *testimonium*—against unbelief. That is not the proper meaning of confessionalism. It would have to be admitted that any such presentation is vain and arbitrary, and could constitute no proper imposition of the gospel challenge on the corresponding subjectivity of *un*belief and its resulting noetic confusion.

Second, there arises the danger of an arbitrary decision as to the *character* of Scripture and its claims on us, whenever it is confessed formally rather than materially. Here the *a priori* nature of the endorsement leads to divisive, man-made extremes with which we are not unfamiliar, just because subjectivity, whatever its guise and however subtly, has always the protec- tionist stance belonging to self-determination. On the one hand, in connection with a futile defensiveness concerning Scripture (the Spirit's own sword!), it may lead to a veneration of the text that refuses to acknowledge either its actual human character- istics or the dynamic freshness of its demands. On the other hand, in connection with an unfortunate defense of the human intellect that confuses autonomy and integrity, it may lead to a statement or confession that proves to be as much a shield for unbelief as an expression of genuine Christian faith. Inevitably, these choices also represent the imposition on Scripture of an independently constructed hermeneutic, visible in a variety of perversions from extreme literalism to what is called the "new hermeneutic." In any form and on every side, conservative as well as liberal, this self-reliance—despite loud denials—is an attempt to achieve control over Scripture, to render it manage- able and to that extent to wrest it from the God who speaks therein. Success could only mean that the Word himself would no longer be fully or clearly heard in the Church.[93]

In contrast to any such incipient or actual error, we must maintain by our confession the humble awareness that Scripture is bound to the living Christ as its real content and the Lord of all genuine experience with it, and that this Lord has himself

---

[93] See Barth, *Church Dogmatics* 1/1. 147; 1/2.1 513f., 522f.; 4/1.1 722f., etc.

constituted and quickened its canonical service to our faith. We must recognize that Scripture is both engendered and assimilated by Christ in his revelation of God. That is, it is Christ who occasioned the word in its origin, who fulfilled the word in his earthly existence, and who is the occasion of its actual termination on man.[94] Then the faith we proclaim will continue to rest directly on the Christ we confess, while the Christ of our confession will remain the Christ of Scripture. Then the full objective reality of his Lordship will be genuinely acknowledged without disjunction between himself and his word. Rather, this testimony will be applied to the bond between Christ and Scripture: to have room for Christ is to have room for his words, and to have room for his words is to have room for him. For Christ, who is the Word of God and the Truth of God, does not reveal God apart from the truths of his own word, nor are these truths truly known apart from himself.[95]

It is in this context that the long-standing confession, *Sacra Scriptura est Verbum Dei*, has real meaning and may be expounded, and in this context that its real bearing on the inerrancy issue can be discerned. Scripture cannot be the word of God other than in its service to Christ, indeed, other than *as* the word of Christ. It is only in Christ that the divine and the creaturely are truly united, and only in connection with the Spirit of Christ that human words can properly be identified as belonging to God and serving his revelation. But that creaturely witness given according to the revealing will and purpose of his Spirit ought, together with Jesus' own words, to be called the word of God and respected as such, is evident in the examination of a variety of texts from both Testaments.[96] 1 Thess 2:13 will

[94] The incarnate Son, as von Balthasar says (*Word and Revelation*, 14), both merges all Scripture in himself and sends it forth from himself, so as to make it fully what it is as the word of the triune God. Thus he also remains the Judge of its significance, as Torrance argues so well.

[95] Jesus made this very plain, as John persistently notes (5:37ff., 6:60ff., 8:31ff., 15:7). See Torrance, *Theological Science*, 146f.

[96] John speaks pointedly of "the word of God and the testimony of Jesus," which he entrusts to his servants by the Spirit (Rev. 1:2, 9f.). Von Balthasar (*Word and Revelation*, 21) indicates that the character of this word derives from the two mysteries of the Trinity—for God has in himself the eternal Word of his own self-expression—and the Incarnation, which guarantees the possibility and rightness of the *human* word about God. The word of Scripture should be seen as the word of the Spirit about the Word that is the Son, for only God can say

prove a helpful example in drawing out the meaning of this significant phrase, which the Church finally attached in a very specific way to the full Christian canon: "And we also thank God continually because, when you received the word of God, which you heard from us, you accepted it not as the word of men, but as it actually is, the word of God, which is at work in you who believe."

It is immediately clear here that it is exactly the human, apostolic word that is the word of God, in that it enjoys the role of providing cognitive direction both to God and from God at one and the same time—a role it fulfills not simply as a message conveyed *on behalf of* God, but as the servant of actual Presence and Power, as the rational medium of the indwelling Christ. Thus we are instructed: "Let the word of Christ dwell in you richly."[97] It is quite obvious, though, that the sense in which the human word does stand as a message conveyed on behalf of God (not merely *about* him) is hardly expendable in this—"you accepted it not as the word of men, but as it actually is, the word of God. . . ." Christ himself, as the mediator between God and man, provides the ultimate paradigm here: "The one whom God has sent speaks the words of God; to him God gives the Spirit without limit."[98] By partaking of his Spirit men became his fellow-messengers, and their words shared in the destiny of his own.

---

what he means by his revelation (p. 62). This, in fact, is the foundation of prophecy and the prophetic office (cf. 1 Pet 1:10-12), not to mention the constitutional cornerstone of the community of God's people, in that God began with the witness of the great prophet, Moses, to communicate a word that would have canonical form and function. Participation by *everyone* in the sacred trust of the word of God and the life it brings to the community is foreseen in many places (e.g., Isa 59:21, Joel 2:28) on the basis of the work of the Prophet who was to come (cf. Luke 3:21-23, 4:18 and the commentary in John 3:27ff., 14:24, 15:26ff.; note then, e.g., Acts 4:31, Col 3:16, 1 Pet 4:10-11). Thus even the proclamation of the Church is often declared by our confessions to be the word of God along with Holy Scripture, if still in distinction from it. Of course, in the NT itself the gospel message as such, whatever its form or application, is most prominently in view where this phrase is used, for the exposition of the good news about Christ is "the word of God in its fullness" and comprises "the whole counsel of God" (Col 1:25, Acts 20:27; cf. 18:11). In general we may say that the word of God, so far as its actual verbal content and character are concerned, is news about God in relation to man that originates from God himself (cf. Luke 1:19, 5:1).

[97] Or "among you" (ἐν ὑμῖν), Col 3:16; cf. 1 Thess 1:5, Acts 12:24, etc.
[98] John 3:34.

To give sufficient account of Scripture as the canonical word of God, then, we must say that it is (1) *a testimonial from certain men*, namely, apostles and prophets, *to and about God*; (2) *the word God has spoken through and among men about himself* (i.e., we are dealing with texts that are to be received as God's own message-bearers); (3) *the word in and through which God himself continues to speak*, in and through which God's personal Λόγος himself confronts us and conforms us to his own image.[99] Each of these senses in which the genitival phrase may be taken must be expounded individually only in light of the concurrent truth of the others if we are not to fall into error. The first two senses—which are really only the two sides of a single coin—will become most immediately engaged in any discussion of inerrancy, while the third sense remains in the Church's every consideration of Scripture the fundamental concern and guiding light.

To expound the first sense is to note that Holy Scripture stands as the full word "which you heard from us," that is, as a word about God which partakes of human history and particularity in culture and language, as a word spoken by men who, though witnesses of the glory of Christ, had this treasure in jars of clay. Their word inevitably shares in their weakness in a variety of fashions, inasmuch as it is truly authored by men. It constantly confronts us with this weakness, to which the Corinthians bore witness—some of whom, with respect to Paul, could see no further than the weakness of both servant and word.[100] But for that they were rebuked, unlike the Thessalonian believers, who more readily recognized the apostolic word for "what it truly is, the word of God." For the apostles (and in their own fashion, the prophets), who were not competent in and of themselves, were made competent for their ministry, we are told,

---

[99] We may expound this phrase by saying that the genitive (θεοῦ, 'of God') can and should be taken in three ways: (1) as simply descriptive, or better, as an *objective* genitive; (2) as a subjective and *possessive* genitive; (3) ultimately, in recognizing Scripture's mediation of God's reconciling and revealing Presence— i.e., in the qualified sense in which the hearing and preaching of Scripture can be for man the actuality of God's personal Address in Christ—as a genitive of *apposition*. Von Balthasar (*Word and Revelation*, 20f.) also employs a threefold analysis which to some extent parallels the analysis I am developing here, while holding these aspects together nicely.

[100] 2 Cor 4:6–7; cf. 13:1f.

a ministry in which they "set forth the truth plainly."[101] They spoke not in fleshly wisdom, nor yet insincerely or with the distortion of human motives, but "before God . . . like men sent from God . . . as God's fellow-workers."[102] In other words, in God's appointment the weaknesses of these messengers did not falsely interpose between God and his audience by any contamination of the message or deviation from the truth. Their weak humanity was so directed toward the true humanity of Christ in which God has chosen to reveal himself that their word was able to stand for his with all the necessary purity. This leads us to the second sense.

The knowledge that it does indeed stand for his (a knowledge, to be sure, that is already part of God's working in and through it) brings us to acknowledge precisely this human word, in all it actually says, with the respect due it "for what it truly is." Just as it stands we will say concerning it that *God has spoken*, even while realizing that we are not yet satisfying the full meaning of that confession, which is also a testimony to the third and fundamental sense. Their word is a distinct word which was given by God *for* men, and thus came *through* men, according to the will and providence of God and the moving power of the Spirit of Jesus. Men spoke ἀπὸ θεοῦ, says Peter, and the human word spoken remains a word ἀπὸ θεοῦ, whatever else may be said of it.[103] At the initiation of canonical inscripturation among the constitutional events experienced by the people of God at Sinai, it was made abundantly clear that divine Lordship would take an articulate form that was to be mediated through men and through written records, and that "living words" could and should be passed on in that manner.[104] Of course, it is only

---

[101] 2 Cor 3:5-6, 4:1-2; cf. Exod 4:10f., Jer 1:4f.

[102] 2 Cor 1:12, 2:17, 4:2, 5:18-20, 6:1, 7, 13:8; "For we cannot do anything against the truth, but only for the truth," said Paul (cf. 1 Cor 4:1).

[103] 2 Pet 1:21. Of course, it should not be supposed that all were "carried along" in precisely the same fashion or degree (see below, pp. 97-100). That would be to ignore both differences of purpose and genre in the biblical materials as well as distinctions which must be allowed between the Old and New Testaments. The OT, in von Balthasar's words (ibid., 13), "served to define exactly the point of mediatorship, the place and the form in which God was to become accessible to man and of service to him," whereas the NT, with a glory all its own, proceeded out of the irrepressible abundance of Christ in his inexhaustible fulfillment of the Old; its inspiration, we might say, is more an "outpouring" (Acts 2:33) than a "carrying along."

[104] Acts 7:37-38. Cf. Meredith G. Kline, *The Structure of Biblical Authority*, rev. ed. (Grand Rapids: Eerdmans, 1975), on the legal or constitutional aspect of

in spiritual connection with Christ that human words can mediate Life, but this connection, in its original reality and ever-present potentiality, is reflected in the sense of belonging to the Lord that is the pervasive self-consciousness of Scripture exactly as a written record. The Law, the Prophets, the Writings, the setting forth of the κήρυγμα and the Apocalypse as well, are all associated with and ascribed to the God who speaks in Christ.[105] This testimony the Church confirms in calling her Bible the word of God and relying on its every teaching as a tributary of the water of Life.

If we are to say neither too much nor too little by this second sense in which Scripture is the word of God, that is, if we are to say what must be said here about Scripture itself and yet leave room for what remains to be said concerning the personal Word of revelation for which this canonical word exists, we must insist that the present statement remains in the realm of the first—that of the pointing word in its simple, scriptural accessibility. We do this exactly in our acknowledgement of the historical fact and mystery of biblical inspiration, for it is just this that we are compelled to admit by the "not as" of 1 Thess 2:13, where the message as the word of God is set against itself as the word of man. It is evident that it is still the human word per se that is being spoken of as the word of God, and equally evident that recognizing the word itself as belonging to God, in and in spite of its humanity, is of genuine significance in one's experience of the divine Power that works through it.

Donald Bloesch is helpful here, reaffirming in *Essentials of Evangelical Theology* that the biblical authors were so guided by the Spirit "that what was actually written had the very sanction of God himself." He speaks of Scripture's dual authorship and contends that Scripture is not only a human witness to divine revelation, but is *at the same time God's witness to himself*. The human word, he adds, could not become revelation unless it already "embodied revelation."[106] In the brevity of his

---

the canonical word, which ought not to be downplayed in going on to recognize the powerful, life-giving function of that word.

[105] Thus 2 Tim 3:15ff. Even Moses the lawgiver, as Stephen tells us in Acts 7:37, "is that Moses who told the Israelites, 'God will send you a prophet like me from your own people.'" It was in the service of that expectation that he passed on living words to be preserved among the people of God.

[106] *Essentials of Evangelical Theology* (San Francisco: Harper & Row, 1978) 1. 52f. "Scripture is not simply a 'pointer to revelation' (as Brunner has asserted),

presentation Bloesch manages to distract us from the point to be made here, however, namely, that a particular word of man about God *is* God's word for and among men and has been marked off as such. He does this by hurrying on to agree with Karl Barth concerning the indirectness of the identity between Scripture and revelation, and the conclusion that "God's Word is consequently not the Bible in and by itself but the correlation of Scripture and Spirit."[107] Now we ought not to quarrel with these latter statements, but to make clear nevertheless that they do not negate, but rather establish, the second sense in which the Bible is the word of God, the sense in which the present perfect significance of the testimony, *Deus dixit*, is plainly applicable to Scripture itself as the concrete linguistic form of God's rational communication with man. Scripture, that is, by virtue of Christ's impact on its origin as well as its disposition, stands with canonical superiority over against every other human word as a word ἀπὸ θεοῦ.[108]

This second sense should be maintained by recognition of the essential identity between words spoken by Christ himself and those spoken by his messengers, there being no distinction here in comprising that which God wills to be spoken among us on his own behalf, and wills himself to speak in making himself known to us. As a matter of fact, the word of the servants is so joined to that of the Master that he now employs no word of his own, except it come through these servants. To his apostles he said: "He who listens to you listens to me"; and "All that belongs to the Father is mine . . . the Spirit will take from what is mine and make it known to you"; and again, "You shall be my witnesses."[109] This is a concrete authorization of human witnesses in connection with the witness of the Spirit of Christ.[110] It may be taken also as a reaffirmation of the validity of the

---

but by the action of the Spirit it is a veritable bearer of revelation," insists Bloesch.

[107] Ibid., 53.

[108] As much is plainly said by Barth also, under the rubric "The Word of God Written" (*Church Dogmatics* 1/1. 99–111), though he has always his larger point (the Word as event) in view.

[109] Luke 10:16, John 16:15, Acts 1:8. In any case, even his own words were not his own, but "just what the Father has taught me" (cf. John 7:16f., 8:25f.).

[110] Berkouwer, *Holy Scripture*, 162. Note that Berkouwer is concerned that we make no mistake about the fact that this is a concrete authorization of human

earlier and distinct, but equally enormous, claim of the Old Testament prophets: "Thus saith the Lord. . . ."

Yet we can be quick to admit that this did not always entail, and that the biblical authors did not uniformly claim for their ministry, the sort of semi-passive experience Christ prophesied about in Matt 10:19–20, for example, or the experience of a Jeremiah or a David (however poetically their claims might be understood). Not all would have considered prefacing their work with something like this:

> The Spirit of the Lord spoke through me,
>   his word was on my tongue.
> The God of Israel spoke,
>   the Rock of Israel said to me. . . .[111]

Nonetheless, the testimony still stands over the entire prophetic witness, which incorporates all the Hebrew Scriptures, that "God spoke to our forefathers through the prophets at many times and in various ways,"[112] and over the apostolic witness: "He has committed to us the message of reconciliation; we are therefore Christ's ambassadors, as though God were making his appeal through us."[113] No practical disjunction can be maintained between that which is said indirectly through messengers, whether angels or men, and that said directly by Jesus. For in the one case as well as the other (indeed, in and because of the other) God spoke to men in the fashion of men, and what was said in

---

witnesses *in their employment as such*, which must not be confused with a merely formal conception of inspiration: "Scripture is the Word of God because the Holy Spirit witnesses in it of Christ. One may no longer understand the God-breathed character formally, not even by means of a general instrumentality; it must be viewed in connection with the reality of the salvation of which Scripture *testifies*." On the other hand, "the kinship of the God-breathed Scripture with the revelation in Christ (i.e., its content) does not mean that it is not related to the words. It explains rather that everything is at stake with these words. . . ."

[111] 2 Sam 23:2–3; cf. Jer 1:6f. with Luke 1:1f.

[112] Heb 1:1. πολυμερῶς καὶ πολυτρόπως can be applied quite safely, I think, if loosely, to a variety of distinctions in the origin, development, character, and function of the biblical materials themselves; the conviction expressed here and in 1 Tim 3:16 remains despite all such distinctions. Notice that the underlying prophetic character of the entire OT Scriptures found recognition in a variety of ways, for example, in the common designation of the major historical books as "the former prophets" alongside "the latter prophets."

[113] 2 Cor 5:19–20.

either case was binding. The speech of God's messengers, in other words, is able to serve him just as his own speech serves him on the lips of Jesus, and it is this that the Church has recognized in its confession of the Scriptures.[114]

What this amounts to, when simply put, is that the entire word of Scripture belongs to Christ and is affirmed by him as his own, having identical value and authority. It belongs, in fact, to revelation, to the togetherness of God and man in Jesus Christ that is shared with us in the Holy Spirit. In truly belonging to revelation this word is a word that is absolutely *true to Christ* and to the counsel of the Father which he has opened to us. It could not be otherwise, for in being granted such a role it has an obligation both to the Truth of God in Christ and to the worldly realities which have been knit together by the Spirit of God into the womb of our knowledge of him. This obligation is satisfactorily met by Scripture, inasmuch as God has determined that the sacred writings should stand rightly related to these worldly realities and to Christ himself (though it is only and ever by grace that this latter relation is actually achieved). It is satisfactorily met because, as men were called to witness to God on behalf of men, their pointing was shaped and sanctioned and appropriated by God as his own gift of words to mankind, by which they might be truly directed to him according to his incarnate Majesty.[115] Their pointing, that is, does not lead astray; it is canonical. Mastered by his Spirit in its human origin, their word is so fitted to God Incarnate in all its diverse contributions that its proper fulfillment is actually found in him. Thus it comes to serve his revelation as he masters its hearers as well.

[114] Cf. Heb 2:1-4; also Deut 5:5, where the principle of representation is clearly established.

[115] On the relationship between the truth of statements, the truth of created being, and the Truth of God, and on the importance of maintaining both the distinctions and the obligations involved here, see Torrance's development of Anselm's analysis in *Reality and Evangelical Theology*, 65f., 126ff. From such considerations comes a clear sense of the propriety of speaking of Scripture as witness and referring regularly to its "pointing" function, as Calvin and Barth were wont to do. And in returning to such basics there is already an indication of the terms in which the reliability of Scripture ought to be put, namely, that Scripture directs us in a completely satisfactory manner, and may everywhere be followed, yet it only *directs* us to reality itself, and need not necessarily—in one sense, cannot (ibid., 66)—attain complete precision everywhere in order to do so successfully. But on this matter there is obviously much more to be said.

Of course, the fact that this human speech serves and partakes in the revelation of God can hardly mean that it *is* that revelation. Rather, in another of Calvin's metaphors, Scripture belongs to revelation as part of the clothing of the Word-made-flesh, and the train of this robe spreads out around Christ in the fabric of history. For he who stands incarnate in the midst of history, as the fullness of revelation in the fullness of time, has clothed himself front and back, as it were, with historical acts and words in the impact of a revelation that penetrates and redeems all of human history. It is only in this clothing that Christ (who still speaks and acts today) comes to men, so that in and through Scripture, in the company of the Church, we too may touch the hem of his garment, or rather embrace Christ himself in the full and splendid garb of the exposition of his promises and their actual fulfillment in him.[116] As for the sometimes troubling assertion with which I began this paragraph, that can be quickly defused if we will only take the trouble to notice that it is not a denial that Scripture contains much information otherwise inaccessible to human inquiry and specially revealed by the Spirit[117]—that in *that* sense it is revelation—or that every passage of Scripture, considered as part of its greater literary and life-context, is a divinely-superintended *result* of revelation, fully suited for the *purpose* of revelation. But as Torrance points out, we must not confuse the truth of statement with the truth of being. Jesus Christ himself is the Revelation of God; when we speak of revelation we ought to be doing so out of a recognition of the fact that God reveals *himself* and not merely truths about himself (theological ground which Barth so justifiably strove to regain, despite the foolish charges often brought against him).[118] Scripture per se is certainly not this revelation, but only its servant. It has therefore the dignity due such a servant, or rather, ambassador. This is a unique dignity, to be sure, exactly because of this servant's participation in the very Presence of the Master, which we must shortly consider.

---

[116] *Institutes* II.ix.3, III.ii.6; cf. John 5:39f., 1 Pet 1:10–12. See also Dogmatic Constitution on Divine Revelation, 2 (*Documents of Vatican II*, 750f.).

[117] See Ps 147:19–20, Dan 2:22, Amos 3:7, 4:13, Matt 11:25, 1 Cor 2:9–10, 14:30f., Eph 3:2–5, etc.

[118] It was on this basis that Barth insisted that the Word of God to man could never be truly conceived as other than an event of free divine grace. Klaas

But before pressing on to speak of Scripture in terms of our actual experience of God in Christ, allow me to say once again that in speaking here of Scripture as belonging to revelation we are talking very simply about what Scripture actually says as written word. We are regarding what it says as the word of Christ and, in him, of God. The Church is entitled, or rather compelled, to insist that this word belongs to revelation whether or not its reading and proclamation are received in the grace of revelation. For though the Scriptures may be known by many only according to the flesh, just as Christ himself often was when his own lips gave utterance, their character and authority do not change. Their words remain the word which belongs to God and is true to God's purposes, and which comes to men on God's behalf. At God's sovereign initiative they have from their very origin been marked off to a priestly service, bearing as it were the inscriptions *Holy to the Lord* and *For Service in the Sanctuary* (namely, Christ and his body, the Church).[119] This second sense in which Scripture is the word of God, so frequently a stumbling block in its bold demands, and just as frequently, perhaps, in what it suffers by way of over-zealous defense, must surely retain its prominent place in the Church's confession. For the Church does indeed accept

> as sacred and canonical the books of the Old and New Testaments, whole and entire, with all their parts, on the grounds that, written under the inspiration of the Holy Spirit, they have God as their author, and have been handed on as such to the Church herself.[120]

Runia, in *Karl Barth's Doctrine of Holy Scripture* (Grand Rapids: Eerdmans, 1962), appropriately begins his work by recognizing this fact, unlike many of Barth's less kind and less competent critics in North America, but never seems really to come to grips with it. When he says that Scripture belongs to revelation, he appears to mean: as "a *selection* of it" (p. 33f.)! He does succeed in pointing out some of the tensions, over-statements, and unwarranted conclusions in Barth's work, along with several of his strengths, but continues to miss the basic issue of which I am speaking here (cf. p. 203).

[119] Cf. Exod 39:30, 41.

[120] Dogmatic Constitution on Divine Revelation, 11 (*Documents of Vatican II*, 756). The references listed with this statement begin with John 20:31, it is interesting to note, doubtless as an indication of the fact that the inspiration of Scripture must be expounded with its material content in view. Of course, differences remain between Catholics and Protestants (not to mention internal differences) over the exact relationship between Church and canon and over the matter of the Apocrypha.

While the precise context and exposition of this affirmation by the Second Vatican Council may not be a matter of fully common understanding, the statement itself stands as the common testimony of the Church down through the centuries. Without recognizing this canonical word in its unalterable sanctity, without this sacred signpost and holy messenger service that is intrinsic to the exercise of Christ's authority over men, the Church could not recognize her God or know herself to be the Church. Apart from the confession that Scripture is the word which God has determined to speak among men in the form in which man himself speaks, "biblical revelation" becomes an empty concept. For the revelation of the divine Lordship that both establishes and governs the Church (and each believer as a member of her) is a specifically *rational* event, a canonical event with linguistic shape.[121]

As a word of man that is also the word of God, then, the Bible stands as direction both to and from God, and revelation is properly said to be biblical. But revelation is never merely rational or linguistic. It is also *event*, and we cannot speak meaningfully of this direction in terms of the loving Lordship that actually shapes our subjection and becomes our personal knowledge of God, unless we have in mind the personal Word who meets us in the words of Scripture. Here is the third sense of the "of God," the depth dimension in which we speak of the divine Word making himself heard in and through Holy Scripture —that is, of the grace in Christ whereby God, whose Person and Act and Word are inseparable, takes up his own appointed human word in the personal Speech of his self-communication. It is here and now in this Lordship that we know Scripture to be living and active and come to recognize the holiness of the servant-form we have been discussing.[122] Here we do not regard mere words, even as the presentation of thoughts which were

---

[121] Barth, *Church Dogmatics* 1/1. 137f.; Torrance provides the most helpful exposition of the rationality involved.

[122] I.e., God chooses to unveil himself in Scripture as speaking Subject and so to present himself as the living Object of the biblical word. It is because of this that we recognize the human word to be the word of God as well as the word of man. Cf. Abraham Kuyper, *The Work of the Holy Spirit*, trans. Henri de Vries (Grand Rapids: Eerdmans, 1979) 56ff., who also develops the fact that God's thoughts are inseparable from his Life, and that Scripture becomes the reverenced

governed by reality and do, in fact, converge upon Christ. If we really mean to regard revelation, we regard the correlation of Scripture and Spirit, the Speaking Presence of the Christ who himself fixes these thoughts for us on the ground of his own Truth so that they are not lost in the crowding flux of other human thoughts and pursuits, who thus distinguishes them from the non-canonical. We regard him who gives himself to us as living Word in the words of his witness, truly causing the words to speak and to find their proper fulfillment in himself. We may speak (in a figure) of Christ inhabiting his word, or rather of God drawing us into habitation in him who has spoken, so that his words become the canon and clothing of genuine revelation. We make reference here to the Spirit mastering the hearer and the disposition of the word, not merely the author and origin of the word.[123]

In view of this present event (one with the inner hearing and vision which on our part is called both faith and understanding) 1 Thess 2:13 tells us that the word of God is "at work in us who believe." We may indeed go to work in the word, following the instructions given to Timothy, but the essence of the situation as Paul sees it is that the word is at work in *us*. As it is put elsewhere, the word of Christ desires to dwell among us richly, for the Word himself, in fact, is at work in us to will and to act according to his good purpose.[124] Clearly what we are contemplating here is *the* sense in which *Sacra Scriptura est*

---

vehicle for that Life as God shares himself with us: "The Holy Scripture is like a diamond: in the dark it is like a piece of glass, but as soon as the light strikes it the water begins to sparkle, and the scintillation of life greets us. So the Word of God apart from the divine life is valueless, unworthy even of the name of Sacred Scripture. It exists only in connection with this divine life, from which it imparts life-giving thoughts to our minds."

[123] Cf. John 6:44–45, 63f.: "The Spirit gives life; the flesh counts for nothing. The words *I* have spoken to you are spirit and they are life" (see Greek text). For the term "Speaking Presence," I am indebted to Northrop Frye, *The Great Code* (Toronto: Academic Press, 1982). The fatal flaw in this stimulating volume, however, is most clearly visible precisely here, in Frye's failure to grasp the significance of the Judeo-Christian doctrine of the Spirit, apart from which the "great code" cannot be cracked. It is very revealing that Frye misses one of the most central and pervasive pieces of imagery in all of Scripture, namely, the Spirit as "the river of the water of life," flowing out from Christ, the Oasis of promise. Thus he finds nothing beyond the substitute ontology of language itself in the "speaking presence" of his vision; he does not recognize Christ.

[124] Col 3:16; Phil 2:13.

Verbum Dei, in the face of which human efforts to control Scripture can only be abandoned to reflection and awe, especially the attempt to compress and confine biblical statements to what is humanly manageable, ignoring the infinite spectrum and depth of living Truth that is revealed for us in Jesus Christ.[125] Οὐ γὰρ ἐν λόγῳ ἡ βασιλεία τοῦ θεοῦ, ἀλλ᾽ ἐν δυνάμει.[126]

And how are we to understand the relationship between the affirmation that the biblical word belongs in its simple humanity both to man and to God, and the affirmation that it has been, and can be, *God speaking*—that is, between the static and the dynamic sense in which the Scriptures are God's κανών, between their belonging to revelation and their "becoming" revelation, as Barth would say? There is indeed a distinction here, but also an indestructible unity, which may be expressed like this: the scriptural word penetrates and indwells, and is known to belong, as and because the Word himself indwells; and the Word indwells and enriches us by means of the scriptural word and not without or apart from it.[127] Thus it is that the Scriptures become a living staff in the hand of a living Lord, in Barth's metaphor, and thus it is that to them the Church must come ever and again to hear her Lord. For there God "opens his own most hallowed lips" to instruct the Church, says Calvin, and *in persona* speaks through them, so that the Scriptures, as witnesses to Christ, really give utterance to what they have to say.[128]

Now because God in this way takes hold of the human word, the Scriptures may be said to participate sacramentally in the revelation of God, in the mystery of the God-Man who is *the* Sacrament, in whom the infinite divine Truth dwells in bodily

---

[125] This point was most emphatically made by Barth, and by Torrance after him; so also von Balthasar (cf. *Word and Revelation*, 22f.). Revelation is certainly articulate, and therefore "propositional," but it must never be supposed that biblical statements can contain or bottle up the Christ-light.

[126] 1 Cor 4:20; cf. 1 Thess 1:5. Deut 5:22ff. suggests something of the profundity of the response evoked when the word is combined with power and heard in the King's own voice.

[127] Cf. Calvin, *Institutes* I.ix.3; notice also the "both/and" in his definition of faith (III.ii.7), whereby together and at once, by virtue of the inner and outer objectivity of the word spoken, Christian knowledge comes to be grounded in reality. See *Theological Science*, 39f., where Torrance raises the necessary distinction (not division) between the Word that is heard—the *concretissimum*, in Barth's terminology—and the words used in its articulation.

[128] *Institutes* I.vi.1, vii.4, ix.3.

form and existence in order to meet and commune with the creaturely.[129] Though we cannot say that biblical words alone participate, yet because God has laid hold of them and spoken by them in such a way as to bind them together with Christ in and for the Church as the special servant of his revelation, they become the mediate standard and judge of every other statement or action which also is granted participation in Christ. God himself has established the Scriptures in this peculiar service as he calls all human speech and action into account before Christ. He has manifested them as the indispensable prism of his divine Light, which by grace shines through them in manifold array, for included in the fact of this array of Light as it strikes the eye is the fact of a carefully-constructed prism fully suited to both Light and beholder in their common worldly existence. Such

---

[129] Torrance (*Theological Science*, 148-50) provides both the terminology and the conceptual framework here, while discussing theological statements, not Scripture per se. It should be clearly noted that this involvement of the word of man in the Word of God is simply involvement with the Person of the Mediator, Jesus Christ. It is not helpful, in my judgment, to follow Barth in speaking of Scripture (and proclamation) as "another form of the Word of God," which will therefore admit of serious analogy to the unity of God and man in Jesus Christ (*Church Dogmatics* 1/2. 501; but cf. 512-13). Many non-Barthians, and especially inerrantists, also employ this analogy, if in a quite different framework and manner! What we are dealing with here is rather a *participation* of human words—sanctioned by God to this end—in the self-communication of the incarnate Word of God, a participation in which Christ does indeed still touch us even from his present hiddenness in the heavenlies. The words of Scripture, whether of Jesus or his spokesmen, are not the creaturely dwelling of the divine Word, nor do they become so in the sense we have in view; there is no *unio personalis* here, as both Barth and Berkouwer (cf. *Holy Scripture*, 196ff.) point out. They are simply the creaturely sound of the Incarnation in the natural form of human testimony. And as the Word of God himself sounds through these words, so that their creaturely intelligibility takes on the divine depth dimension which is their ultimate goal, they are but the opening of the Incarnation doorway through which we are drawn into the fellowship there taking place, having heard the "Welcome!" as it is pronounced by Christ on behalf of the Father in words the Spirit has chosen to use (see John 14). That event is, as it ever has been, the outward thrust of the communion between God and man that is grounded in the Incarnation into the divine harvest of humanity, in connection with the rational instrumentality of Scripture (which interpenetrates with the dramatic instrumentality of baptismal and eucharistic participation in Christ, and like these finds fulfillment only in a free act of grace). To be sure, in this event human words *partake* of the hypostatic relation between Christ's humanity and deity in mediating his Presence (Torrance, ibid., 148), for they are granted a role in the self-communication of him who in his own unity of Person, Act, and Word has permanently united himself to creaturely reality and to the speaking of just such words as these. That, if you like, is the mystery of Scripture, but then not so much of Scripture as of Christ.

participation of human words in the Lordship of the divine Word is an integral feature of the Incarnation, as I have said, implicating Scripture in the self-authenticating authority of Christ. Torrance points out concerning the Truth of God in Jesus that:

> It belongs to the nature of this Truth to be at once Person and Message, to be personal Being and yet communicable Truth. If it were only a communicated truth we would be thrown back upon ourselves to authenticate it, but if it were only a Person we would be thrown back upon ourselves to interpret Him. But because He is Person and Message in One, He is the Truth who both authenticates and interprets Himself.[130]

It may be said again, therefore, that the Church must always be prepared to confess Christ in terms which include a clear affirmation of Scripture, while affirming Scripture only in connection with the living Christ.[131] To do so is to allow the full impact of the Incarnation to prevent any limitation (i.e., usurpation) of Christ's Lordship through detachment of Person from Message or of "revelation" from the Person of God. These dichotomies, however varied the intent behind them and no matter where the emphasis is placed, progressively deposit everything into the breach they create, or rather into the breach between reality and the autonomous reason that insists upon them.[132] There is, in fact, but *one* obligation in view in the Church's confession of Christ the Word and of the biblical word of Christ: *obedience to the Christ of the Scriptures.* The Church recognizes both that all authority resides in Jesus himself, and that its knowledge of him is verbally mediated in and through canonical literature; it can afford no divorce here. The Scriptures

---

[130] Ibid., 147. In his most recent book, *The Mediation of Christ* (Grand Rapids: Eerdmans, 1984), Torrance speaks of the long construction process in which God labored to provide permanent structures of thought and speech about himself, "hammered out by the Word of God on the anvil of Israel," as he says, and committed to the Scriptures—apart from which "Jesus himself would have remained a bewildering enigma" (p. 28).

[131] "One must speak of the Christ *of Scripture*. Whoever dissolves this unity and thus divides the one true faith not only attacks the certainty of faith, but does so by suspending and secularizing the intent and meaning of faith in Scripture" (G. C. Berkouwer, *Holy Scripture*, 103. Cf. Luke 11:27–28).

[132] See Torrance, *Reality and Evangelical Theology*, 15ff., for the analysis of liberal and fundamentalist aberrations in these terms.

are thus known to have a genuine authority which nonetheless lies not in themselves, and not simply in the various realities to which they refer, but ultimately in the Light that shines through them. They have a derivative authority that is no less binding for being derivative, an authority by which they are constituted in their canonical status as the transparent medium of a Light that commands their every facet.[133]

What then will suffice in all this except to say that to stand under Christ is indeed to stand under the word of Christ in Scripture? Surely these two are but one posture where they are not mere posturing, where to stand under the Scriptures means to submit again and again to the living Lord who quickens them to penetrate mind and spirit with the Light and Truth of God embodied in himself. The many ramifications of this cannot be ignored. Considered from this point of view it will be apparent that the Scriptures are not a static intellectual authority but a focused witness, centered on Christ, and a functional witness, with a goal toward which they tend, namely, the knowledge of God in Christ. In that case we will often be found speaking with doctrinal and hermeneutical relevance of the *scopus* of Scripture, of the Mark or Object on which one fixes the eye through Scripture.[134] But in view of Christ's authority in

---

[133] Cf. Rev 19:9b–10. Scripture itself does not pass judgment on the rightness of our statements, actions, or motivations independently of Christ and in his place; that is not what is, or ought to be, meant when we speak of testing doctrine and life against Scripture. As Torrance puts it (ibid., 95): "In no way can the light of the Scriptures substitute for the Light of Christ, for they are entirely subordinate to his Light and are themselves light only as they are lit by his Light." We must not focus on the Scriptures as if they were Christ, but rather attend to that to which they direct us, especially himself. "This is not to resist or impugn the authority of the Holy Scriptures," he says (p. 135), "but on the contrary to let them serve the ultimate Authority of God himself. . . . Faith and certainty do not rest on biblical authority as such, far less on ecclesiastical authority, but on the solid truth that underlies all the teaching of the Holy Scriptures." Thus Christ remains the judge of Scripture's significance and of our understanding of it; as Kenneth Hamilton comments in *Words and the Word* (Grand Rapids: Eerdmans, 1971) 82, it is he, and not we, who must say what Scripture means.

[134] Greek: σκοπός, Phil 3:14 (the wording I have chosen here is taken from H. G. Liddell and R. S. Scott, *A Greek-English Lexicon*, rev. Henry Stuart Jones [Oxford: Clarendon Press, 1968]). See Berkouwer, *Holy Scripture*, 178f., who notes that in reflecting on the nature of Scripture's authority we ought to be concerned "with the fact that Scripture is not composed of a number of isolated words, theses, and truths expressed, but a centered witness" (i.e., to Christ). We should not then reject every differentiation between the character and claims of various Scriptures, for that rejection is not implied by a proper respect for

and through the Bible, we will speak also and unashamedly of the full scope and diversity of the scriptural witness in its capacity as an entirely compelling and *canonical* witness to the work of God in time and space. For Scripture serves to illuminate with uncompromising authority all those realities with which and in which Christ wishes to engage us. These realities may indeed outstrip their verbal pointers, but they do not outstrip the Authority with whom we have to do in Scripture. Nor do they turn to show themselves in such a way as to undo what he has already said about them: "Heaven and earth may pass away, but my words will never pass away."[135] We will therefore confess that the Church knows itself to be properly ordered by its Lord in thought and deed only when it stands under the biblical word as a word of unmitigated authority and constant relevance in Christ's self-interpretation for the world, and interpretation of the world in relation to himself. We cannot allow that any contrary word has properly entered into the true facts and order of the realities being addressed, for such a word has not responded to the Lordship of him who speaks in Scripture. It has failed to focus clearly on Jesus Christ.

All this must certainly be applied with full force to the problems that concern us in the debate about Scripture's trustworthiness within the Church's recent discussions on biblical revelation. If Scripture cannot be detached from Christ, it cannot be detached from his authority. If it cannot be detached from his authority, it cannot be detached from his reliability. Certainly one cannot produce an adequate answer to the question of biblical reliability, or properly address the doctrine of Scripture at all, without focusing first of all on the Person of Jesus Christ and on the will of the Spirit to make him known in and through the documents of Scripture. The Scriptures must never be loosed in any inquiry from their role as servants to Christ in the twofold movement of his revelation of the Father and his restoration of man and his world to the harmonious Truth of their Creator. Jesus Christ is the Word spoken in Scripture and

---

inspiration. Berkouwer adds: "The fear that this idea of goal . . . will lead to an arbitrary [form/content] dualism and to an attack on the authority of Scripture is not only based on a misunderstanding, but also contradicts the seriousness and depth of the biblical message."

[135] Matt 24:35.

the Word who speaks in Scripture, and what must be emphasized just here is that he cannot speak except out of his own lordly truthfulness, though he speak in ever so many ways and on ever so many occasions out of the humility of his painful identification with fallen man and through feeble spokesmen like his brethren, the apostles and prophets. Their word is his word, and his word has the right both to our attention and to our "amen." It is therefore a most serious thing to indulge in negative criticism of the Bible. As Berkouwer says, "one can never legitimately devaluate Scripture while intending to pay attention to the content of the message."[136] Or, we might say, one can never legitimately devaluate Scripture while intending to pay attention to Christ. The sanctity in which the human writings in the Bible have always been held by the community of faith, which openly confesses them as ἱερὰ γράμματα, duly recognizes their authoritative service as his message-bearers, as *God's* message-bearers. Failure to see that the Scriptures must be clearly distinguished from teachings and traditions taught by men on their own authority, and that they cannot be broken, stands rebuked by Christ himself.[137] History testifies that through the continual illumination of the same Spirit who inspired the Scriptures the Church has shared the attitude of Christ on this matter.

In this confidence and in this process lies the epistemological relevance of the Holy Scriptures, or more profoundly, of the doctrine of the Holy Spirit.[138] The Holy Spirit both *directs* man toward the objective Reality of God Incarnate (by means of a faithful inscripturated witness), and also *creates room* in man for Christ and his word (by a work of re-creation on the subjective pole of knowledge, man himself). As the Spirit of the Father and the Son he draws men into the articulate fellowship that the Son has with the Father, a fellowship that embraces the biblical word,[139] such that a man enters into true and confident knowledge of God and of the world in relation to him through the grace of God's own Presence in connection with Scripture.

[136] Ibid., 103.

[137] Matt 15:1–9. Thus we must recognize the indispensability of both the static and the dynamic senses (or aspects) of the commitment to Scripture as *Verbum Dei*.

[138] Cf. Torrance, *Theological Science*, 52ff.

[139] The significance of Luke 2:41ff., e.g., which recounts Jesus' early hungering after the Scriptures, should not be lost on us here.

Thus obtained, the knowledge of God in Christ calls forth the confession, "God speaks," and this is found on reflection not to differ at all from the longer version: "God speaks in Scripture." The Scriptures, in fact, are always present in one form or another where God speaks to man in the Spirit's witness to Christ, for the Scriptures are the means by which God sets us and keeps us in the Truth. This fundamental fact of biblical teaching and of experience with God then allows one of the most basic principles in the valid pursuit of knowledge to come clear, namely, that knowledge of self and of the world has come under the judgment and refinement of the Light of Christ through the active penetration of the biblical word. The knowledge of God and man and world that is opened to us in Christ through Scripture must be allowed to serve as the master-context of all other knowledge, for it is knowledge that finds immediate justification in God himself. At the same time it is important to note that this master-context in no way suggests an essentially deductive approach to knowledge or a preconceived authoritarianism; rather it provides a definite impetus toward open-ended growth and refinement of human knowledge in exploration not only of Scripture, but also of the cosmos and its history, which commands our respectful attention just because it has its existence in Christ and for his sake. In fact, biblical knowledge in the Spirit provides the most essential ingredients for human intuition and understanding in this task—an organic, "light-sensitive" coherence and confidence.[140]

We need not hesitate to point out that because this coherence is not founded in ourselves, but is ours in a living relationship with God shaped by the Scriptures, there is no self-destructive

---

[140] Ps 36:9; cf. Eph 5:13f. It is most unsatisfactory, however, when actual exploration of reality is supplanted by a mental reconstruction of the cosmos through the misuse of Scripture as servant to foundationalist procedures (need the name of Gordon Clark be mentioned here?). Science of every sort is then subjected to an abstract reasoning which is completely out of step with both science and Scripture, for these are intended to assist man in *discovering* the character of creation via the process of devoted personal involvement with it. Reality, in either its spiritual or material aspects and possibilities, cannot be known in any other way. Statements and propositions, whether biblical or otherwise, are like roadmaps—they are altogether unable to reproduce the road exactly or to substitute for the experience of traveling on it. They do, however, guide the traveler, and the biblical roadmap is altogether indispensable for real penetration of the cosmos and its meaning.

inadequacy in it, whether of finite relativity or of spiritual darkness. It leaves us with no fear of coherence-shattering contradictions in the universe itself, in the Scriptures, or between the two, for with Christ there is no self-contradiction. But neither is there any *self-security* in knowledge allowed us here, not even in the Scriptures, for all that is known or thought to be understood is constantly called into question by the radical authority of the God with whom we have to do and by the worldly realities which derive the authority of their existence from him. That is to say, Christian knowing is firmly founded in the personal Objectivity of the God who makes himself known in Christ, but our knowledge is constantly undergoing refinement in a process of individual and corporate maturation before God and the cosmos itself.

This admission leaves us with no empty promise or with the prospect of eventual loss of objectivity and clear direction, as some suppose, precisely because the Scriptures *are* God's canon and because they *serve* us as such. Because they stand before us in their creaturely objectivity as God's unalterable word of direction, and because they speak to us in God's own self-revelation, the relativity of our human knowing is constantly encountered and encircled, channeled and molded, by God himself. With such a footing we do not walk in the trackless wastes to which one is led by a methodology that would ascertain any aspect of reality in opposition to, rather than with the aid of, Scripture. Nor do we trifle with the word of God by adjusting it to our own procedures and conclusions by means of a self-directed hermeneutic. Scripture commands our unwavering regard as the unique Word of Truth. Though its priority does not negate our responsibility to any part of what is disclosed to us in the rest of our interaction with the world, it does serve the judgment as to whether or not disclosure has been properly achieved, and whether or not our methods (including our openness to the biblical texts) are adequate. If we proceed on the basis that the scriptural word and reality itself are always in harmony in Christ, then any apparent lack of harmony must be due to dullness in our hearing of Scripture or weakness in our present grasp of the realities concerned.[141] At all events, *Scripture*

---

[141] To know him in whom τὰ πάντα συνέστηκεν is indeed to realize that only in him and by his word can human thinking remain in touch with reality

cannot be gainsaid, for Christ cannot be gainsaid. Next to him we must always ask: "Where is the wise man? Where is the scholar? Where is the philosopher of this age?" For the foolishness and weakness of God, we are told, is wiser and stronger than human wisdom and strength.[142]

In dealing with these matters we need to keep in mind the point made earlier that man is both relativized and established by revelation. He is relativized by the absoluteness of the God who confronts him in Christ, and established by the messianic identification of God with man that results in concrete leadership and articulated direction in human knowledge and behavior. This means, with respect to the fundamental epistemological issues before us, that the relativized mind of man is obligated to Christ, for he is the Bond between the thinking subject's freedom to the truth and the compelling rule of the truth. He is such because he is the Truth of God for man and speaks what he hears from the Father, and in him no conflict between open integrity and unshakable verbal authority can be admitted. It means with respect to the Scriptures, if the Scriptures belong to Christ, that their role is a ruling role. Scripture, says Barth,

> must have unconditional precedence of all the evidence of our own being and becoming, our own thoughts and endeavours, hope and suffering, of all the evidence of intellect and senses, of all axioms and theorems, which we inherit and as such bear with us. . . . To try to hold together and accept *pari passu* both the testimony of the Bible . . . and the autonomy of our own world of thought, is an impossible hermeneutic programme.[143]

And on no account, it must be added, dare we think to avoid such conflicts as may arise by seizing Scripture in part or in

---

and consistently refrain from substitution of false interpretive principles which have a distorting impact on perception of reality. Human judgment is truly refined only as it taps οἱ θησαυροί discovered in Christ (Col 2:3), only when it learns to feel the pull of his gravity as it traverses creation. I am reminded here of one of Martin Heidegger's little sayings in *Poetry, Language, Thought* (by which, of course, he meant something quite different): "As soon as we have the thing before our eyes, and in our hearts an ear for the word, thinking prospers."

[142] 1 Cor 1:18–25.

[143] *Church Dogmatics* 1/2. 719, 721.

whole in order to shake loose a truer canon within or behind this canon. For to shorten the Shepherd's staff, as it were, to meddle with it at all, implies a denial of the Shepherd's hand upon that staff and a wandering from the Church's confession. The very fact and concept of canon forbids any such attempt and renders it self-contradictory.[144]

In the last analysis nothing is, or should be, more clearly recognized by the faithful than the absolute authority belonging to revelation, an authority that knows no boundaries either before or behind. The Scriptures' mediation of this authority is recognized in the fact that God speaks to the Church in Scripture, and the Church's testimony here resists every dismemberment and every attempt to weaken either the "God speaks" or the "in Scripture." It rejects every effort to liberate Christ from the word of his chosen spokesmen, or to seize the humanity of this word as if it were not the word by which man himself is seized and called to account. God in Christ has bound the Scriptures to himself, and the Church along with them. The Church does not stand under Christ because it has first found other reasons to stand under Scripture, nor does it stand under Scripture because it has found other reasons or means to stand under Christ. Rather, Christ reveals his own Lordship by speaking through this witness, constantly surrounding the Church with Speech from God's Throne, so to speak, with the care and concern of his own guidance and assurance. The Church echoes its "amen" by acknowledging the biblical canon and relying on its witness, and by conforming to the boundaries its Lord thus imposes on those who would make progress in the paths of truth.

Now the implications of all this to the inerrancy question are perhaps obvious, but not so altogether obvious as some

---

[144] Similarly, Hartmut Gese (*Essays on Biblical Theology*, trans. Keith Crim [Minneapolis: Augsburg, 1981] 32) remarks: "In the light of tradition history, it is nonsensical to try to find a so-called canon within the canon, a concept that completely contradicts the essence of the canon." Says Barth (*Church Dogmatics* 1/2. 517): "If in their concrete existence and therefore in their concrete speaking and writing the witnesses of revelation belong to revelation, if they spoke by the Spirit what they knew by the Spirit, and if we really have to hear them and therefore their words—then self-evidently we have to hear all their words with the same measure of respect." Berkouwer (*Holy Scripture*, 103) insists that "every reflection on Scripture and on the canon must terminate in the reminder of the danger of this canon's fading away. The danger is that we then, whether aware of it or not, would replace it with a canon of our own creation."

might imagine. At any rate, it is time to consolidate the efforts of the present chapter by speaking directly to some of the questions raised in earlier sections.

*   *   *

Conclusion to Part 1

The inerrancy question cannot be approached in a manner relevant to the Christian Church unless it is considered within the context of the Church's actual knowledge of Christ. The significance and authority of the Scriptures derive from no other fact than their service to his lordly Presence, so that any attempt to examine their character independently, or to answer this question in a fashion not understood to be a response to the divine Word who speaks in Scripture, must be regarded as entirely superfluous. This is what is meant by "working under the Word." But if Christ has bound the Scriptures to himself, and in the Spirit bound the Church to Scripture in its knowledge of him, indeed, if the Church knows only the Christ of the Scriptures and the Scriptures of Christ, then surely no answer to the inerrancy question can be countenanced that is not part of an overwhelming affirmation of the Bible's right to our allegiance. Such an answer would destroy the integrity of the Church in view of its acknowledged obligation to the divine Lordship revealed in Christ.

Of course, this means that we are already working under the biblical word in our very approach to the inerrancy issue, but it hardly means that we are working in a self-made circle. That charge is valid only in the case of those who are willing to divorce Scripture from Christ (or Christ from God!) and attempt a formal demonstration of biblical authority—it may be applied against both the classical method and rationalistic versions of "presuppositionalism."[145] The confessional method makes no such attempt; rather, it is beholding the lordly Reality who

---

[145] This charge is frequently bandied about with very little understanding, though it is most often found in use by adherents of the classical method against presuppositionalists. There is, in fact, an entirely necessary circularity underlying any valid penetration of reality, inasmuch as true thought is grounded in visionary fashion (extra-linguistically) according to the light of reality itself, and is only a reflection of that light. An *artificial* circularity exists wherever basic argumentation fails to recognize its utter dependence on this light (see Torrance,

claims the Church's allegiance, and noting that the way of his revelation is the way of his Voice in and through the biblical word. Quite properly, then, it regards the essential epistemological function of Scripture in Christian thinking as the drawing of every thought into captivity to Christ, such that all knowledge of reality must submit to the direction and refinement it receives in the believer's dialogical relationship with God.

With the autonomy of human thought laid to rest by the canonical service of Scripture to the articulate Presence of God, the broader terms of the inerrancy issue can also be laid to rest: the practical infallibility of the Bible cannot be an open question. That is the primary contribution of asking the inerrancy question epistemologically. A true hearing of Scripture and an adequate grasp of worldly realities will not reveal genuine contradiction if Scripture is the word of the Lord; we must therefore approach that which appears to generate real conflict (within the Bible or in connection with it) with the dissatisfaction of one who has failed to hear properly or to penetrate the realities involved. To shy away from this task is to open a gap

---

"The Framework of Belief"; also *Theological Science*, 34–36). The classical method falls prey to this artificiality despite the empirical ties it cultivates, because it refuses to rest finally on the grace-character of the Light of God in Christ, the ultimate Reality with which it is concerned; it prefers rather to rest Christ on its own arguments about a book. Its false circularity appears even on the surface when one observes that the infallibility of Scripture is actually derived directly from its "general reliability" (see n. 11 above), for on this approach the Christological foundation on which the argument pivots cannot be appealed to *in and through* Scripture *on its own irreducible ground*, but only *in* Scripture. The same problem faces the presuppositionalist, however, insofar as he rejects the "activist" distinction between the Word of God and the verbal objectivity of Scripture, attempting to lock up his case on the level of words and ideas, in conjunction with a fatal abstraction known as "the mind of God." Many valid insights, only inconsistently perceived with regard to their proper grounding, can be observed going astray at this point. Where Scripture *per se*, as a mere compendium of statements and concepts, is thought to be absolute and self-attesting, a false circularity must again be admitted. Thought cannot attest its own fundamental relation to reality, no matter how crucial its concerns or incoherent its contrary; it must be attested by the reality to which it bears witness. In the dialogue between these approaches a common dualist outlook evidently prevents each from grasping the other's point, while both stumble over the ultimate unmanageability of the Word of God and the sword of the Spirit. As Barth says, "the Bible must be known as the Word of *God* if it is to be *known* as the Word of God." Therein lies the proper circularity belonging to the doctrine of Scripture in conjunction with the doctrine of God and his grace; it is a circularity rooted in the present Reality of the revelatory Speech-Acts of God (see *Church Dogmatics* 1/2. 534f.; also Torrance, *Theological Science*, 50f.; *Reality and Evangelical Theology*, 16ff.).

between Christ and Scripture and to deny the verbal objectivity of his divine Lordship, which is to return altogether to the sphere of self-determination. This we cannot afford to do, if the Church is to remain the Church. The very foundation of the community of faith is built around the cornerstone of the verbal aspect of our Lord's Presence, and the rule of his Word cannot be separated from the canonical form already assimilated to it at Sinai. Scripture simply cannot be disengaged from the absolute intellectual authority belonging to the revelation of God in Christ.

Barth, of course, to whom I have more than once appealed, did take another tack here in the first volume of the *Church Dogmatics*. Though he spoke plainly of "the authority and normativity of Holy Writ," and though he would later write: "If we accept the witness of Holy Scripture, then implicitly we accept the fact that, quite irrespective of the way in which they were humanly and historically conditioned, its authors were objectively true, reliable and trustworthy witnesses"[146]—though he clearly asserted the need for subordination of our own thoughts and convictions in coming to Scripture and rejected any attempt to make distinctions within Scripture—he nonetheless argued that we ought not to vainly imagine an infallible Bible, "an idle miracle of human words which were not really human words at all." Rather, he said, we should come to the Scriptures in order to take part in the real miracle by which "they have still spoken the Word of God in their fallible and erring human word."[147] Now insofar as Barth was valiantly attempting to reassert the proper understanding of verbal inspiration as but one moment in the unbroken circle of revelation in the Spirit, insofar as he was stressing the sovereign grace of God's Word over against the naturalistic tendencies of even the most supranaturalistic orthodoxy of the post-Reformation period, we can applaud his boldness.[148] This boldness nonetheless carried him forward beyond the demands, indeed, beyond the

---

[146] 3/3. 201: " . . . It is not merely that we recognize their opinions to be good and pious, or appreciate their part and significance in religious history. We perceive rather that it pleased God the King of Israel, to whom the power of their witness is pledged as to the Lord, to raise up these true witnesses by His Word and work."

[147] See 1/2. 528ff.

[148] See 1/2. 514ff., where Barth discusses the "secularization of the whole conception of revelation."

allowances, of his own most important insights. By speaking of theological contradictions and uncertain traditions in the Bible one disrupts the real bond between Christ and the Scriptures determined by the Incarnation, not to mention the avenue of continuity between Christ and the community of faith in the knowledge of God. By insisting on the fallibility of the biblical witness one weakens the real bearing on human minds of the realities belonging to the Incarnation in its historical setting, and suggests as well a limitation to the practical Lordship of the reconciling and redeeming God over fallible and erring servants. This unnecessarily complicates the miracle of the Word of God, which remains no less a matter of grace for the inspired fitness of the prophetic and apostolic word as it points us to Christ.[149] Further, it can only cloud the witness of the Church. Precisely because incarnate Grace has determined to approach us by means of the biblical witness, we must not permit ourselves to posit any disjunction between the actualities involved in God's encounter with man and the biblical perception of same. That would be to neglect the entirely essential relationship between the verbal pointing, as the means of revelation, and the actual content concerned, the space-time Lordship of Christ. What such a view risks achieving is not the greater respect for sovereign grace that Barth was seeking, but rather a lessening of its impact and the establishment of a second stumbling block alongside Christ.[150]

---

[149] In other words, the doctrine of infallibility *need* not be associated with the secularization of Scripture and revelation, or the resisting of the sovereignty of grace; on the other hand, it *is* required if content and form are not to be ripped asunder in considering the miracle of the Word of God as heard in the words of weak human servants. But by "infallibility" I do not mean perfect inerrancy, and it is the sentiment and viewpoint there expressed against which Barth is actually directing his attack (see 1/2. 529). The idea of infallibility unfortunately seems for Barth to get caught up in the question of divine perfection over against human imperfection (cf. p. 508). Perhaps I should add that there is, so far as I can tell, some conflict in Barth's own statements on the question of establishing actual error in what the Bible has to say. In any case, in practice, as in the overall thrust of his comments, it would be difficult to distinguish his position from that of one holding to the sort of infallibility I am talking about. And certainly the underlying concerns he was working with in *Church Dogmatics* 1/2 continue to be relevant, though they could well afford to be balanced by the perspectives set out in his little essay, "The Humanity of God," and other later writings.

[150] Cf. Berkouwer, *Holy Scripture,* 209f., who appears to be taking issue with Barth. Note that on p. 265 he affirms the confession of Scripture's God-breathed infallibility, and adds that this "is not added to reliability as a miraculous novelty, but *coincides* with it" (emphasis mine).

We are at no risk of such an error if we faithfully maintain the genuine unity of the three senses in which *Sacra Scriptura est Verbum Dei*, if we refuse for any reason and at every point to divide between Christ and the Scriptures in our approach to either. When we acknowledge instead that the Scriptures, even in their human weakness, are the unfractured prism of God's Light, we make plain the fact that to stumble over Scripture is really to stumble over Christ as the Scriptures point to him, to reject his Light. Conversely, to be faithful to Scripture is to be faithful to Christ—which can mean nothing less than to be obedient![151] The oneness of allegiance to God and faithfulness to Holy Scripture has been known to the community of faith from its very inception; the infallible authority of Scripture is indeed a first-order doctrine. To abandon the intellectual aspect of this authority—"inerrancy" in its broader terms—to make the transition from the reliability of Scripture to its unreliability, in Berkouwer's words, would be a step entirely inimical to all genuine Christian theology. It would constitute ethical, as well as intellectual, rebellion against the Lordship of Christ in his dialogical relationship with the Church.[152]

When we come to the narrower terms of the inerrancy debate, however, the situation is far less clear. Certainly the Scriptures are fully reliable in their service to Christ. Certainly they point us to him accurately and without disfiguring distortion through every contribution of every passage. Certainly also they do this without so much as a hint of any anti-incarnational distinction between worldly truth and religious truth.[153] The

---

[151] This point found timely expression in Francis Schaeffer's final book, *The Great Evangelical Disaster* (Westchester, IL: Crossway Books, 1984) 61, 63. "It is *obeying* the Scriptures," he said, "which really is the watershed" (emphasis mine).

[152] See Berkouwer, *Holy Scripture*, 265, 209. Berkouwer recalls Bavinck's testimony to "the 'ethical significance' of the battle over Scripture carried on through all ages," in connection with the *skandalon* of Christ in which Scripture participates. I must concur with this serious view of the issue, and the reader will recognize that I am leaving many matters of dispute to the force of present considerations.

[153] Schaeffer and others have concerned themselves a great deal over this distinction, of course, and rightly so, though with questionable penetration of the real issues (even of basic matters like the relationship between subjectivity and objectivity). It is the Incarnation which renders such a distinction completely naïve, not to mention its contrariety to the very notion of canon and whatever else may count heavily against it in practical terms. "One of the most startling features about the Old Testament Scriptures is the way in which they

Scriptures speak truthfully about every worldly reality they choose to address in the service of divine revelation. How could they speak for Christ otherwise, and how could he speak through them in fulfillment of their witness to him? Christ does not fulfill that which leads us astray from himself, and his Presence among his people is always made known precisely in the concreteness of their temporal history. The straight does not fit the form of the crooked, nor the crooked the form of the straight; the Scriptures, which belong to Christ not in part but in whole, could never be anything other than the Word of Truth. With all of this we ought to agree. But does this mean total perfection in the biblical texts? Obviously not.[154] Does it mean the *total* absence of factual error? Not necessarily.

We must take seriously the *two-way* implications of the fact that glad submission to the revelation of divine Lordship is the only proper context for the asking of the inerrancy question, and that our one obligation is to this Christ of the Scriptures whom we have come to know. We must not seize Scripture in order to determine or defend its character in our own way, lest we set out on self-appointed agendas and battles which only distract us from the glory of God shining through it. If we come to Scripture in order to hear the living Word of God—or returning to Calvin's metaphor, in order to see Christ rather than merely to wear the biblical spectacles—we will be content to confess the character and rightness of these spectacles according to their actual purpose and function. The yardstick by which we measure Scripture will be the *scopus* of Scripture; its actual nature and dynamic in serving Christ will determine our description of it.

Once again, in view of what has already been said, this yardstick cannot be supposed to introduce distinctions into

---

represent the Word of God as becoming physically implicated with Israel in the very stuff of its earthy being and behaviour," remarks Torrance (*The Mediation of Christ*, 25).

[154] For then indeed they would not be human. A. Kuyper (*The Work of the Holy Spirit*, 64, 78) observes correctly that the Scriptures "show many seams and uneven places" and "in many aspects do not make the impression of absolute inspiration." But that does not matter. "The chief virtue of this masterpiece," he said, "was so to enfold God's thoughts in our sinful life that out of our language they could form a speech in which to proclaim through the ages, to all nations, the mighty words of God." Nevertheless, there are important implications here for the inerrancy issue which will bear further attention.

Scripture (i.e., to have an active, rather than a descriptive, function). We must continue to be quick in confessing the total Lordship of Christ in and through all of Scripture. But in asking what this Lordship requires of Scripture as direction to and from Christ, we are not called on to presume anything more or less than that the reader will never be *mis*directed. It would be very difficult indeed to maintain that a total absence of factual error is necessary in order for the Scriptures to fulfill their service, even in every textual nuance of that service. And the fact that the Holy Spirit has attracted and molded the words of malleable earthen vessels to the Truth of God in Christ displayed within the manifold truths of creation and history, and has therefore claimed these words as his own and marked their messages as both true and relevant for all of time, does not make it immediately self-evident that he has purified them from even the "innocuous inaccuracies"[155] common to the speech of men in virtually every sphere save mathematics. Such a conviction would have to be shown to have arisen from the biblical testimony itself, or from the absence of any evidence to the contrary in the text.

The narrower, debatable terms of the inerrancy issue certainly require careful qualification according to the restrictions determined by the divine Lordship of which the broader terms must speak; yet they cannot be supposed simply to merge with the broader terms. Unfortunately, the proper affirmation of Scripture belonging to the primary concern of the inerrancy question is often surreptitiously allowed to obscure legitimate problems within the narrower terms of the debate. The argument responsible for this might take the following syllogistic form:

Premise A: God is excluded from the class of beings who lie or err (John 17:17).
Premise B: All Scripture is spirated by God (2 Tim 3:16).
Conclusion: All Scripture is excluded from the class of literature which includes lies or error.

There is, of course, a certain validity to this argument. But alongside the tendency here to withdraw from the empirical

---

[155] Kuyper; see Berkouwer, *Holy Scripture*, 244f.

context of the text itself, there is also a problem in the second premise which requires the argument and its conclusion to be revised. The problem centers on the word "spirated," or rather on the Greek word θεόπνευστος, which I shall deal with in the next chapter. The real implications of this inerrancy argument go no further than the implications of θεόπνευστος, which is actually no further than the broader terms of the debate. The question concerning absolute errorless purity therefore still remains.

We must be careful in all this, as we have been warned from several quarters, to resist the temptation to canonize our own views about the canon. The narrower terms of the inerrancy debate ought to be acknowledged and viewed as second-order discussion, not as a watershed issue. Some have found it difficult to make this distinction, but it is nonetheless required if the Church's crucial confession of the Word of Truth is not to get bogged down in wrangling about words.[156] By now, of course, it is already clear how a doctrinal commitment to infallibility and an openness to alternatives regarding the accuracy of certain textual phenomena can be allowed to stand together, that is, how the broader and narrower terms of the debate can be maintained in their own integrity, yet successfully interrelated. When we are resting on the self-evidencing Lordship of Christ we are compelled to confess our full submission to Scripture, *but we are also freed from any concern about a grudging retreat from biblical authority.* Fear and defensiveness are removed, and a proper measure of openness therefore remains.

This is the secondary contribution achieved in asking the inerrancy question epistemologically. When it is Christ himself on whom we are resting and whom we are seeking to see and hear, we are able to show the utmost respect for the text by which he addresses us without taking offense at the marks of its humanness (which are only reminders of *incarnate* Grace). For, in any event, we are not concerned so much with the statements or words themselves, but with the realities to which they are

---

[156] It is unfortunate that Francis Schaeffer, for example, apparently did not pick up on the clue provided in his own reformulation of the Church's "watershed" issue (see n 151 above). Seeing Scripture in terms of its purpose and function provides for just such a distinction to be meaningfully held without jeopardizing the evangelical commitment to Scripture.

intended to direct us. And we would be very remiss, as Torrance makes plain in *Reality and Evangelical Theology*, to treat the statements by which revelation is mediated to us with a false and inappropriate sort of respect that unwittingly robs the living Christ of the absolute attention due him. This we might do by separating form from function and failing to regard the text at all times in terms of its service to Christ—an error naturally accompanying the dualistic epistemology underlying the main problems of the inerrancy debate.[157] But in that case it would not even be clear that there is anything to be gained or lost in the debate, for it is Christ himself who is, and who must be, all in all.

The doctrine of biblical authority must be focused, like every other doctrine, on the majesty of Jesus Christ. All Christian thinking is the outworking of the hearing of faith διὰ ῥήματος χριστοῦ,[158] and a first-hand recognition of his majesty. Thus,

---

[157] Wherever there is a tendency to divorce the empirical and the theoretical there is a natural tendency to lose sight of the actual dynamics of the object in view, either in its internal, character-constituting relations or in its external environment. This is especially dangerous where Scripture is the object of attention, in that it is a priestly document intimately related to Jesus himself, and as such is constitutionally bound up in a uniquely bidirectional movement between God and man, according to which it performs its canonical service and apart from which it cannot be comprehended. Observing the argument Carl F. H. Henry carries on with James Barr (see Henry's discussion of "functional authority" in *God, Revelation and Authority*, vol. IV [Waco: Word, 1979] 98ff.), it would appear that people on all sides of the inerrancy issue are capable of suffering from a sort of perspectival inertia that prevents them from recognizing the dynamic character of biblical authority. Certainly Barr need not fear that he has too much respect for the text (!), but he does need to come to grips with the formality that biblical authority takes on precisely in its mediation of Christ's ministry. On the other hand, once Scripture's canonical service to Christ is what chiefly occupies us in our regard for the Bible, we can indeed maintain "a more relaxed attitude" about infallibility, as Barr would have us do, without stepping out from under the tutelage of the text itself. That is, we can hold to infallibility without developing a fixation that gives "an infallible Bible and a set of rigid evangelical beliefs primacy over God's self-revelation which is mediated to us through the Bible" (Torrance's criticism in *Reality and Evangelical Theology*, 17). Such stagnation of biblical authority, formalized in terms of exhaustive inerrancy, tends toward bibliolatry. There is a warning for us here in Luke 4:14ff., where those who knew the Scriptures best and treated the scrolls with the greatest of dignity, were offended at the actual Lordship—so humble in form— of him for whom the scrolls existed. The demonized man, who also attended synagogue, expressed the prevailing attitude best of all: "Ha! What do you want with us, Jesus of Nazareth?"

[158] Rom 10:17.

even our thinking about Scripture must be carried out under the instruction and correction of the divine Word who makes himself heard just there and in that way. The posture of independent judgment must be eagerly abandoned as we confess the commanding Presence of Christ realized in the Church by the Spirit in connection with the biblical word. The importance of this unique foundation cannot be overestimated in responding to the inerrancy issue; on it depends the stability and practicality of our doctrine of Scripture and deliverance from the excesses at both poles of the current debate. The basic affirmation of full authority in Scripture arises here without the least hesitation or reservation, while no self-directed rigidity is necessary or appropriate in discussing textual problems. This is the double-edged implication of the Truth of Christ for the inerrancy debate. With incarnate Majesty as our foundation, in the true strength of an *a posteriori* confession, any trace of a Maginot-line mentality disappears. With the rejection of autonomy and self-sufficiency there is also a rejection of fear and insecurity. These are cast out together, for it is the vestiges of the former that introduce the latter into the believer's attestation of Scripture, comprising a double-mindedness that is not free to the rule of Christ—a double-mindedness that has meant in some cases a dangerous ignorance of the shield of faith, and in others, abandonment of the open field of the Christian calling for the narrow confines of an imaginary citadel. What is lacking either way is the appropriate insecurity of quite another sort: the humble recognition that we are to walk as those *constantly* called into account by our Lord.

With these things in mind, then, and with the parameters of faith clearly before us in canonical form as the Word of Truth under which we stand with complete confidence, we are free to explicate inerrancy in terms of its biblical reference points without any hidden agenda. We are free to handle honestly the data before us and to make such revisions within the narrower terms of the debate as may be necessary. It is time now to ask the inerrancy question exegetically, if you please, pointing out both certain questionable interpretations and some false inferences which have exaggerated the doctrine and propelled the discussion down the path of mere disputes about words.

Part 2
Disputing about Words

3 | Exhaustive Inerrancy: A Doctrine Not Addressed

A large portion of evangelicalism, particularly American fundamentalism, rests its case for the character and veracity of Scripture with the postulation of complete biblical inerrancy. It is in hopes of maintaining this position, or rather in fear of the consequences of failing to do so, that many become embroiled in disputes over the validity of the tiniest details of Scripture, regardless of their significance or insignificance. In these disputes the Church's focus is inevitably shifted to the words of Scripture and away from what Scripture actually has to say—making the length of Pekah's reign, as Clark Pinnock once put it somewhat hyperbolically, a matter of much greater concern than Paul's theology or Jesus' teaching.[1] That shift is highly detrimental, as is the thinking behind it, and the sharp disagreements to which it leads are not infrequently a cause for shame.

"Complete inerrancy" is perhaps not the best terminology here, for even that may be taken to say less about the nature of inerrancy than what is commonly intended. While various qualifications have been suggested to clarify what can be considered an error, of course, "exhaustive inerrancy" might better indicate both the nature and extent of the purity to which proponents of this position are committed on behalf of the biblical text. Essentially, Scripture is considered to be a body of information which, if analyzed into a series of propositions (both stated and derived), would contain no errors of any kind.[2]

---

[1] "The Ongoing Struggle Over Biblical Inerrancy," *JASA* 31 (1979) 72.

[2] "The vast majority of Fundamentalists and Evangelicals alike hold to a belief in the inerrancy of the Scriptures in their original autographs as the proper view of biblical inspiration. Most conservatives base their position on the teaching of the Scripture itself and trace the formulation of the plenary-verbal inspiration concept to the crystalization of that position by Warfield and the Princeton theologians of the nineteenth century. To Fundamentalists, the inerrancy of Scripture is ultimately linked to the legitimacy and authority of the Bible. We view the Bible as being God-breathed and thus free from error in all its statements and affirmations. To us the question of the inerrancy of Scripture was

This definition of inerrancy represents an unacceptable shortcut in the process of refining and explicating the doctrines of inspiration and infallibility. It does, however, involve a claim that the position is virtually demanded by Scripture's own statements, which would reverse this criticism. But such a claim has a very questionable foundation. I will therefore devote this chapter to an exegesis of the key texts to which appeal is commonly made in order to demonstrate that exhaustive inerrancy is no concern of those passages. In so doing, much of a positive nature will also be gained for our larger discussions.

2 Timothy 3:16

All Scripture is God-breathed and is useful for teaching, rebuking, correcting and training in righteousness. . . .

This is certainly the primary text in the minds of most, speaking as it does to both the origin and purpose of Scripture. Several things must be noted about this passage in order to ascertain its implications for the inerrancy question, and the key word here (θεόπνευστος, God-breathed) deserves a close examination, if the reader will bear with me for a few pages.

Perhaps it is unnecessary for present purposes to enter at any length the discussion over the attributive or adjectival function of θεόπνευστος, the lack of an article with γραφή, and the collective or distributive use of πᾶσα. That Paul's reference is to Scripture as Scripture can be granted here, that is, his meaning in context is clearly not "Scripture as a whole," nor could it possibly be "certain portions of Scripture, namely, those that are inspired." A. T. Hanson is conscious of the necessary sense of the passage when he says:

> To produce the meaning, "the whole Bible," one would have to have πᾶσα ἡ γραφή. Thus πᾶσα γραφή can mean only one thing here, "every passage of Scripture. . . ." From this it follows that we must prefer the translation: "Every passage of Scripture is inspired and is profitable. . . ." Admittedly there is nothing in either grammar or syntax to prevent us taking it as many editors

settled long ago"—Ed Hindson, "The Inerrancy Debate," *Fundamentalist Journal* 1 (1982) 25.

do: "Every inspired passage of Scripture is also profitable" . . . but considerations of sense must surely weigh against this. If the author wrote "Every inspired passage of Scripture is also profitable . . . ," he was implying that there could be an uninspired passage of Scripture, but this is precisely the view that he is opposing. He is claiming that every passage in Scripture is inspired and may therefore also be used for various purposes, paedagogic, apologetic, and devotional.[3]

θεόπνευστος, then, may certainly be understood to qualify Scripture per se. But when it is asked, "How exactly does it qualify Scripture?" the questions become more difficult. B. B. Warfield's *The Inspiration and Authority of the Bible* stands as a thorough and classic work in this area, but even his analysis does not answer the question satisfactorily.[4] By virtue of its monumental status it will provide a suitable basis for interaction throughout much of this chapter, however.

Warfield's discussion of θεόπνευστος is essentially a rebuttal of Cremer and Ewald in their attempts to achieve a sense for the word somewhat different from the traditional purely passive one. He discusses each of the word's rare early occurrences to demonstrate that the passive sense is always primary, with this conclusion:

> We cannot think it speaking too strongly, therefore, to say that there is discoverable in none of these passages the slightest trace of an active sense of θεόπνευστος, by which it should express the idea, for example, of "breathing the divine spirit," or even such a quasi-active idea as that of "redolent of God." Everywhere the word appears as purely passive and expresses production by God. . . .[5]

> If then, we are to make an induction from the use of the word, we shall find it bearing a uniformly passive significance, rooted in the idea of the creative breath of God.[6]

[3] A. T. Hanson, *Studies in the Pastoral Epistles* (London: S.P.C.K., 1968) 44. Hanson also denies that Paul might have meant to refer to every book of Scripture: "As Schrenk says: 'γραφή for a single book of the Bible is completely absent from the New Testament, though it is a very frequent usage in Hellenistic Judaism.'"

[4] B. B. Warfield, *The Inspiration and Authority of the Bible*, ed. Samuel G. Craig with an introduction by Cornelius Van Til (Philadelphia: Presbyterian and Reformed, 1970).

[5] Ibid., 272.

[6] Ibid., 275.

To say that there is not "the slightest trace" of an active sense may indeed be a little strong, but the evidence pointing in the general direction of Warfield's attention to the passive sense and to origin is not without force, as Ewald also apparently recognized:

> The main object of Ewald's earlier treatment of this passage, to be sure, was to void the word θεόπνευστος of all implication as to the origination of Scripture. By assigning to it the sense of "God-pervaded," "full of God's Spirit," he supposed he had made it a description of what Scripture is, without the least suggestion of how it came to be such; and he did not hesitate accordingly, to affirm that it had nothing whatever to say as to the origin of Scripture. But he afterwards . . . saw the error of his position, and so far corrected it as to explain that, of course, the term θεό-πνευστος includes in itself the implication that the words so designated are spoken by the Spirit of God or by men inspired by God—in accordance with what is repeatedly said elsewhere in Scripture, as, for example, in II Peter i.21—yet still to insist that it throws its *chief emphasis* rather on the nature than the origin of these words. And he never thought of denying that in the circles in which the word was used in application to Scripture, the idea of the origination of Scripture by the act of God was current and indeed dominant. Philo's complete identification of Scripture with the spoken word of God was indeed the subject under treatment by him. . . .[7]

Not content with Ewald's progress, Warfield furthers his case for the idea of origin by noting that "compounds of verbals in -τος with θεός normally express an effect produced by God's activity." He demonstrates this by adjoining a list of some 75 examples out of the 86 he found in the sixth edition of Liddell and Scott.

> If analogy is to count for anything, its whole weight is thrown thus in favor of the interpretation which sees in θεόπνευστος, quite simply, the sense of "God-breathed," i.e., produced by God's creative breath. . . . Surely there was no conception more deeply rooted in the Hebrew mind, at least, than that of the creative "breath of God. . . ."[8]

Warfield concludes, then, by saying:

[7] Ibid., 287.
[8] Ibid., 281–85.

From all points of approach alike we appear to be conducted to the conclusion that it [theopneustos] is primarily expressive of the origination of Scripture, not of its nature and much less of its effects. What is θεόπνευστος is "God-breathed," produced by the creative breath of the Almighty.[9]

All of this—a very brief condensation of Warfield's lengthy but well-known exegesis—is to demonstrate that his excellent foundation does not produce a fully satisfying description of theopneustos. Even if we grant that source constitutes the word's *primary* signification (a conclusion which needs some qualification), in what *way*, to what *extent*, and for what *purposes* is God the source of Scripture?

To demonstrate that these are not the idle questions of sheer obduracy, I would like to make further comments about this key word, theopneustos. To begin with, it is a New Testament *hapax legomenon*, and does not occur in the Septuagint. What is more, it may actually have been coined by Paul on this occasion. Whether Paul's use of the word is the earliest known usage depends on whether or not an excerpt in Plutarch from Herophilus (born ca. 300 B.C.) preserves his very words.[10] At any rate, we do not have the light of any powerful tradition back of the word. The strongest of associated etymological factors, perhaps, are the parallel compounds with θεός which were mentioned above. These may normally stress divine origin or divinely-produced result, but will not assist much further.

So far there is nothing to urge a very specific concept upon the reader, except that the adjective θεόπνευστος or God-breathed *appears* to be an appropriate construct for attaching the formation of the very words of Scripture to God himself. That, in fact, is just how the word is often understood, with obvious ramifications for the nature and application of the doctrine of inerrancy. But upon examining its other early occurrences, this thought is nowhere to be found. In the Plutarch reference it qualifies certain dreams; in Pseudo-Phocylides the reference is to "the speech of theopneustic *wisdom*;"[11] in the fifth book of the

---

[9] Ibid., 296.

[10] See ibid., 248–63; *Plutarch*, De Placitus Philosophorum (Moralia 904:2).

[11] See P. W. van der Horst, *The Sentences of Pseudo-Phocylides* (Leiden: Brill, 1978), 201–2. Note, however, that the reference may be an interpolation which actually refers to Scripture.

Sibyllines it refers to streams (the sources of the Kyme which serve the sibyl?) and to all theopneustic things (μέγαν γενετῆρα θεὸν πάντων θεοπνεύστων);[12] in the Testament of Abraham it modifies "ointments" (and, as Warfield observes, to some extent parallels the accompanying phrase σινδόνι θεοῦφαντῷ 'God-woven burial cloth').[13]

In his only partially successful endeavor to prove the purely passive sense of θεόπνευστος, Warfield in fact demonstrates in his own interpretation of these passages that the word maintains a certain ambiguity and may also be translated 'God-provided', 'God-pervaded', or simply 'divine'.[14] This is evident in looking at specifically Christian and later usages as well. Consider, for example, Nonnus's paraphrase of John 1:27, where he refers to Christ's sandals as theopneustic.[15] Or note Warfield's suggestion concerning the application of the word to a man: "What it would seem specifically to indicate is that he has been framed by God into something other than what he would have been without the divine action."[16] One might well ask whether this thought might suffice in 2 Tim 3:16. Admittedly, these usages can hardly be read back into Paul, but surely the point has been made that the word need not necessarily be understood as "spirated" in the sense of phonetic speaking activity, and that the idea of nature is clearly in view along with that of origin.

Concerning the supposed intimate connection between God and every individual word of Scripture, however, the thought of Philo on inspiration must be taken into account. Warfield quotes this admission even from Ewald:

> It is certainly undeniable that the new expression θεόπνευστος . . . is intended to say very much what Philo meant, but did not yet know how to express sharply by means of such a compressed and strong term. . . . This term includes in itself the implication that the words are *spoken by the Spirit of God,* or by those who are inspired by God. . . .[17]

---

[12] See Eduard Schweizer, "Θεόπνευστος," *TDNT* 6, 454.
[13] *Inspiration*, 268.
[14] Ibid., 266-71.
[15] See ibid., 269 (Warfield includes the Greek text).
[16] Ibid., 271.
[17] Ibid., 279; citing Ewald, *Jahrbuch für biblische Wissenschaft*, 9, 91.

After touching on Philo's "complete identification of Scripture with the spoken word of God," Warfield notes with disapproval Cremer and Holtzmann in their differing attempts to find a less extreme view of Scripture in the New Testament (though Holtzmann admits a Philonian concept of inspiration in 2 Tim 3:16, but denies the epistle's Pauline origin). Warfield was of the opinion that

> whatever minor differences may be traceable between the general New Testament conception and treatment of Scripture and that of Philo, it remains a matter of plain fact that no other general view of Scripture than the so-called Philonian is discernible in the New Testament, all of whose writers . . . consistently look upon the written words of Scripture as the express utterances of God, owing their origin to his direct spiration and their character to this their divine origin.[18]

A. T. Hanson adds his voice to the Philo connection, recalling that in *Die Pastoralbriefe* by Martin Dibelius (revised by H. Conzelmann) it is "shown clearly" that the phrase ἱερὰ γράμματα (2 Tim 3:15) comes from Philo, being his "regular method of referring to the LXX."[19] As for θεόπνευστος, he says:

> we can say with confidence that though Philo does not use it, it exactly expresses Philo's idea of the relation of Scripture to the authors of Scripture. What theopneustos implies is that the author of Scripture is possessed by God and therefore what he writes is inspired by God.[20]

He notes Philo's use of words such as καταπνέω and ἐνθουσιάζω for inspiration, together with his descriptions of the prophets, such as this of Samuel: " 'not really on the human plane at all, but somehow possessed and mastered by the divine frenzy.' "

---

[18] Ibid., 288–89. Following is a selection from Philo: "Now with every good man it is the holy Word which assures him his gift of prophecy. For a prophet (being a spokesman) has no utterance of his own, but all his utterance came from elsewhere, the echoes of another's voice. . . . The name only befits the wise, since he alone is the vocal instrument of God, smitten and played by His invisible hand," *Philo*, vol. 4, Rev. Div. Her., 259; trans. by F. H. Colson and G. H. Whitaker, The Loeb Classical Library (London: William Heinemann and Cambridge, MA: Harvard University, 1953) 417.

[19] See Hanson, *Studies in the Pastoral Epistles*, 42.

[20] Ibid., 45.

And this of Moses: "'He became possessed by God, being inspired (καταπνευσθείς) by the Spirit which usually visited him, he uttered oracles (θεσπίζει) and prophesied. . . .'"[21] A similarly radical comment found in Origen might be mentioned as well. Warfield, in adducing several quotations from the fathers in his discussion of the passive significance of θεόπνευ-στος, includes this unusually extreme example:

> But if "the words of the Lord are pure words, fired silver, tried as the earth, purified seven times" (Ps. 2:7) and the Holy Spirit has with all care dictated them accurately through the ministers of the Word [μετὰ πάσης ἀκριβείας ἐξητασμένως τὸ ἅγιον πνεῦμα ὑποβέβληκεν αὐτὰ διὰ τῶν ὑπηρετῶν τοῦ λόγου] let the portion never escape us, according to which the wisdom of God is first with respect to the whole theopneustic Scripture unto the last letter . . ."

(whereupon Origen makes reference also to Matt 5:18).[22]

But surely there is something not quite right in this consensus concerning a Philonian concept of inspiration in 2 Tim 3:16. First, what modern scholar is satisfied with an interpretation that imposes either a dictation theory or an "unconscious instrument" theory on the whole of Scripture? And we must remember that all of Scripture is precisely what Paul is dealing with here. Second, the Scriptures do not support such an idea elsewhere, nor do they offer any suggestion that inspiration entails but a single mode. Third, Hanson himself mentions Schrenk's suggestion that in primitive Christianity the writers' personalities were emphasized more than in Judaism, with Jeremias going even further to draw a distinction between Palestinian Judaism and the Diaspora (as represented by Philo).[23] Fourth, even Philo apparently recognized *some* distinctions in biblical materials and corresponding modes of inspiration behind the prophet who delivered the material.[24] At any rate, we should insist that

---

[21] Ibid., cf. 44–45. These particular references may be found in the Loeb Classical Library: *Philo*, vol. 5, De Somniis I:254, 429; and *Philo*, vol. 6, De Vita Mosis II:250, 575.

[22] *Inspiration*, 274.

[23] Hanson, *Studies in the Pastoral Epistles*, 46.

[24] "Of the divine utterances, some are spoken by God in His own Person with His prophet for interpreter, in some the revelation comes through question and answer, and others are spoken by Moses in his own person, when possessed

Philo and Origen (and any in their camp) have discredited their conclusions in these matters through imaginations untempered by Scripture itself, and that their views should not be read into the biblical text.[25]

Clearly we require another perspective on the term θεόπνευ-στος. Perhaps we can find a clue to its significance in Job 32:8 and 33:4, where the Septuagint employs similar terminology: πνοὴ δὲ παντοκράτορός ἐστιν ἡ διδάσκουσα ('the breath of the Almighty is that which teaches'). The reference is to the Spirit of God as the Teacher of wisdom to the creature made in his image.[26] The notion of the Spirit as the Giver of special gifts of

---

by God and carried away out of himself. The first kind are absolutely and entirely signs of the divine excellences, graciousness and beneficience. . . . In the second kind we find combination and partnership: the prophet asks questions of God about matters on which he has been seeking knowledge, and God replies and instructs him. The third kind are assigned to the lawgiver himself: God has given to him of His own power of foreknowledge and by this he will reveal future events. Now, the first kind must be left out of the discussion. They are too great to be lauded by human lips. . . . Besides, they are delivered through an interpreter, and interpretation and prophecy are not the same thing. The second kind I will at once proceed to describe, interweaving with it the third kind, in which the speaker appears under that divine possession in virtue of which he is chiefly and in the strict sense considered a prophet," *Philo,* v. 6 (De Vita Mosis II:188-91; 543). Philo's most extreme comments are generally found in a context dealing with predictive prophecy (cf., e.g., De Specialibus Legibus I:64-65; vol. 7, 137).

[25] "For when the light of God shines, the human light sets. . . . This is what regularly befalls the fellowship of the prophets. The mind is evicted at the arrival of the divine Spirit, but when that departs the mind returns to its tenancy. Mortal and immortal may not share the same home"—*Philo,* vol. 1, Rev. Div. Her., 264-65. This is entirely out of step with Paul's pneumatology (cf. 1 Corinthians 2, Romans 8, etc.). Kleinknecht makes this assessment: "The NT, though not unacquainted with enthusiastic spiritual phenomena, judges these and all kinds of μανία critically by consciously avoiding the religious vocabulary which profane Greek customarily uses in general synonymity with πνεῦμα [so also Philo]. . . . Only in the apologetic and post-apologetic writings are the Greek expressions again used in Christian statements about the Spirit (πνεῦμα, *TDNT* 6, 358-59). See also Schweizer, "Θεόπνευστος," 454-55.

[26] Cf. Robert Gordis, *The Book of Job* (New York: The Jewish Theological Seminary in America, 1978) 367; Marvin H. Pope, *Job* (AB; Garden City: Doubleday, 1965) 212. Pope comments: "The spirit of God gives both life, xxvii 3, xxxiii 4; Gen ii 7, and wisdom, or any special ability . . . ." Note also Job 35:10-11, 36:3-4, 22—"God is exalted in his power. Who is a teacher like him?" The Job references make clear that the breath of God has the very broadest associations as the life-giving and energizing Power behind human existence and human accomplishments; there is nothing fixed or narrow in the notion of the Spirit as quickening Agent, and nothing specifically verbal or phonetic in the idea of the "breath" of God, though a clear focus is maintained on the

wisdom is common in the Old Testament, surfacing explicitly with reference to such diverse figures as Bezalel, Daniel, and the messianic King; it is even more pronounced in the intertestamental period.[27] The same association finds frequent expression in the New Testament, especially in Paul,[28] and it is just this connection which highlights the logic of 2 Tim 3:13-17: the sacred writings are able to give us wisdom because they are the product, not of evil men and imposters, but of men taught by the Spirit; they are theopneustic because it is the *wisdom of God* which their authors have learned and expressed under the tutelage of the Holy Spirit, whose ministry in such things Paul acclaims in 1 Cor 2:12-13.[29] θεόπνευστος describes the documents themselves in just the connection that θεοδίδακτος (also Pauline terminology) might describe the men who write them. The allusion to the creative Breath of God should not be understood with a literalistic bent, as bearing on the sphere of biblical phonetics or the spiration of words as such. It is far more plausible to understand it as a reference to the personal teaching ministry of the Spirit that accounts for the actual content and

---

thought of God's wise instruction (cf. Job 33:14ff.). Job 32:7-8 reads as follows in the Hebrew text:

אָמַרְתִּי יָמִים יְדַבֵּרוּ וְרֹב שָׁנִים יֹדִיעוּ חָכְמָה
אָכֵן רוּחַ־הִיא בֶאֱנוֹשׁ וְנִשְׁמַת שַׁדַּי תְּבִינֵם

Job 33:4 reads:

רוּחַ־אֵל עָשָׂתְנִי וְנִשְׁמַת שַׁדַּי תְּחַיֵּנִי

while the LXX has Πνεῦμα θεῖον τὸ ποιῆσάν με, πνοὴ δὲ παντοκράτορος ἡ διδάσκουσά με.

[27] See Exod 31:3, Isa 11:2, Dan 5:11-12—"There is a man in your kingdom who has the spirit of the holy gods in him. In the time of your father he was found to have insight and intelligence and wisdom like that of the gods." Cf., e.g., Wis Sol 7:24-27—"For wisdom is . . . the breath of the power of God [ἀτμὶς γάρ ἐστι τῆς τοῦ θεοῦ δυνάμεως], and a pure influence flowing from the Almighty. . . . And in all ages entering into holy souls, she maketh them friends of God, and prophets" (*The Septuagint Version with Apocrypha: Greek and English*, trans. Charles Lee Brenton [Grand Rapids: Zondervan, 1978]). See also 7:15-16, 9:17: "And your counsel who has known, except you give wisdom and send your Holy Spirit from above?" The author of Wisdom does get rather carried away, abandoning canonical restraint for his own variety of wisdom speculation, but for better or worse there was a growing identification between Spirit and wisdom; see J. Coert Rylaarsdam, *Revelation in Jewish Wisdom Literature* (Chicago: University of Chicago, 1946).

[28] See, e.g., Acts 6:3, 1 Cor 12:8, Eph 1:17.

[29] "We have not received the spirit of the world but the Spirit who is from God, that we may understand what God has freely given us. This is what we speak . . ." (see below, pp. 109-11); cf. 2 Pet 3:15-16: "our dear brother Paul also wrote you with the wisdom that God gave him."

wisdom of these documents, and for their ability to lead us into a right relationship with God.[30]

It is time now to stress emphatically what has begged to be heard from the beginning. Especially in discussing a *hapax legomenon*, "context is king." Paul himself provides the only sure elaboration of the significance of being theopneustic, namely, that the theopneustic writing is thereby unfailingly profitable. Paul is interested in the purpose and function of Scripture. He guarantees its quality and satisfactory performance by appealing to its divine origin, but his main point overall remains its effective function. The appeal to origin serves to preclude a *deceptive* function or *misleading* result. A semantic analysis may assist here, as an abbreviated means of displaying the contextual development of his statement:[31]

13a	Evil men and imposters will go from bad to worse	
b	[They will be] deceiving	- *Manner of 13a*
c	and being deceived	- *Manner of 13a; Complex cause-effect with 13b*[32]
14a	But you abide in the things you learned	- *Contrast to 13a; Conclusion of 14c, 15a*
b	and became convinced of	- *Comment on 'things learned'*
c	Remembering from whom you learned them	- *Grounds for 14a*
15a	[Remembering] that from childhood you have known the sacred writings	- *Grounds for 14a*
b	They are able to make you wise for salvation	- *Comment on 'writings' (collectively)*[33]
c	through faith in Jesus Christ	- *Manner of 15b*
16a	Every passage of Scripture is theopneustic	- *Reason for 16b*

[30] "The adjective *theopneustos* . . . does not imply any particular mode of inspiration, such as divine dictation. Nor does it imply the suspension of the normal cognitive faculties of the human authors. . . . The sacred Scriptures are all expressive of the mind of God; but they are so with a view to their practical outworking in life" (Colin Brown, "Scripture, Writing," *NIDNTT* 3 [Grand Rapids: Zondervan, 1978] 491).

[31] For explanation of this method of analysis, see John Beekman and John Callow, *Translating the Word of God* (Grand Rapids: Zondervan, 1974) 281–312. The following is a modified application for a narrower purpose.

[32] I.e., there is a two-way relationship here, such that each is in part a result of the other.

[33] The semantic relations in v 15 are somewhat complex and difficult to determine with certainty. I have avoided some of the questions in this simplified construction (as elsewhere in the present analysis).

b	They are profitable for teaching reproof, correction, training in righteousness	- *Comment on 'writings' (distributively)*; *Result of 16a; means of 17a*
17a	So that the man of God may be adequate	- *Purpose of 16b (and 14a)*[34]
b	equipped for every good work	- *Explanation of 'adequate'*

This sketch of course is subjective in part, but it will suffice to establish the contextual flow. The comments on the value of the Scriptures (15b, 16b) underline Timothy's experience with them, and support the admonition (14a) to stick by the Christian teachings which have grown out of them in response to the Christ-event. The recognized texts of the community of faith are offered as preventive medicine in facing conditions outside and on the fringes of that community (13); the facts of v 16 make possible effective abiding (17). That Scripture is God-breathed ensures its *relevance* (it is profitable) and its *reliability* (for teaching and correction). It is this nature of Scripture as profitable and reliable that allows it to function as a weapon in the struggle against the deception of ungodly men. It is evident that it is not the *mode* of production, then, but simply the *fact* of the product's divine Source and Superintendent that is in view here in the assertion that Scripture is theopneustic. Ungodly men, who pursue knowledge only on their own and for their own ends, will be ever learning and never able to arrive at the truth (7, 13). The man of God, on the other hand, will abide and make progress in the truth—a dynamic concept involving the man and his lifestyle, not just his intellect (9-10)—because his understanding is grounded in the knowledge which the Spirit delivers to him in the Scriptures. The full quality of every passage *as a contribution to teaching, rebuking, correcting and training in righteousness* is guaranteed in that they are all provided by God for that purpose. Nothing more or less is told us here. In interpreting this passage, we cannot loose θεόπνευστος from its bond with ὠφέλιμος, nor ὠφέλιμος from its bond with θεόπνευστος.[35]

[34] I.e., this is the purpose both of the inspiration which shaped the Scriptures and of the activities appropriate in their employment. It should be noted here that everything following v 15a remains part of the grounds for the instruction given in v 14a.

[35] Edward W. Goodrick, writing in the silver anniversary issue of the *Journal of the Evangelical Theological Society* ("Let's Put 2 Timothy 3:16 Back

With these things in view, we may still say that Warfield is partially correct when he concludes that "we appear to be conducted to the conclusion that [θεόπνευστος] is primarily expressive of the origination of Scripture. . . ." But he is misleading when he jumps without justification to what appears to be a modal predication that the Scriptures owe their origin "to God's direct spiration."[36] He speaks much more appropriately when he says of 2 Tim 3:16: "In a word, what is declared by this fundamental passage is simply that the Scriptures are a divine product, without any indication of how God has operated in producing them."[37] Of course, in making this admission Warfield would still defend the use of "direct spiration" as a figure to completely identify the very words of Scripture as words spoken by God. To do this, he turns (as do most) to other passages for support. Indeed he must, for of the threefold question asked concerning inspiration: "In what way, to what extent, and for what purposes is God the source of Scripture?," only the last appears to find a full answer in this passage or in the word itself. The second receives only a partial—though very important—answer (πᾶσα γραφή), and the first, no answer at all.

2 Peter 1:21

For prophecy never had its origin in the will of man, but men spoke from God as they were carried along by the Holy Spirit (ὑπὸ πνεύματος ἁγίου φερόμενοι ἐλάλησαν ἀπὸ θεοῦ ἄνθρωποι).

---

in the Bible," *JETS* 25 [1982] 486), makes a similar point: "When I emphasize the fact that the whole sentence hinges on *ōphelimos* I most certainly do not want to leave the impression that I see no role for *theopneustos*. The word is there, but it serves *ōphelimos*."

[36] *Inspiration*, 296, 289. The admission that the focus is on Scripture's origin, by the way, does not mean that we must reject Barth's insistence that the discussion of *theopneustia* per se cannot be limited to the (admittedly important) point in the circle of revelation where the biblical word emerges. We can still agree that the doctrine of inspiration must rather *in the final analysis* be a consideration of the free grace whereby Scripture is "given *and* filled and ruled by the Spirit of God," actively outbreathing and spreading abroad the knowledge of God (cf. *Church Dogmatics* 1/2, 504, 517; emphasis mine). Thus we can also listen much more sympathetically to Ewald and Cremer than does Warfield. In any case, the attachment of θεόπνευστος to ὠφέλιμος demands that we consider source, quality, and function all at once in our regard for Scripture, and that we deduce nothing from or about one of these that is not called for by the others.

[37] Ibid., 133.

What does this passage add to the understanding of inspiration as it might bear on inerrancy? Michael Green finds it interesting that

> in this, perhaps the fullest and most explicit biblical reference to the inspiration of its authors, no interest should be displayed in the psychology of inspiration. The author is not concerned with what they felt like, or how much they understood, but simply with the fact that they were bearers of God's message. The relative parts played by the human and divine authors are not mentioned, but only the fact of their cooperation.[38]

It can be agreed that no discussion of the psychology involved is to be found, and while some prefer to emphasize that men spoke in cooperation with the Holy Spirit, others make a point of the Spirit's activity in bearing them along. The point of the passage is certainly with the latter emphasis, though no evidence is given to warrant connection with the mindless instrumentality postulated by Philo and connected with certain pagan prophecies (or even with unusual biblical examples like that in the Saul narratives). As in the previous passage, it is simply a matter of causing the profitability and reliability of the biblical word to stand out in connection with its divine origin against the doubts and perversions of false teachers. Nonetheless, a brief discussion of the significance of φερόμενοι and the reference of the previous verse to προφητεία γραφῆς is in order here.

On φερόμενοι Warfield remarks:

> It is not to be confounded with guiding, or directing, or controlling, or even leading in the full sense of that word. It goes beyond all such terms in assigning the effect produced specifically to the active agent. What is borne is taken up . . . and conveyed . . . to the "bearer's" goal, not its own.[39]

Timothy Phillips, for one, writing in the *Journal of the American Scientific Affiliation*, criticizes this "rigid interpretation" of φερόμενοι. He notes that the meaning of the word "normally extends far beyond Warfield's restrictive interpretation to include figurative senses—for instance, those implying mere guidance,

---

[38] Michael Green, *The Second Epistle General of Peter and the General Epistle of Jude* (TynNT; Grand Rapids: Eerdmans, 1976), 91.
[39] *Inspiration*, 137.

direction or leadership."[40] A quick glance at the *Theological Dictionary of the New Testament* or a lexicon will confirm the word's broader potential, though Phillips' use of "normally" seems odd, and the force of the passage remains, perhaps, with the stricter sense (especially in view of the τοῦτο πρῶτον with which Peter introduces his statement).[41] In any event, Phillips appears to overlook the larger context when he argues for a mere guidance that produces sufficient, if dim, light for the path. This hardly suits Peter's attention to central messianic prophecies respecting both advents of Christ.

On the contrary, Warfield was correct, I believe, in postulating a further special divine activity here, while also pointing to the universality of the providential government of God and to the fact that within this providence "the production of Scripture is . . . a long process, in the course of which numerous and very varied divine activities are involved. . . ."[42] Certainly, to Peter or to any Jew of sincere faith, the prophetic word was never a matter for doubt *for the very reason* that men spoke *from God*.[43] And surely the detailed messianic prophecies fulfilled in Christ's

---

[40] "The Argument for Inerrancy: An Analysis," *JASA* 31 (1979) 82.

[41] BAGD analyze φέρω into four semantic fields: (1) bear, carry—a. lit.; b. fig. (e.g., the bearing of sin); c. endure; d. bring along; (2) bear, produce (lit. and symb.); (3) move out of position, drive, and pass. of same—a. lit., by the wind; b. fig., of the Spirit [here they include 2 Pet 1:21b]; (4) bring (on), produce—a. fetch a thing, utter a word; b. bring or lead people (e.g., "they brought Jesus to the place called Golgotha"). LSJ (pp. 1922-24) provide a more extensive breakdown, with additional categories or subcategories that include these: (1) to bring or carry with one, involve; (b) to give one's vote, appoint or nominate, pass.—enroll (φερομένου μοῦ ἐν τῇ συνοχῇ, "since I am [enrolled] in prison"), med.—choose, adopt (ταύταν φ. βιοτάν); (c) to carry off (e.g., booty), gain, win; (d) to lead or stretch toward (i.e., of a road or tract of land) and metaph.—to lead or tend to an end or object, to point or refer to, to incline. On the passive, LSJ have: "Pass. is used in most of the above senses:—special cases: *to be borne* or *carried* involuntarily; esp. *to be borne alone by* waves or winds, *to be swept away* . . . ; simply, *move, go*. . . ." (Neither listing is exhaustive.) BAGD thus favor Warfield's stronger rendering, but LSJ indicates a wide variety of metaphorical usages that might allow for the more flexible idea of choosing, inclining, leading. Nonetheless, it is primarily a matter of degree, and the force attributed to it by Warfield reads well and suits the context. Given the conscious, cooperative element in the work of God's prophets, however, the "bearing" need not take on a mechanistic character. A play on words should perhaps be considered as well, φερόμενοι being suggested by ἠνέχθη.

[42] *Inspiration*, 154-58.

[43] This despite its being "made more certain" in the actual light of its fulfillment in Jesus Christ (1:19). On the translation of βεβαιότερον see Joseph B. Mayor, *The Epistle of St. Jude and the Second Epistle of St. Peter* (reprinted;

first coming, for example, cannot be imagined to have been mere insight, no matter how providential.

Warfield, however, was probably wrong in not distinguishing the additional divine involvement he had in mind from the general requirements for the creation of theopneustic literature—regarding which the weaker sense of φέρω might indeed be adequate in a variety of material without in the least diminishing the verdict: ἀπὸ θεοῦ. In fact, Warfield has not given the context its due either, in assuming that the present reference to προφητεία γραφῆς (and the bold sense of φέρω suggested here) was meant to be understood distributively as addressing the origin of any and all Scripture. One ought to recognize the particularity of Peter's focus on the Christ-event, and on the second coming and its practical implications, bearing in mind the parallel in 1 Pet 1:10–12, where this restricted interest is exceedingly plain in his reference to the prophets.

In any case, even the bolder interpretation of φερόμενοι in no way necessitates a view of inspiration that is happily expressed by the imagery of God's direct spiration of every word of the text; rather, it accords well with a moderate view such as the one being developed in this study. The prophets are carried along by the Spirit as they speak so that we too may be guided and carried along by the Spirit as we receive their messages and live out the truth of which they speak. A firm but simple concern for the genuineness of the biblical word much more readily answers to Peter's assertion about the "bearing along" than does any fanciful application to the interests of exhaustive inerrancy.

Matthew 5:18

"I tell you the truth, until heaven and earth disappear, not the smallest letter, not the least stroke of a pen, will by any means disappear from the Law until everything is accomplished."

Wishing still to defend exhaustive inerrancy exegetically, some would turn to Matt 5:18 for support. But this verse should be understood simply as a hyperbolic figure; the smallest letter

---

Minneapolis: Klock & Klock, 1978) 107f.; on the sense of the passage cf. Paul J. Achtemeier, *The Inspiration of Scripture: Problems and Proposals* (Philadelphia: Westminster, 1980), 108f.

or stroke refers to that which appears least significant and easiest to avoid. (Taken literally, this phrase would place the entire matter on the level of textual criticism, an altogether absurd thought!) Christ explains his meaning in the following verse: the insignificant letter or stroke represents the sanctity of each and every commandment as a functional part of the Mosaic covenant. The commandments were in no sense to be relativized or dismissed, being divinely ordained even to the least of them; yet this was something even the Pharisees had attempted to do (cf. Mark 7:13). This passage does have some relevance to the consideration of Paul's statement in 2 Tim 3:16, but not as an elaboration of it. It serves rather as an illustration, indicating the sanctity of πᾶσα γραφή down to its smallest instruction.

"The Holy Spirit says . . ."

Turning to a group of passages with more serious potential to help refine the concept of inspiration and indicate its bearing on the inerrancy construct, it becomes evident that there *are* verses suggesting a direct identification of scriptural statements as the words of God. Under the rubric " 'It says:' 'Scripture says:' 'God says:' " Warfield lists many such passages and divides them into two primary classes, with this comment:

> . . . together, they make an irresistible impression of the absolute identification by their writers of the Scriptures in their hands with the living voice of God. In one of these classes of passages the Scriptures are spoken of as if they were God; in the other, God is spoken of as if he were the Scriptures; in the two together, God and the Scriptures are brought into such conjunction as to show that in point of directness of authority no distinction was made between them.[44]

Leaving aside Warfield's ill-advised language and the charge of bibliolatry he unnecessarily invites, we ought to applaud his insistence that the Scriptures cannot be separated from the authority of God. But we must ask whether this particular biblical device for recognizing that fact implies that every individual word and detail contained in Scripture is a verbalization belonging to the perfection of truth in the mind of God. Once

[44] *Inspiration*, 299.

again it would be very difficult to show that any such extended, mechanical correspondence is in view. Certainly the typical examples mentioned by Warfield do not involve the sort of material that would even raise such considerations—e.g., "You spoke by the Holy Spirit through the mouth of your servant, our father David: 'Why do the nations rage and the peoples plot in vain?'" or "So, as the Holy Spirit says: 'Today, if you hear his voice, do not harden your hearts . . .'"[45]—they are prophetic words, interpretive words, rhetorical and sermonic words. And perhaps we ought to keep in mind the similar idea in our Lord's promise to his disciples: "But when they arrest you, do not worry about what to say or how to say it. At that time you will be given what to say, for it will not be you speaking, but the Holy Spirit of your Father speaking through you."[46] What is there here to suggest a Philonian view of inspiration, as Warfield would have it? What is there here that is not answered to by postulating nothing more specific than a divine message sovereignly provided, humanly mediated, and accompanied by God's authority? Surely the point in attributing these passages of Scripture to the Holy Spirit is not to indicate an exhaustive *co*-spiration, as it were, of "a compact mass of words,"[47] from which we ought to deduce an exhaustive inerrancy. Rather, it is simply evident that a genuine *in*spiration is in view, that Scripture does indeed belong to God and speak for him, that the creative and unfathomable instruction of the Holy Spirit has produced via human authors a word, a message, which God claims as his own.[48]

[45] Acts 4:25, Heb 3:7; cf. Acts 28:25f., where Paul says: "The Holy Spirit spoke the truth to your forefathers when he said through Isaiah the prophet: 'Go to this people and say, "You will be ever hearing and never understanding. . . ." For this people's heart has become calloused. . . .'" It will be observed from this example that some of the OT citations attributed to God actually had the form of divine quotations in their original context. Some, however, did not, and it might also be observed that while the author of Hebrews is especially fond of ascriptions to divine authorship, instances like these can be multiplied throughout the NT, as Warfield demonstrates.

[46] Matt 10:19-20.

[47] Cf. Warfield, *Inspiration*, 147.

[48] We may speak with justification of *in*spiration, whether thinking of the divine impulse in the authors of Scripture or of the product of their pens—we might even speak of *ex*spiration, when thinking of the outbreathing of the Word of God in and through Scripture—but no one ought to imagine that the doctrine of inspiration refers to God's *co*spiration (i.e., formation) of every word

The book of Exodus offers a helpful analogy, I believe, respecting this very matter. When Moses hesitated in his mission to Egypt because of his lack of eloquence, the Lord responded: "Who gave man his mouth? . . . Now go; I will help you speak and will teach you what to say." But Moses continued to balk, so that the Lord countered with this: "What about your brother, Aaron the Levite? I know he can speak well. . . . You shall speak to him and put words in his mouth; I will help both of you speak and will teach you what to do. He will speak to the people for you, and it will be as if he were your mouth and as if you were God to him."[49] A little later he says: "See, I have made you like God to Pharaoh, and your brother Aaron will be your prophet."[50] The thought here explicitly parallels the most radical of possibilities in prophetic inspiration, yet it is plain that what is in view is instruction in, and faithful reproduction of, a *message*. In this case, in fact, to think of word for word correspondence destroys the sense of the story; it is *Aaron* who has the eloquence, not Moses. It is plain, then, that one can be altogether true to the strongest of language identifying Scripture with the speaking of the Holy Spirit without going beyond the idea of the Spirit's power to teach and to guide the biblical authors into accurate communication of his own messages to men.

To be sure, the New Testament quotations of Old Testament Scripture present a variety of prophetic material in all the authority and relevance of its divine Source, drawing sometimes on a paragraph or two and sometimes on a mere word or phrase.[51] God has indeed spoken in the prophets, and we ought to let the New Testament model of respect, along with the last two passages we have looked at, inform our understanding of

---

of Scripture. Even to reduce the present discussion to an argument about "co-spiration" must surely seem absurd to many, but when the word θεόπνευστος is used in conjunction with the references under consideration in order to generate a view of Scripture that fancies something like a divine "mouthing" of the words themselves, it becomes necessary in order to make clear to others how far these fancies, often unwittingly held and wrongly attached to conservative or orthodox views, have drifted. That there is widespread difficulty here is indicated by the relatively straightforward affirmation of the Chicago Statement (article VI) "that the whole of Scripture and all its parts, *down to the very words of the original*, were given by divine inspiration" (emphasis mine).

[49] 4:10f.
[50] 7:1.
[51] Cf. John 10:34–35, Gal 3:16.

πᾶσα γραφή in its theopneustic character. We must not fall into the trap of supposing that the divine messages are sometimes poorly mediated or think that we can confine inspiration to the general thrust of a passage; the particulars obviously cannot be left out of account if we are to take "The Holy Spirit says . . ." seriously. At the same time, it is not well-inferred from this commitment that every passage and every particular must be treated exactly alike in respecting its participation in the divine authority of τὰ λόγια τοῦ θεοῦ.[52] On the contrary, this naturally varies according to genre and purpose, as we shall see. The New Testament use of the Old offers no justification for treating any and every sort of biblical detail alike, for its employment of previous Scripture, in however detailed a fashion, always revolves around the meaning and significance of the portion quoted.[53] This is no small point for this entire study, and becomes very significant in examining the next passage.

John 10:35

" . . . *and the Scripture cannot be broken*" (καὶ οὐ δύναται λυθῆναι ἡ γραφή).

I mentioned in Chapter 2 that the one reference which appears to come close to a biblical statement on inerrancy is John 10:35. We must look at the context of this statement,

---

[52] Despite Warfield's handling of the matter—he remains paralyzed by Philo—none of the scriptural references to τὰ λόγια τοῦ θεοῦ (Acts 7:38, Rom 3:2, Heb 5:12, 1 Pet 4:11) suggests any leveling of biblical passages to "a compact mass of words" like some gigantic and tedious pagan χρησμός (cf. *Inspiration*, 147f., 295, 326). While I see no reason to deny the appropriateness of τὰ λόγια τοῦ θεοῦ as a designation for canonical Scripture per se, it is in any case the Law given to Moses on the mountain that is primarily (not exclusively) in view when Scripture speaks of the oracles of God, except in 1 Pet 4:11—where analogy is being made to prophetic speech in the Church, an analogy that could hardly be drawn on Warfield's view!

[53] That it does so with serious objectivity is of course a claim which has been superficially rejected by any number of scholars, who are only too willing to find in the NT exegetical methods differing only slightly from those of the apostles' contemporaries. But the apostles' more or less radical departure in *substance* from the interpretations of their contemporaries is a sufficient clue to the inadequacy of this view, and careful exegesis has continually demonstrated their profound and circumspect attention to the textual meaning of previous Scriptures in the light of further revelation.

though it is of no concern here to demonstrate the exact progression of Jesus' argument as he responds to the Jews' accusation of blasphemy. It is enough to know that he predicated of Scripture an indefectible authority; for while this verse may well include an element of mockery, Warfield is doubtless correct in dismissing any attempt to suggest that Christ was merely hanging the Jews with their own rope and not actually approving the statement about Scripture. Warfield admits that there is a vein of satire running throughout the passage, yet the argument from Scripture, he says,

> is not *ad hominem* but *e concessu*; Scripture was common ground with Jesus and his opponents. If proof were needed for so obvious a fact, it would be supplied by the circumstances that this is not an isolated but a representative passage.[54]

Granting, then, that the Lord considered the Scriptures inviolable, it nonetheless remains to indicate what sort of inviolability it is to which he referred. Two observations are important.

The first concerns the meaning of λυθῆναι and the point of Christ's appeal to the character of Scripture. λυθῆναι as it occurs in this verse is often translated 'to be broken', but this has frequently proved misleading. Arndt and Gingrich classify this occurrence under a heading based on these meanings: *destroy, bring to an end, abolish, do away with*; and with respect to commandments, laws, and statements—*repeal, annul, abolish*.[55] While many want to see in John 10:35 an affirmation that "every statement of Scripture stands immutably, indestructible in its verity, unaffected by denial, human ignorance or criticism, charges of errancy or other subjective attack,"[56] that is not quite the point of saying that Scripture is οὐ δύναται λυθῆναι. Christ was not concerned here with the factual verity or accuracy of Scripture, but with the authority of its voice and the binding nature of its testimony.[57] The rendering of *The New English*

[54] *Inspiration*, 140.

[55] BAGD, 484.

[56] R. C. H. Lenski, *The Interpretation of St. John's Gospel* (Minneapolis: Augsburg, 1943) 767.

[57] It should be noted that in Matt 5:17-20 καταλῦσαι is contrasted with πληρῶσαι, 'to fulfill'; cf. Raymond E. Brown, *The Gospel According to John: I-XII* (AB; Garden City: Doubleday, 1966) 403f., who is following Jungkuntz. Cf. also John 7:23.

Bible,[58] "Scripture cannot be set aside," commends itself as an accurate and suitable translation which leads the reader in the proper direction. Such a statement is indeed relevant to the inerrancy discussion in its broader terms, but can hardly be used to support the position of exhaustive inerrancy—not, at least, when the second observation is made.

The second observation is this: those who with Warfield employ this passage in an attempt to justify the opinion that Christ and the New Testament authors "appeal indifferently . . . to every element in Scripture" are quite mistaken.[59] It is true that Ps 82:6, the passage to which appeal has been made, does not normally bear heavy traffic, and that Christ focuses on a single word at that. But in doing so he is appealing to a prophetic judgment involving nothing less than a divine interpretation and appraisal of a very significant office among his people (that of judge or magistrate). The single word "gods," by which he makes his point, is an extremely noteworthy appellation and is pivotal in its own context, making sense of the entire Psalm. Klaas Runia also takes note of this: " . . . the word 'gods' is no less than the key word in this Psalm."[60]

Warfield therefore goes astray when he says:

> Now, what is the particular thing in Scripture, for the confirmation of which the indefectible authority of Scripture is thus invoked? It is one of its most casual clauses. This means, of course, that in the Savior's view the indefectible authority of Scripture attaches to the very form of expression of its most casual clauses. It belongs to Scripture through and through, down to its most minute particulars, that it is of indefectible authority.[61]

This sort of argument, with its temporary laying aside of exegetical acumen, is all too common. Runia is worth quoting

---

[58] Oxford University Press, Cambridge University Press, 1970.

[59] *Inspiration*, 140.

[60] *Karl Barth's Doctrine of Holy Scripture*, 185. Without it, as Runia says, "the Psalm not only wholly loses its point, but one of the most decisive indications of the very special place and function of the magistrates has disappeared from Scripture." It was their exalted role as representatives of divine justice that formed the basis for the judgment pronounced against these judges in Psalm 82 (cf. James 3:1).

[61] *Inspiration*, 140.

at some length on the point at issue here. Jesus and the apostles, he says, never appeal to the Old Testament in the abstract,

> as to a kind of divine oracle-book, but always to the divine record of God's saving acts in the past, to the divinely given proclamation of the history of salvation, to the Old Testament as the book of the prophecy of Christ. Unfortunately this has been too often neglected by orthodoxy. The attitude of Jesus and the apostles has sometimes been described as a more or less mechanical, undifferentiated appeal to a book which in all possible respects is sacred and infallible. When, for example, Warfield in his defense of the doctrine of verbal inspiration (which we also hold) says that Jesus in John 10 appeals to one of the "most casual clauses" of Psalm 82 . . . this is a serious misrepresentation of Jesus' attitude. . . . No, Jesus does not use the Scriptures indiscriminately.[62]

The proper attitude toward Scripture, the attitude of Christ, is visible in another good rendering of John 10:35 in Raymond E. Brown's commentary: "the Scripture cannot lose its force."[63] This translation (along with that of the *NEB*) properly represents the kind of inviolability in view, and to this inviolability the Church must remain committed without squabbling about lesser things. It is, after all, precisely this perspective that allows us to say with Francis Schaeffer that *obedience to Scripture* is the real watershed issue for the Church today.[64]

Comments on Other Passages

Having examined the passages above, it is possible to make brief reference to two or three others which are sometimes entered in the debate in support of exhaustive inerrancy.

John 17:17. Some point to the statement, "your word is truth," as the positive counterpart of John 10:35, supposing that together with 2 Tim 3:16, etc., a very simple and direct case can

---

[62] *Karl Barth's Doctrine of Holy Scripture*, 185.

[63] *The Gospel According to John: I–XII*, 402. I.e., λυθῆναι would be understood in the sense of 'to be dissolved' or 'slackened' or 'dismissed' (see LSJ).

[64] This assertion, of course, only underlines the need for the Church and its teachers to face the hermeneutical and theological challenges of the day boldly, for if the Scripture is to be obeyed and thus fulfilled, if its force is to be properly

be made for the witness of Scripture to its own complete inerrancy. But once again this is a violation of context, for neither the contents of biblical texts nor even the idea of biblical literature are actually under consideration. The focus here is on the total divine Address in and through Jesus Christ which brings about knowledge of God, that is, salvation.[65] Of course, it would not do to disembody this Address (or John's kerygmatic concern in recording it) from the constituent verbal messages received and preached in connection with Christ, for that too would be unfaithful to the context and doubtless to v 17 itself.[66] Yet this very bond between Word and words makes it clear that in the eventual application of the verdict of John 17:17 to Scripture, to the canonical truths through which God works to sanctify men to himself in Christ, it is always *communicated message* that is in view.[67] Here as well, then, only the broader terms of the inerrancy debate can possibly come into play.

Psalm 12:6 and parallels.   These passages certainly have a place in discussing biblical claims to trustworthiness. In Ps 12:6, 2 Sam 22:31, and Prov 30:5-6, for example, canonical material appears to be directly in view, and each describes the word of the Lord as "flawless." It might be tempting to seize on these passages as justification for the doctrine of exhaustive inerrancy, but for the fact that the obvious frame of reference in each case is *the faithfulness of God in his instruction and his promises,* a faithfulness that is proven out in personal experience by obeying the instructions and relying on the words of promise. When we speak here of biblical trustworthiness, therefore, we cannot pretend to be speaking of the issues involved in the narrower

---

felt, then it must be understood and the hearer must be brought to stand in the way of its impact. But this labor itself must be carried out with a humble and discerning spirit, in honest submission to the counsel of the Lord (cf. Jer 8:8f., 23:16ff.).

[65] Vv 1-5 indicate the significance of all that follows in the passage.

[66] See esp. vv 6-8; also vv 14, 20.

[67] ἐγὼ δέδωκα αὐτοῖς τὸν λόγον σου, said Christ, and others will believe through their message (διὰ τοῦ λόγου αὐτῶν). This λόγος which Christ gave and the disciples kept was communicated, of course, in many constituent messages and sayings (ῥήματα, v 8) flowing from the Truth in which and by which men are sanctified.

terms of the inerrancy debate.[68] We speak instead of something much greater.

1 Corinthians 2:6–16. Walter Kaiser, in an article reviving much of Godet's exegesis, has doubtless renewed some bibliological interest in this text.[69] 1 Corinthians 2 does in fact have something to contribute to discussions of inspiration and inerrancy, but not by addressing the matter and mode of biblical inspiration directly, as Kaiser would have it. Rather, the passage touches on the reality and value of revelational knowledge in a much broader context—that of the experience of every Christian—and in so doing provides a useful parallel for discussing inspiration. Again, context must be allowed to control exegesis, and a moment or two may be taken to discuss this final example.

Paul's argument here is subsidiary to his correction of the Corinthians' ironic spiritual and intellectual pride (expressed in their division into rival schools), on which he embarks immediately in the early chapters of the epistle. As chap. 2 begins, he is gently pointing out that he had especially avoided anything approaching a wisdom style or frame of reference in the Corinthian context, not only because the Gospel is not like secular wisdom (1:17), but also because he was conscious of danger to them in the early going. They in particular needed to be grounded in humility and a display of the power of God (2:1–5). To make their spiritual problem even more plain, he goes on to point out a couple more things of which they ought to be aware. First, Paul does indeed talk wisdom with some folk, namely, those who are mature (2:6ff.). Second, the Corinthians, unfortunately, *still* cannot be numbered among them (3:1ff.). With this backdrop we can ask how Paul develops his argument and how he makes use of the idea of revealed wisdom to serve his purpose in correcting the Corinthians. He does not do this, as Kaiser suggests, by establishing his personal authority over

---

[68] The context of Prov 30:5–6—*if* these verses are viewed as a response to vv 1–4—may broaden the focus beyond the reliability of divine guidelines, predictions and promises, having in mind the whole sphere of biblical wisdom, but that would still not take the matter beyond the practical concerns of satisfying, trustworthy *understanding* (בִּינָה). In any case, the overall point I am making in this paragraph is clearly established in the parallelism of Ps 33:4.

[69] "A Neglected Text in Bibliology Discussions: I Corinthians 2:6–16," *WTJ* 43 (1981) 301–19.

them through an appeal to his *special* revelational insight.[70] He does not do it in the almost gnostic fashion of exalting himself as the inspired agent of a revelation designed, presumably, for a distinct class of people called "the perfect." On the contrary, rather than appealing to a special apostolic inspiration, he appeals to the special process of participation in revealed wisdom *that is intended for every believer.* His point is that—precisely because such sharing in the genuine wisdom of God is practically available to all believers through the Holy Spirit—it is to the Corinthians' shame that they obviously have not recognized and laid hold of the real thing (3:1-4).

Kaiser's contrast between ἡμεῖς and ὑμεῖς quite misses the point.[71] ἡμεῖς in 2:6-16 is not primarily editorial for Paul as an apostle (note the temporary change from the usual κἀγώ), but stands ultimately for proper, normally-functioning Christians. The ὑμεῖς of chap. 3 is not a reference to the Corinthians as lay-people, so to speak, but as carnal. ἡμεῖς is the "we" of God's children versus the "they" of the world; that is, it includes everyone who recognizes that he both lives and thinks spiritually, not according to the sophistication of the world, but according to the sophistication of Christ. In principle it included the Corinthians, but sadly, in practical terms it did not. On Kaiser's view, oddly enough, it properly *excludes* all except inspired spokesmen. This stands the passage on its head, so that it no longer presents the positive potential of the Christian's spiritual mind to grasp and apply divine wisdom. Instead, it is seen as presenting a negative distinction, a spiritual boundary, in order to find in the passage a discussion that will uphold a technical view of inspiration.[72] Ironically, this approach obscures a more significant insight into how the revealed wisdom recorded in Scripture can actually function in the mind and life

[70] Ibid., 311f. Kaiser's discussion is worthy of more space than I can allow here; in the main it will be more helpful simply to present an alternative to his position and leave the reader to compare the two.

[71] Ibid, esp. 314-15, 319. The sort of distinction he wants to develop between apostles and the rest of the Church forces him to regard Eph 1:17, e.g., as referring to "only a secondary and derivative revelation"—whatever that may be!

[72] Ibid., 316. In his words, we have here "one of the most precise statements on the mode of inspiration, i.e., the connection and method by which the divine Spirit and the human author interacted in the transmission and recording of these 'deep things of God.'" He goes on to quote Godet: "'To teach things

of the believer, who is equipped by the Spirit in connection with the apostolic teaching to speak spiritually about spiritual matters (2:10ff.).[73]

What does this passage contribute to bibliology, then? Simply this: what is true of mature believers is true *a fortiori* of the authors of Scripture as God's appointed spokesmen, that is, in the measure and manner required for their varying roles in the revelation of Christ. Their writings present *Spirit-taught wisdom,* and present it accurately in appropriate words. Without direct reference to canonical literature, the present passage provides a larger frame of reference for inspiration that is very amenable to the understanding of theopneustic literature developed earlier, one that is focused on meaningful and reliable communication instructing man in the mind and will of God, rather than being oriented essentially to individual textual phenomena.[74]

Adjusting the Focus

None of the passages we have examined can be said to concern itself with the question of exhaustive inerrancy over which many of today's conservative evangelicals are struggling. Very clearly, however, they do combine to address in no uncertain terms the more crucial questions about the fundamental authority and relevance of Scripture facing all of Christendom. The work of the Spirit in the origin of Scripture is acknowledged throughout as undergirding the biblical word with an authority

---

which the Spirit has revealed, terms are not made use of which man's own understanding and ability have discovered. The same divine breath which lifted the veil *to reveal,* takes possession also of the mouth of its interpreter when it is *to speak.*'" He denies that this implies dictation.

[73] This I consider to be a fair paraphrase of πνευματικοῖς πνευματικὰ συγκρίνοντες. I take πνευματικοῖς to refer to λόγοις, which is the central term in the verse (it is elliptical in the previous phrase) and maintains the flow of thought and language much better than would an anticipation of ὁ πνευματικός (v 15). ἐν [λόγοις] διδακτοῖς πνεύματος is not best understood as putting emphasis on individual words, but simply on the content and actual communication of that which the Spirit wills to be said. The sense of this saying, then, is that the Spirit enables us to speak legitimately and genuinely, making spiritual sense in all matters about which God is pleased to teach us in connection with Christ (v 12).

[74] To say this, however, is not to support any arbitrary distinction between πνευματικά and other matters addressed by biblical writers.

that comes from God himself, who wills to speak in just this fashion. All of these passages thus testify to the reliability of the word of God, though each contributes in a different way: 2 Tim 3:16 guarantees Scripture's serviceability as an infallible guide to the righteous man; 2 Pet 1:21 guarantees its prophetic certainty; Matt 5:17-18, if you like, indicates the value and authority of even the smallest scriptural contribution to the instruction of God's people; passages introduced by "the Holy Spirit says . . ." remind us that God has indeed chosen to address us in the words of Scripture, which bear his messages to us; John 10:35 makes clear the indefectible authority of that which is written, while Ps 12:6 and parallels underline God's faithfulness to us in all that is offered there. In every case (including John 17:17 and 1 Cor 2:6-16) the context makes perfectly plain that there is a primary focus on the power and the right of that which is taught by the Spirit in connection with Christ *to function as an intellectual and practical authority leading to righteousness*: "Sanctify them by the truth; your word is truth."

This concern is indeed intellectual in part, requiring that conformity to Christ be governed by thinking that is yielded to the truths of Scripture, in and through which the Truth himself is revealed in ever-increasing clarity.[75] But because this concern is not *merely* intellectual, but expressly purposeful and life-oriented, that is, prophetic, it should not surprise us that Scripture does not describe its own reliability in terms that embrace every level of textual phenomena and every question we might pose. That could hardly be thought necessary, if due attention is given to the fact that it is in its function as the Word of *Life* that Scripture is given to us as the Word of Truth. This is the light in which Scripture must ultimately be viewed and received as reliable—a pattern set for us in 2 Timothy 3.[76] The Scriptures were introduced into a cursed and sinful world for the sake of correction and redemption, to serve the grace of God in

---

[75] In that it is Christ himself who ultimately comes into view here, we could just as easily translate John 17:17 in terms of the concrete personality of the divine Λόγος: "Sanctify them in the Truth; your Word is Truth."

[76] 2 Tim 3:15-17 may serve as a convenient paradigm for representations of the nature of Scripture and its reliability, because it concerns itself with the soundness of Scripture in relation to its purpose and result, and in so doing, speaks of the divine foundation of every portion. Nonetheless, this model passage should not be viewed in isolation from the contributions of the other related passages.

Christ. According to Berkouwer, therefore, we ought not to formalize our view of the biblical witness to redemption by setting forth the infallibility of Scripture in terms of inerrancy (as it is commonly conceived, at least), for that would reflect a lopsided emphasis on abstract information rather than on purpose. Berkouwer comments:

> It is not that Scripture offers us no information but that the nature of this information is unique. It is governed by the *purpose* of God's revelation. The view of inspiration that forms the basis of the misunderstanding of this purpose considers "inerrancy" essential as a parallel characterization of reliability; that is a flight of fancy away from this purpose.[77]

When shortcuts are eschewed in refining the doctrine of the reliability of Scripture, and when the biblical texts contributing to this process are seen in context to be directed toward this very

[77] *Holy Scripture*, 183–84; for clarity's sake I would substitute "exhaustive inerrancy." It might also be pointed out that of course *all* speech, canonical or no, is purposeful; the point is simply that Scripture's very special, dominating purpose must be taken into account in characterizing its reliability. Certainly when we examine the biblical record of communication between God and man, the inherently purposeful and functional character of language is evident from the beginning, just as in our own experience. First we discover that God's personal Word is both active and deliberative (Gen 1:1–24, 26). Then in his communication with man we do not encounter a mere transmission of data about the cosmos, but rather performative address, command and warning (1:28, 2:16–17). Man's speech also appears first as performative address in naming the animals. Satanic use of human language likewise makes its entry as the means to a very specific end, in this case the proliferation of rebellion through deliberate untruth. We may note as well that God's response in the ensuing situation takes the form of three questions obviously designed, not to increase knowledge, but to elicit confession; these are followed again by a performative use of language in cursing creation (3:1–19). In other words, it should be obvious that the information which speech conveys is always subject to larger purposes and goals (as indeed the Genesis record itself is) and must not be judged for adequacy or accuracy apart from a thoroughgoing respect for both the dictates and flexibility of the service for which it was intended. In the case of Scripture, it ought to be recognized that its divine service to Christ certainly imposes a very high standard of reliability on the information it conveys, but to imagine a technical or exhaustive standard could only *distract* one from the earthy, inspiring dynamic of Scripture as it leads men into the truth. Paul Achtemeier (*The Inspiration of Scripture*, 58, 74), who admits that the "unwillingness to acknowledge any lordship, moral or intellectual, other than that of Scripture is perhaps the greatest strength of the conservative view of the nature and inspiration of the Bible," also suggests that "diversion of attention from the Bible's witness about God's saving acts to questions about the precise accuracy of minor details" is perhaps its most serious defect.

concern with function rather than mere formal description, it becomes clear that an emphasis on absolute errorless purity apart from the demands of Scripture's serviceability in speaking for God is misplaced. A change is needed. But in adjusting the focus here we need to guard against a view that presses the purposeful character of Scripture into a false distinction in reliability between its central saving message "and all of the difficult surrounding material which supports that message."[78] That could only achieve from the other side the same reprehensible dichotomy of form and function already rejected, and the same separation between Christ and the Scriptures! At any rate, it would not be true to 2 Timothy 3, etc.; everything that is being said in Scripture is indeed reliable because it is all "God-breathed" or Spirit-taught, and because it is the linguistic servant of God's communication with men. Scripture has no less need for reliability in its parts because of the direction and purpose that provide the unity of its message as a whole. Quite the reverse; if the constituent messages are to support and contribute at all, they must contribute truthfully.[79] Nevertheless, adjust our focus we must, if we have read into the key texts any indication of a formalized, *exhaustive* inerrancy. That is a doctrine not addressed, and a commitment not necessary in order to acknowledge Scripture's faithful service as both a divine and a human witness to Christ (a matter which I will pursue further in the next chapter).

---

[78] Jack B. Rogers, "A Third Alternative," in *Scripture, Tradition, and Interpretation*, ed. W. Ward Gasque and William Sanford LaSor (Grand Rapids: Eerdmans, 1978) 87. Rogers indicates such a distinction in an article supporting Berkouwer, though he does not apply it directly to the question of reliability. Has Berkouwer himself—despite his strong rejection of using the idea of goal to serve "an arbitrary dualism" that leads to an attack on the authority of Scripture—partially skirted this issue in stressing somewhat one-sidedly the relationship of biblical reliability to the moral question of erring in the sense of "swerving from the truth and upsetting the faith" (*Holy Scripture*, 181)? J. I. Packer (*Beyond the Battle for the Bible*, 140-42) seems to think so, while commending Berkouwer overall.

[79] Packer (ibid., 38-40) shows the balance which some lack when he warns against the danger of any principle "which has the effect, whether intended or not, of hindering Holy Scripture from exercising authority over the church." He indicates the importance of the positive affirmation that Scripture is the means and instrument whereby God "teaches his people everywhere and at all times all that they need to know in order to serve him acceptably"; the inspired texts are "the God-given presentation of God's own message."

The exegetical work of this chapter has indicated that Scripture does not, in fact, address the narrower terms of the inerrancy debate. It does not do so directly, nor does it do so implicitly by providing a full answer to the threefold question raised above regarding inspiration: The *purpose* of inspiration is expressed in terms of reliable direction for the sake of righteousness, and nothing more specific is offered; the *means* of inspiration is left largely to the realm of mystery, and that is where it must be left; the *extent* of inspiration is clearly indicated as co-extensive with the canonical text, but is not specifically related to the words as such but to the messages they contain and to the purposes with which they are bound up. The matter of God's relation to the text, therefore, and of its participation in the perfection of his own knowledge, is not clear beyond the fact that the meaning and significance of every passage is a sovereign gift from out of his own truthfulness, and carries his authority. On the other hand, the broader terms of the debate are clearly addressed in the fact that Scripture is treated in this way as a word from God for men, a word that cannot successfully be set aside or overruled. That is why the syllogism mentioned in the previous chapter (p. 79) is not entirely without significance in responding to the questions raised by the inerrancy debate and in expressing the Church's commitment to the Christ of the Scriptures. But that is also why the syllogism must be corrected, for it assumes too much of the word θεόπνευστος and the concept of inspiration—as if more were needed!

Certainly we ought to accept the implications of the divine authorship of Scripture via the teaching ministry of the Holy Spirit, however demanding and unpopular such a stance may have become, acknowledging that the expression of the human authors is entirely adequate to the instruction their Teacher would offer and free from distortion of it. To suggest any other attitude toward Scripture is to depart from that which the Scriptures have always demanded and received from the community of faith, and to depart from the understanding of Christ and Paul and Peter and John and the author of Hebrews. It is also to malign the Spirit's ministry. At the same time, however, we have no call to turn this confidence in the scriptural word into a concern with every individual word and detail of the text *beyond its contribution to the message constructed*. As we have seen, such a focus on the words themselves is not justified by Paul's description of Scripture as theopneustic or by the other biblical statements often put forward. If "God-breathed" could be shown to mean that every word of the biblical text was formulated directly from the mind of God, then inerrancy would have to be defined in quite strict a fashion (still allowing, of course, for some cultural expression and the like). But as this cannot be shown, the syllogism representing the argument pressed by inerrantists within the narrower terms of the debate rests on an underlying equivocation, which turns "word" or message into words or details on an exhaustive scale. The tendency to overlook this equivocation ignores the moderation suggested by the fact that God both determined the messages we would hear, and that they would be delivered through the servitude of history and human authors.

What then shall we do with the syllogism, where for one reason or another it is necessary to repeat our confession of the infallibility of Scripture in terms of inerrancy? That means of expressing our conviction about the truthfulness of the Bible can still be useful, so long as it is constructed with reference to the functional, communicative purpose of Scripture and the practical Lordship of Christ, indicating the sanctity of what every passage has to say rather than the sanctity of a body of isolated data.[80] The following suggestion is an improvement, I think, which clarifies the affirmation of inerrancy in its broader terms without making any commitment regarding the disputes within the narrower terms of the debate:

> *Premise A*:   God is excluded from the class of beings who lie or err.
>
> *Premise B*:   The communicative design of every passage of Scripture is the product of the Spirit of God as well as of the human author.

---

[80] Carl Henry (*God, Revelation and Authority*, 4. 176), whose position at times appears very conservative indeed, even dependent on the sort of equivocation to which I just referred, nonetheless wisely comments: "The term inerrancy needlessly becomes a spectre if one ignores the referential frame in which it is intended. Everett F. Harrison asserts that while *the fact of inerrancy* is properly deduced from the teaching of Scripture, its form is to be defined inductively from an examination of the content of Scripture." Harrison's statement in particular ("Criteria of Biblical Inerrancy," *CT* 20 [1958] 17) is able to point us in the right direction here, one which I will pursue further in chap. 6.

> *Conclusion*: The communicative design of every passage of
> Scripture is without deception or error.

By "communicative design" I mean that which each portion has
set out to say, and has actually said, in its context. That is, I do
not mean design in the sense of *int*ent as opposed to *cont*ent,
which would in fact say nothing at all. This will receive further
clarification as we continue. Meanwhile, it can be remarked that
this revised syllogism, as a means of indicating the fact that
Scripture is unfailingly profitable (not merely always well-
intended), comes into a more natural harmony with John 10:35
as interpreted above, expressing one implicit aspect of Christ's
confession of biblical authority. It is on the basis of the sort of
confidence he modeled there, which still arises out of the actual
knowledge of God received by the Church in and through
Scripture, that the simple "it is written" comes to stand with all
the weight of divine authority behind every passage of canonical
Scripture. This testimony is, at root, much greater than that
which a simple assertion of the Bible's formal veracity could
ever express.

4 | Exhaustive Inerrancy: A Needless Struggle

Despite the exegetical facts of the previous chapter, some still prefer to struggle on with the defense of exhaustive inerrancy. Under the influence of the epistemological misconceptions discussed earlier, they often feel compelled to construct logically a much stricter understanding of infallibility than Scripture itself demands. They are thus themselves seemingly prepared to take the risk of setting up an additional *scandalon* alongside Christ, turning the "it is written" into an unnecessary occasion for stumbling in a human attempt to preserve its connection with the divine authority it attests. This defense, constructed as it is by means of several faulty inferences, can be effectively cross-examined in relatively short order—though some treat the arguments of inerrantists a little too lightly, perhaps, under the impact of allegedly overwhelming, but often quite debatable, contrary evidence. In any case, it will not be necessary to touch on more than three or four basic points.

Language and Communication

Is exhaustive inerrancy necessary for accurate message-bearing? The answer to this question obviously depends on the nature of the material at hand. There is a great breadth of material in Scripture, of course, and some parts of it more technical than others, but Scripture is written to and for the people of God and cannot generally be characterized in technical terms. We do not look, then, for mathematical precision in Scripture, but how should we indicate the sort of accuracy we rely on? How does "people-language" function in communication? While a wide variety of considerations in linguistic philosophy and the social sciences might be brought into play here, along with discussions of referential and commissive uses of language, of the literal and the metaphorical, etc.,[1] for present purposes it will suffice to attend briefly to semantic structure as it bears on the role of individual units of signification. (This will also provide an opportunity to begin demonstrating what is meant by "communicative design.")

In a very instructive article on idiomatic translations, John Beekman outlines some of the features of semantic structure in written communication.[2] All translators agree that "communication consists of a form-meaning composite." Grammatical and lexical forms and categories vary from language to language, but underlying the grammatical-lexical structures belonging to messages composed in the various languages is "a semantic structure which is near-universal." In semantic analysis, as he puts it, "the focus of attention shifts from grammatical to semantic units, such as components of meaning, concepts, propositions, semantic paragraphs, sections."[3] But aside from his concern that these aspects of written communication be properly appreciated in their application to translation, Beekman addresses himself to their possible implications for inerrancy, proposing that an easing of certain tensions might be found therein. The aid which he offers he refers to under the rubric "functional inerrancy":

> Throughout this paper, there has been an emphasis on meaning over form. . . . That which is most important in these composites . . . is not so much the form but rather its function or meaning. Minor variations in form do not impair function. . . . My concern is that the number of unresolved problems [in Scripture] is so small and inconsequential that these problems should not receive the concentrated attention so often given to them. Moreover, low probability solutions give the impression that inerrancy stands or falls upon the eventual success of explaining these remaining problems. Would it not be better to shift the focus to the inconsequential nature of these remaining problems and emphasize that each is functionally inerrant even apart from final explanation?[4]

---

[1] See, e.g., G. B. Caird's helpful volume, *The Language and Imagery of the Bible* (Philadelphia: Westminster, 1980).

[2] "Idiomatic Translations and Some Underlying Theological Questions," *Notes on Translation* 68 (1978) 2–23.

[3] Ibid., 2–6.

[4] Ibid., 13. I.e., the inerrant meaning-function of the text should not necessarily be strictly identified with all constituent information content (stated or implied).

Beekman illustrates with an example drawn from Matt 3:17 and its parallels in Mark 1:11 and Luke 3:22. Whereas Matthew reads, "This is my Son," the parallels read, "You are my son." He points out that while both οὗτός ἐστιν and σὺ εἶ refer to the same individual, "from the standpoint of concepts we do have a difference in *information content* . . . and there is a difference in the referential *purpose*, since one makes a reference *to* Christ [and] the other makes a reference *about* Christ."[5] To that extent, these accounts do not agree.

> However, from the standpoint of the proposition, the purpose is unaffected. Functionally, each proposition . . . accomplishes the purpose of the author in this immediate, specific context, i.e., to show the unique relationship that existed between God the Father and Jesus. Thus, it can be claimed that, even though there are concepts within the propositions of these verses that are at variance . . . yet this does not affect the function of the proposition.[6]

Beekman then enlists the support of Charles Hodge, who wrote concerning such minute variations in the biblical records: "These matters have no more to do with the totality of the text than a tiny streak of sandstone appearing here and there in the marble of the Parthenon would affect the entire building."[7] Beekman does not fail to note, though, that individual concepts can be very crucial to the function of a proposition, as indeed a tiny crack can be very crucial if it opens at a point of stress in the structure. Thus, he says, "to claim that problems arising from differences in concepts used by authors are minor and incidental is based on the relative importance of the concept in the total meaning of the proposition to be communicated" (an essentially exegetical determination).[8]

[5] Ibid., 14. For a synopsis of his terminology, see the chart on p. 3 entitled "Semantic Structure of Written Communication."

[6] Ibid. Of course, many proponents of redaction criticism, even within evangelical circles, would simply argue outright that the biblical authors have taken considerable (but legitimate) freedom in certain areas to recast their material in light of their larger narrative and doctrinal purposes. This remains a matter of no small debate on certain touchy points, as the events involving Robert Gundry and his commentary on Matthew have demonstrated.

[7] *Systematic Theology*, 1. 169.

[8] "Idiomatic Translations and Some Underlying Theological Questions," 14. One might recall here the discussion of Psalm 82 in the previous chapter.

We are all aware, however, that there are difficulties in the text on a larger scale than the example chosen. Perhaps we may profitably expand on this sort of thinking in light of semantic structure involving total discourses. The process of analyzing the information content and the role of each semantic unit does not stop at the propositional level. There are units which go on up to the paragraph and section and beyond, until the total discourse has been analyzed. In exegeting larger semantic units, watching for the development of theme and for textual indicators of "what is focal or emphatic and . . . essential for topic and theme control,"[9] we should allow such considerations to modulate application of the inerrancy commitment. More will be said in another place, but the overall point to be made here is that meaning and message involve a two-way relationship of lesser and greater semantic units. The latter are not possible without their constituents, but it is the latter which, as context, help to narrow and select the meaning of the former, providing them with textual significance. While meaning may at times hinge on a single word or detail, it more commonly turns on semantic units much larger than this, often on units larger than the sentence.[10] The details, the tools, the everyday "scenery" employed in communication for a variety of purposes, need not always be considered essential to the message itself and its authority, unless the larger units of meaning clearly point back to them.[11]

[9] This wording is taken from Beekman's definition of "prominence," a technical term referring "to the fact that one constituent in each semantic unit is more focal, i.e., of greater significance" (ibid., 8).

[10] Kenneth L. Pike (*Language in Relation to a Unified Theory of the Structure of Human Behavior* [The Hague: Mouton, 1967] 484) challenges Hockett's view that "'a *sentence* is a grammatical form which is not in construction with any other grammatical form; a constitute which is not a constituent.'" He notes that "hierarchical structure does not stop with the sentence, nor begin with it. Rather it must begin with the total language event in a total cultural setting. . . ." Pike looks to a theory of language that recognizes the complexity of linguistic integration internally and externally, and works with the trimodal analogy of particle, wave, and field (see p. 511, n 1). Certainly the complex meaning-structures of language ought to produce caution on *both* sides of the inerrancy debate in attempting to apply the doctrine of infallibility to actual textual information or detail.

[11] In "The Semantic Structure of Written Communication, Part I" (prepub. draft, 4th rev., 1979) 18, Beekman and Callow write that "every communication unit is considered to have a purpose, i.e., no information is included in the discourse without some purpose. Experience indicates, however, that a purpose that can be stated propositionally, a purpose with definite content to it, seems

We may focus on the sentence or proposition (the most basic communication unit), but even then only within a hierarchy of considerations imposed by larger semantic units and higher levels of linguistic integration.

Now the purpose of the author—that is, the message he is constructing—is the final court of appeal in indicating the role and significance of any proposition or group of propositions, and thus in determining the leeway with which its constituent information content can be treated without dissolving the purity, soundness, or force of the message. But we must note well that it is *he* and not *we* to whom the appeal must be made; each constituent part of the message must be granted the significance given it by the author if we are to respect the fact that he speaks to us in God's place, and that God speaks through him. At any rate, to be concerned with the author's service as messenger means to focus on the point or purpose of a proposition in its total semantic context, that is, to determine message at every point according to the communicative design of the text. This often renders exhaustive inerrancy irrelevant, and we should not hesitate to say so.[12]

Before leaving the discussion of language and communication a second point is worth touching on, as an illustration on a very basic level (with well-defined parameters) of the flexibility that ought to characterize our considerations of the Word of Truth. Modern linguists and translation theorists are increasingly conscious of *both* the universal capacity of language to

---

normally to be discernible from the section level upwards. . . . The purpose of units below the level at which a purpose can be discerned is simply *to contribute to the higher-level purpose*" (emphasis mine). The exact contribution such a unit is intended to have, it seems to me, can only be judged by looking at it both forwards and backwards, as it were, i.e., in view of what it *offers* to add and in view of what in context it is *invited* to add.

[12] Let me offer an illustration: If it were shown, say, that the genealogy of Genesis 5 had canonical purposes—e.g., the perpetuation of a sort of "hall of fame" of significant ancestors leading up to Shem, a remembrance of pre-flood longevity, a theology of human mortality ("and he died"), etc.—which did not demand perfection in the record itself, would it matter if this record, though included in the canon, were in fact inaccurate in a variety of details? What I am saying is not the same thing as saying (rather foolishly, in my opinion) that Scripture may inerrantly reproduce erring records, for I am concerned directly with what the text is specifically designed to communicate. Broader considerations than those raised by the present illustration may even be in order here, for biblical traditions in general, as Paul Achtemeier points out (*The Inspiration of*

convey messages and its corresponding inability to convey them with precisely the same inherent impact or preservation of detail. I quote from Kenneth L. Pike to illustrate the point:

> Transcultural communication must be granted as possible . . . [and] more than a crude approximation must be possible; the communication must be in some sense transculturally *effective*. . . . It should be observed closely, however, . . . that there is inevitable category slippage in translation, and that this poses certain problems for the translator. . . . On the other hand, he is tied to "additions" of categorical distinction. . . . This factor demands that the translator make judgments about the marginality of some of the categorical elements.[13]

The meaning-complex of a text, despite careful design of the new surface structure, cannot in fact be reproduced so as to have precisely the same information or impact potential. Yet God's word, his messages for us, are translatable; on this we must insist. The canonical expression in Hebrew, Aramaic, or Greek is God's chosen and standardized form of those messages, but they can also be expressed in other languages (or indeed differently in the same language to some extent, as they are and were in preaching). In actually attempting that expression, however, it becomes obvious, as Pike points out, that each text is a tapestry interwoven with significant elements and insignificant elements, some of which are expendable in the functioning of that text.

Translation theory thus serves to clarify from yet another standpoint that the unerring Word of Truth is such as *living message,* not as a body of isolated data which must be preserved.[14] It is a sad commentary that of the same people who

Scripture, 125), are not "primarily concerned with historical fact so much as they are concerned with the significance of those past events for the present, and the promise they hold for the future. It is for that reason that such traditions can err in factual matters, statistics and the like without in any way compromising their truth as *traditions.* Given the nature of tradition, it is sheer perversity to want to find statistical accuracy in them, and to want to judge their value and validity by the presence or absence of such elements." (I cannot follow Achtemeier all the way in this matter however; more will be said on such things in Part 3.)

[13] "The Linguist and Axioms Concerning the Language of Scripture," *JASA* 26 (1974) 48.

[14] This consideration only balances, it does not deny, that other hard (but rewarding) reality of which every student of biblical languages has assured

hold to a very strict concept of inerrancy there are many who pay little attention to the problems of language and culture and hermeneutics, and who are scarcely concerned with effective dynamic equivalence in translation (who rather reject it), while ironically upholding their Bibles as though they were the very *words* of God. When they counter by simply pushing their claim back to the original languages and manuscripts, they appear to gain a tighter hold on the authority of Scripture, but lose its subjects—we do not have the original manuscripts and the vast majority of people today are entirely unable to read even the adequate (but imperfect) copies we have, never mind to read them with the ability of those for whom they were originally intended. No, if we claim to have the word of God today, we must admit that there are in fact certain kinds of expendable details in that word which do not compromise the speaking of God in and through it. The very interdependency of canon and proclamation ought to make this plain in the first place.[15] There is, in any event, nothing in the analysis of language and communication that supports fixation on a strict or exhaustive view of inerrancy. Perhaps the next question lies closer to the root of this claim.

Scripture and Certainty

Is exhaustive inerrancy necessary in order to prevent skepticism? Would the presence in Scripture of any sort of error at all

---

himself, namely, that the biblical message is at times quite dependent for its clarity on a grasp of the details of its original expression, or at least of their significance.

[15] One of the strengths of Barth's discussion of the Word of God is his sensitivity to this interdependency (cf. the summary statement in *Church Dogmatics* 1/1. 136); of course, he did not deal with these matters as I am dealing with them. My point here is simply that the "increase" of the Word, as Paul and Luke often refer to the progress of the gospel, has always been wrapped up in the actual proclamation and dissemination of the biblical message, in which the scriptural word itself flowers into a hundred different forms on a hundred different occasions. In other words, the canon only functions as canon insofar as it serves a living testimony to Christ. But then we are forced to admit the already obvious conclusion that there is nothing sacred about the very *form* of Scripture other than its stabilizing service to the actual *content* of its message, and suddenly we must face the fact that some disputes about this or that minor element of the text—including some questions about accuracy or veracity—are unable to demonstrate any final relevance.

undermine the whole process of theology, not merely by establishing a precedent leading to eventual erosion of confidence in biblical truth, but by denying to Scripture the power (i.e., the right) to serve as a *principium* for Christian thought? The basic issue here has largely been dealt with in the discussions of chap. 2, but further comments are in order respecting this particular question, to remind us of the manner in which Scripture serves theology and the Christian hope.

It must be denied immediately that the Bible can function under any circumstances as a *principium* for our knowledge in the technical sense of the word. Timothy Phillips, in the article mentioned earlier, charges that the inerrancy debate too often centers on "ancillary issues such as what constitutes an error, inerrancy's historical support, or purported errors in Scripture," while assuming all along this much more problematic idea (and for that reason sustaining an inflated view of its own importance). As Phillips sees it, those issues

> are secondary and even evasive because the very ground of the discussion, the inerrantist's precise framing of biblical authority, is not directly confronted. The fundamental issue rather is whether it is correct to assert that the most crucial problem facing theology is inerrancy, inasmuch as an inerrant Bible is "the foundation of our Christian thought and life, without which we could not . . . maintain the confidence of our faith and surety of our hope."[16]

Such an assertion rests, says Phillips, on the "underlying and dubious presupposition" of *foundationalism*. Nicholas Wolterstorff describes the goal of foundationalism as the formation of "a body of theories from which all prejudice, bias, and unjustified conjecture have been eliminated." "To attain this," he says, "we must begin with a firm foundation of [non-inferential] certitude and build the house of theory on it by methods of whose reliability we are equally certain."[17] But that is not the way of Christian knowledge, nor indeed of knowledge in general.

Foundationalism, says Wolterstorff, although the classic theory of theorizing in the western world, is dead. Nor can the

---

[16] "The Argument for Inerrancy: An Analysis," 80 (his quotation is from Warfield, *Inspiration*, 127).

[17] Nicholas Wolterstorff, *Reason within the Bounds of Religion* (Grand Rapids: Eerdmans, 1976), 24.

Bible resurrect it, for whatever one may suppose about the character of biblical revelation and its propositional content, it cannot be held that it is open to men to acquire indubitable understanding of this content. The Bible, therefore, cannot function as a *principium* even for strictly theological thinking.[18] In any case, I hasten to add, the whole dualistic, rationalistic mode of thinking epitomized by foundationalism is altogether inimical to genuine Christian thought, which is rooted in actual involvement with reality and with the living God. Truths have never been the foundation of theology, nor could they be; genuine theology is founded and controlled by the grace of divine revelation and therefore by the Truth himself. All this should not be taken to mean that it is of no consequence whether or not Scripture is true, but only that genuine knowledge does not find its justification in these theoretical terms and the pseudo-perfectionism they engender, and that the Bible therefore should not be examined from that perspective.

Yet the arguments of many inerrantists for both the importance of inerrancy and the necessity of a strict view of inerrancy do give the appearance of resting on just such a foundationalist vision of the Bible. Warfield writes:

> Though, then, in the abstract, we may say that the condition of the validity of the Christian teaching and of the Christian hope, is no more than the fact of the supernaturalism of Christianity, historically vindicated; practically we must say that the condition of the persistence of Christianity as a religion for the people, is the entire trustworthiness of the Scriptures as the record of the supernatural revelation which Christianity is. . . . That the church may have unsullied assurance in the details of its teaching, —that the Christian man may have unshaken confidence in the details of the promises to which he trusts,—they need, and they know that they need, a thoroughly trustworthy Word of God in which God himself speaks directly to them all the words of this life.[19]

----

[18] Ibid., 52–58.

[19] *Inspiration*, 122. Phillips ("The Argument for Inerrancy: An Analysis," 81) observes: "When it becomes apparent that the inerrantist defines the problem of biblical authority within the epistemological context of foundationalism, the unique stresses characteristic of inerrancy are illumined. For instance, because Scripture is interpreted as theology's principium, the character and range of its truthfulness is predetermined."

Edward J. Young appears to get in even deeper, prefacing one of his major works with this comment:

> Despite all that is being said and has been said to the contrary, the doctrine of inspiration is of the utmost significance and importance. If the Bible is not infallible, then we can be sure of nothing. The other doctrines of Christianity will then one by one go by the board. The fortunes of Christianity stand or fall with an infallible Bible.[20]

This sort of reasoning has foundationalist tendencies all right, though that does not make either Young or Warfield a full-fledged foundationalist;[21] we must ask what the real concern of these men is.

Careful examination of such quotations and their contexts reveals that their primary concern is not so much a system of indubitable knowledge as the ability to return time and time again to all that Scripture has to say, without reservation as to its value and reliability.[22] With this we ought to be concerned, in spite of our rejection of any rationalistic attempt at a system of indubitable knowledge, precisely because it is God who has established Scripture as the avenue of his own Word. What we must not do is suppose that our confidence is attached *to the book itself or to a system of ideas,* and so slip into a theoretical mode of thought that has difficulty escaping charges of rationalism and foundationalism. We must remember that our confidence comes from God, that it is grounded by faith in his self-revelation, that when we come to Scripture we are coming not to a compendium of truths from which our theology is simply deduced, but to the Truth himself who instructs us truthfully in matters ultimately too wonderful for us, as the psalmist says.[23]

---

[20] *Thy Word is Truth* (Grand Rapids: Eerdmans, 1957), 5.

[21] It is obvious, in fact, that they were not, as Warfield's stress on induction and Young's emphasis on the testimony of the Holy Spirit make clear. Yet the dualist/rationalist tendencies surviving in each create tensions which surface in the form of foundationalist concerns and procedures.

[22] "The Christian man requires," says Warfield in the same place, "and thank God, has, a thoroughly trustworthy Bible to which he can go directly and at once in every time of need."

[23] Ps 139:5–6, 17. "The personality of the Word of God signifies," says Karl Barth (*Church Dogmatics* 1/1. 157–58), "not any diminuation of its verbal character, but the sheerly active obstacle to reducing its verbal form to a human system, i.e., to using its verbal form to lay the foundation and raise the structure

In that case we will face no temptation to pre-determine the character of this book as one of pristine perfection, in order that we may not be frightened by the signs of its frailty or be forced to admit that we cannot lean on it. Instead we will only say that in this book we have confidence that we will never be misdirected, however often our own thoughts may go astray. We will say that God gives himself for us to lean on in and through Scripture, and that we therefore attest the truth of Scripture in this sacred service as the bearer of his own self-attesting Word. This much we can say, indeed, we are unable to say otherwise with integrity. Yet once again we are free to recognize in the text its adequacy to the Authority with whom we have to do without having to postulate in advance its error-free perfection in all things.[24]

Inspiration and Expectancy

Perhaps it is only fair, however, to turn over the coin for a moment and consider the fact that the currency of inspiration does indeed bear the insignia, "In God we trust." In spite of all the rush these days to defend critical methodology as essentially profitable and constructive when sanely practiced, and the willingness to tolerate those signs of weakness in the biblical records which may sometimes be unearthed, *can it not be asked with a certain seemliness whether exhaustive inerrancy might be reasonably adduced just because of "the high level of expectation"*

---

of a human system." Both Warfield and Young (not to mention a host of limited inerrantists) lose sight of the personality and irreducible authority of the Word of God in their treatment of the Scriptures, and in their perception of the sort of confidence that pertains to Christian doctrine as learned from Scripture.

[24] I.e., we will confess that God has spoken and still speaks everywhere in this book, and thus constantly renews his direction and authority over our thinking—that Scripture in this definite, but limited and non-technical, sense is made to serve as a foundation or framework for our thought—but we will not find it necessary to defend the idea that God "is the Author of every word thereof" (E. J. Young, *Thy Word is Truth*, 269) in the most literal sense, which can only serve a vain attempt to find our security in Scripture per se. While we thus also reject the idea that an error anywhere in inspired Scripture calls our entire faith into question (ibid.), we must nonetheless insist on something that Phillips, for one, seems to overlook—namely, that a true message, though containing certain indications of human weakness, perhaps, and very often imperfectly comprehended by its readers as well, is much superior to and more useful than a partially falsified message (however well or poorly understood). We can hardly allow that God's speaking is any way *disrupted* by untruth; nor can we fall back at this point on the fanciful distinction between revelational and non-revelational matters in the messages his spokesmen have delivered.

produced by the doctrines of revelation and inspiration? It might indeed, but for three facts.

First, God *chose* to employ the earthen vessels of human authorship, men of varying skill, gifts and opportunities (and none with technical assistance or the modern mindset); he chose to employ time-bound cultures, community documents, and much that bears no marks of the miraculous. This hardly means that relative perfection was therefore placed beyond the grasp of inspiration, as some falsely contend; it only means that we have no warrant for presuming upon it. That Holy Scripture "shows so many seams and uneven places" (as Kuyper puts it) in matters not pertaining to the inerrancy issue ought to be warning enough not to appropriate indiscriminately the high level of expectation Scripture is constantly recreating for the attentive reader. For reasons difficult to discern, the force of the simple fact of Scripture's obvious and undisputed imperfections in areas other than factual error seems to be largely lost on strict inerrantists. But this fact, however insignificant next to the compelling beauty of Scripture on the whole, is devastating to their position nonetheless. If one sort of harmless imperfection can be "God-breathed," why not another? Only errors that actually *mislead* the trusting reader in his pursuit of the truth of a matter about which the Bible is speaking take us to a new level of imperfection on which the canonical function and God-breathed identity of Scripture is rendered problematic.

Second, the equally indisputable defects of the Bible's transmission—its textual corruption and uncertainties, limited though they be—make doubly plain the fact that God's speaking does not require the sort of perfection exhaustive inerrancy has in view, that canonical Scripture can afford to embrace a variety of minor flaws without becoming suspect in its power to function as canon. And if I may expand on a point made earlier in this chapter, we must deal with present realities if we intend to say anything intelligible about Scripture as canon. In any case, it could hardly have been the original autographa, of which some inerrantists are overly fond of speaking, that Paul was thinking of when he advised Timothy to be faithful to the God-breathed Scriptures he had known from childhood, or that Christ had in mind when he spoke of the unbreakable, not-to-be-set-aside Scriptures to which the Pharisees were responsible. (How could one be responsible to non-existent autographa—particularly when for some books there may never have been anything recognizable as "an original autograph"?) What is more, in the former case the reference was doubtless to the Septuagint. The fact that no fuss was raised about all its deviations from the Hebrew text indicates that God is quite prepared to identify an imperfect text as his own, or at least shows where the emphasis did and must lie, namely, on the function of the text as dynamic message-bearer. The fact that exhaustive inerrancy must appeal to manuscripts that no longer exist is evidence of its own irrelevancy. At best such a position involves a completely unnecessary attempt to vindicate God's reliability, a somewhat presumptuous move if God has taken no steps of his own to do likewise in this matter.[25]

The third fact I leave to the next section, though it too may be handled with great brevity so far as my purposes here are concerned. In any case, many have written with greater knowledge and cogency on these very issues, though some, to be sure, have allowed their own arguments and assumptions to drift much too far in the opposite direction![26]

Evidence and Honesty

Finally, we must turn again, and turn directly, to that aspect of the Church's exposure to Scripture which has occasioned the inerrancy debate (though it is not responsible for the debate's refractory nature). We must ask a question which has never been far from view and refuses to go away just because one

[25] Greg Bahnsen ("The Inerrancy of the Autographa," in *Inerrancy*, ed. N. L. Geisler, 161), after surveying some of Scripture's own references to the use of copies and existing texts, states: "What these things show us is that the *message* conveyed by the words of the autographa . . . is the strict object of inspiration. Therefore, because that message was reliably reflected in the copies or translations available to the biblical writers, they could be used in an authoritative and practical manner." Just so! And because that is all that concerns us about the written word, the ultimate veracity and functional authority of those messages might quite conceivably leave room for certain imperfections or errors in the original text even as in the copies, without jeopardizing anything crucial to the integrity of the word of God at all, despite Bahnsen's arguments to the contrary. If infallibility is so important to the Church, and it is, we are quite rightly asked to stick to the practical question of the infallibility of *our* Bibles (as Clark Pinnock and others have requested), though that insistence does not disallow all distinctions between the original text and imperfect copies or translations thereof.

[26] On present concerns see, e.g., Dewey Beegle, *Scripture, Tradition, and Infallibility*; Paul Achtemeier, *The Inspiration of Scripture*.

might like it to, a question whose answer is obvious to the vast majority of those who have given serious attention to Scripture: *Do the biblical phenomena, inductively examined, support the idea of exhaustive inerrancy?*

The answer here (and this is the third fact I had in mind) would be extremely difficult to give in the affirmative, though it is no concern of mine to prove the negative. For long lists of problem passages—often debatable, but assuredly *long*—the reader will have to turn elsewhere; likewise for any analysis of proposed solutions. I will simply say that, given the lack of any compelling reason to scrutinize and re-scrutinize the many difficulties in the biblical text that fall within the narrower terms of the inerrancy debate, to juggle facts or conjure up solutions, or even to refuse a decision and await further light, we need not be overly concerned about encountering that sort of list. Indeed, surface difficulties in the text need not bother us at all, except where the message-function is impaired; honesty to the "anomalies" is possible. Where an apparent conflict in information is perceived, it is usually not long before one can observe this conflict receding to complete insignificance by looking through the lens of a renewed focus on what the text(s) have actually set out to say. This promises to be a more fruitful course of action than pulling on the gloves in order to defend exhaustive inerrancy![27]

I will present one example as an illustration: Matthew and Mark both record that the criminals who were crucified with Christ "also heaped insults on him," together with the Roman soldiers, the Jewish chief priests, scholars and elders, and even those who were passing by. Luke, however, having carefully researched everything, indicates that one of the two robbers was conscious of Christ's righteousness and came to his defense.[28] It is possible, of course, that the thief began by cursing and came to a change of heart. But functionally considered, such speculation (and only partially successful harmonization) is unnecessary.

---

[27] Conflicts arising from actual biblical messages about this or that will also be resolved by the same procedure, though in such cases resolution is never to be reached by leaving room for supposed errors. This conviction and the perseverance it prescribes never disappoints, but always rewards, the student of Scripture and of the matters of which Scripture speaks.

[28] It is interesting that Luke's source(s) was also sufficiently close to notice that the soldiers were joining in this mockery of a crucified "King." This fact and the matter of the saving of the thief are recorded by Luke alone (23:36f.; cf.

All three evangelists wanted their readers to know that Christ went to the cross rejected by ruler and ruffian alike. Luke had an additional purpose, to point out the gracious authority of Christ on behalf of the prisoner and the oppressed, even—perhaps especially—at the height of his own weakness and Passion.[29] Both purposes are achieved, both messages are true and historical and without real conflict, though Matthew and Mark might well have simply assumed that the second thief shared in the mocking words of the first.[30] This example demonstrates the superior ability of functional inerrancy to handle the data honestly while keeping the focus of the exegetical discussion where it belongs.

*   *   *

Conclusion to Part 2

In the last two chapters I have shown that a strict view of inerrancy has no solid base of support in Scripture and that it is not called for by careful reflection on other lines of evidence. If this be so, then a change of direction is necessary in many conservative circles. For when exhaustive inerrancy is set in the place of, and treated with the respect due, the doctrine of biblical infallibility, the Word of Truth is done damage in the house of its friends and wrangling about the words of Scripture replaces worship of the Lord who speaks by them. We must let the Bible establish its own character, determining both our commitment to its truthfulness and our openness to irregularities in the text. Without doubt this adjustment is difficult to many and requires a serious pondering of the issues raised in Part 1 (issues worthy of consideration for a number of reasons). It is nonetheless essential if "the battle for the Bible" is to retain any integrity,

---

1:3). John was also standing nearby (John 19:26), of course, but he chose not to include the incident at all.

[29] Notice Luke's programmatic addition to the other synoptics at 4:16f., which initiates this very theme.

[30] Both of these gospel writers quite probably witnessed the crucifixion, though standing at some distance (Luke 23:49). It should be noted that the harmonization mentioned above *formally* resolves the factual conflict with Luke, but does not resolve the conflicting impression left by Matthew and Mark about the second thief. On my proposal neither aspect of the conflict amounts to the kind of error that disrupts biblical infallibility or reliability.

instead of becoming a vain war for the honor and security of the conservative evangelical.

For all that, however, the arguments of Parts 1 and 2 unite to affirm that the openness of which I have just spoken is not left open-ended, not on both ends, at least. Every aspect of the biblical text must be considered responsible to the purpose of God to speak truly therein, and our response to the text must confess the full authority of its message in all its multiformity, indeed, in everything that it would say to us. This remains the right the Bible claims for itself, despite the fact that God did not choose to take up every element of human participation—in either the authoring or the preserving or the hearing of this literature—into his own divine standard of perfection.[31] Certainly, then, there will be a good bit of wrestling both with Scripture and with apparently sound judgments that nonetheless run contrary to Scripture, thus requiring thoughtful refutation. That sort of thing is hardly a needless struggle, but there should be no evidence of panic or desperation in such a struggle, only submission to the Lord and hard, scholarly work. Wrestling, I might venture to say, is a very different and much more profitable venture than wrangling.

Of course, the balance I am seeking here leaves us still with many questions, but the answers to these questions are essentially hermeneutical in nature. Refining the doctrine of infallibility and working with the broader terms of the inerrancy construct is, in the end, *a practical matter relating to our actual understanding of the biblical text.* Part 3 will attempt to develop in a small way the main themes of what has been suggested thus far, and in particular, to ask the inerrancy question hermeneutically. Right off the top, however, a chapter must be devoted to the question of where the real battlefields lie, if exhaustive inerrancy has proved to be only a diversionary skirmish. The Lordship of Christ over the Church through Scripture leaves no more room for careless ambivalence in our acknowledgment of Scripture than it does for reactionary conservatism.

---

[31] Some have mistakenly imagined that this idea might pose problems when applied to Jesus' own words. But it is not sin to have an incomplete knowledge of natural things. If Christ spoke and acted as other men in areas which did not obscure his expression of the things revealed to him by the Father or disrupt the true theocentricity of his knowledge and moral consciousness, this is no cause for concern, but rather another sign of his solidarity with us. Today's "mustard seed" fuss is of less consequence than the seed itself.

Part 3
A Faithful Confession

5 | The Real Battle

A faithful confession of Scripture in our regard for the Christ of the Scriptures does entail a willingness to set that confession over against contrary tendencies in both scholarly and popular thought. Of course a great deal could be said about the latter, but it is largely the former which occupies us in the present discussions of Scripture's reliability. While it is hardly feasible to attempt to visit every front on which the intellectual and practical authority of Scripture is attacked or every area in which it is quietly undermined, a few of the strategic support bases for such unhappy maneuvers can be pointed out in a brief tour of three significant challenges facing those who would hold to an evangelical view of Scripture. The standard to be raised is that of Christ's living authority over the rest of humanity's best efforts to interpret the character of Scripture or the relative values of its parts. Against any display of autonomy in such efforts we must vigorously protest, for autonomy only cuts us off from Christ.

Rejecting Empirical/Rationalism

When we speak of a *faithful* confession, what else do we mean to underline except our desire to be truly *responsive* to the God who has found us in Christ? The besetting sin behind so many of our problems in the doctrine of Scripture, as I think I have already made clear, is that distancing of ourselves from our Lord which takes place in a formal approach to the Scriptures. When the bond between Christ and the Scriptures is left un-broken, we do not come to the authors of Scripture to argue or to judge or even to approve; we do not come in our independence. We come in silence.[1] No other response is appropriate as the fundamental mode of our hearing. "He who has ears to ear, let

[1] Cf. Dietrich Bonhoeffer, *Christ the Center*, trans. Edwin H. Robertson (San Francisco: Harper & Row, 1978) 27.

him hear" does not rule out our difficult questions, our inquisi-
tiveness, our dialogue, our witness. It simply founds all this in
the profound silence of respect for that Man who speaks as our
God. In the matter at hand perhaps the most unhappy fact of all
is that even the defenders of biblical authority often speak out of
the noise of man's own clamoring after self-assured knowledge,
till the Voice of Christ in the very word they are defending is
smothered in a wave of human rationalization.[2]

Is this not mere secularism in religious clothing? What was
it that prompted Clark Pinnock to charge that "stress on the
Spirit is noticeably lacking in the literature of inerrancy"?[3] Is
not the reason for this lack to be found in the fact that man is
always inclined to speak *before* he will listen, to establish
himself before he will submit to being established by Christ?
The real threat to the Church's recognition of the authority of
Scripture lies as much in the camp of inerrancy as it does in that
of inerrancy's opponents. It lies with all who espouse the
methods of empirical/rationalism or who in any fashion exercise the adamic independence and autonomy of thought in their
approach to Scripture. It lies with them because they reduce
Christ to a correspondingly distant and dependent Lord, and
Scripture to an object of their own disposal. It lies with them
because to this extent their focus is not on the Truth himself
through the Holy Spirit; they have been seduced into grasping
after truth of statement apart from the truth of being—*God's*
Being—and in that wrenching of the truth to their own ends
(even its supposed protection) they are in danger of losing even
that which they have. It lies ironically with those who, in their
haste to close the back door on the smallest inconsistency in the
biblical phenomena, rush through the house leaving the front
door fully ajar to all who would subject the word of God, yes,
and God himself, to the priority of human judgment.

---

[2] For theology generally, writes Eberhard Jungel in the first foreword to
God as the Mystery of the World (p. vii), the great danger exists "that God will
be talked to death, . . . silenced by the very words that seek to talk about him."
Cf. Hab 2:18–20.

[3] "A Response to Rex A. Koivisto," *JETS* 24 (1981) 154. There has, in fact,
been a widespread and general breakdown in genuine trinitarian thought that is
only slowly being corrected in many circles; certainly it is not the *triune* God
who requires the sort of defense many inerrantists offer.

I have already noted that when the pagan principle of independent judgment is affirmed even in the face of the knowledge of Christ, then the possibility of requiring Scripture to defer to that judgment, the possibility of withdrawing approval at some point from the very instrument by which that knowledge comes, is also affirmed. Daniel Fuller once challenged Pinnock on just this matter (in a now somewhat dated exchange):

> My biggest difficulty with your position is that I cannot see how you can make such an emphasis on the validity of the inductive method . . . and then deny the right of reason and criticism to be sovereign. . . . Induction, as I understand it, means letting criticism control all aspects of the knowing process from beginning to end.

Fuller went on to describe his own outlook at the time:

> . . . I am not saying that the Bible cannot err in revelational matters while it can where historical control is possible. . . . All I am saying is that if it errs where historical control is possible in matters germane to "the whole counsel of God" which "makes a man wise to salvation," then all the Bible becomes questionable. I sincerely hope that as I continue my historical-grammatical exegesis of Scripture, I shall find no error in its teachings. But I can only affirm inerrancy with high probability. . . .[4]

Certainly such an approach threatens the purity of the Church's response to the Christ of the Scriptures, whether or not one is presently an inerrantist and whether or not one is prepared to draw drastic conclusions about the whole Bible should he suppose himself to have found one significant error. The immediate, practical problem is that one's reading of Scripture is not free to the present rule of Christ if one's own critical ability must "control all aspects of the knowing process from beginning to end." Not that attention to the historical questions associated with Scripture or the genuine devotion to scholarly

---

[4] See Daniel Fuller and Clark Pinnock, "On Revelation and Biblical Authority," *JETS* 16 (1973) (reprinted from *Christian Scholar's Review* 2 [1973] 330-35) 67-69. Fuller was not a full inerrantist even at that time, but Pinnock was. It might also be helpful to note that Pinnock has since become a leading opponent of the idea that one error renders all of Scripture suspect.

research thus engendered are an actual threat to Christ, of course, or to Christian truth; but they can be made into a threat to the believer and to the proclamation of the truth. Because of a footing in human self-sufficiency and lack of concrete respect for the Spirit in terms of the sanctity of the word he has chosen to speak, we are led all too often not to the shedding of naïve or defensive distortions of Scripture, which is the proper goal of scholarly examination, but to further, more complicated distortions. The imposition of our own critical and cultural baggage on the writers of Scripture has led time and again to unnecessary detours on the path of truth, and for many, to dead ends of disbelief and self-government.[5] Robert Reymond counters that

[5] We must recognize, as we are now commonly reminded, that the student of Scripture inevitably brings with him—imbedded in his interpretive methods and engrained in his very outlook—selective criteria for understanding and assessment of the text, just as the text itself inevitably presents a selective and interpretive view of reality that requires to be understood as such. But in the hoped-for fusion of horizons the question remains as to the right of the biblical word to speak altogether out of its canonical authority despite its entry into a new knowledge context. The question is not whether the student of Scripture, and the scholar in particular, has something to contribute to the renewed hearing of an ancient word, or even whether the text as well as its audience must undergo a sort of self-adjustment in the process, but whether the scholar is *in a position to actually correct or deliberately impose upon the text* in view of other knowledge he supposes himself to have attained and the methodology he has derived in the process. The answer which presupposes the canonical reality, i.e., the answer of the Church, can only be "No!" Fuller, e.g., appears to assume just such a stance, however, one obviously shared by his colleague, Paul Jewett, who a short while later found himself in a position of dispute with the apostle Paul on certain women's issues, posing some rather thorny problems for those around him. Quite obviously a great deal is at stake in this matter of who will correct whom; in the best and most practical terms that is what the inerrancy issue is all about. Ray S. Anderson (*On Being Human* [Grand Rapids: Eerdmans, 1982] 116) is helpful when in another context he gently questions Jewett—who of course believed that he was only correcting Paul with Paul (no pun intended)— asking whether it is right to appeal even to some transcending theological principle over against the actual statements of Scripture: "Is an abstract concept such as 'analogy of faith' more inherently theological, and therefore more normative, than the words which denote the concrete event of creation and revelation itself? Why is it necessary that Paul be 'wrong' when he teaches that wives must be subordinate to their husbands, despite the fact that this is expressed in the language and thought-forms of his own tradition and culture? Is it because the concept of subordination has itself become culturally despised and incapable of restoration in its essential theological sense? If so, this might be a premature conclusion, and a dreadful expedient with far more serious implications than has been bargained for." He goes on to say: "Theology's difficult task is to clarify—and perhaps even resurrect—biblical concepts, not to substitute more congenial alternatives." As far as I can see, this is the spirit in which even

"the Christian's life should be one grand doxology to God," that his intellectual life, too, should be lived under the Lordship of Christ.[6] Is that not the proper impact of the Church's personal knowledge of its living Lord?

Clark Pinnock likened Fuller's situation to life on a slide, doctrinally speaking. "He gives us a slope, not a platform," was his complaint; though it was to become obvious that Pinnock's own inerrancy platform provided something of a grade, leading to considerable modification in his position and a search for a new approach.[7] Some years later, in response to growing criticism that on the one hand the need to redefine inerrancy makes a farce of it, and on the other, that so much fancy exegetical footwork is necessary to maintain it, Pinnock admitted:

> For those who like myself are sensitive to both these criticisms the appeal and attractiveness of the inerrancy category lessens considerably. It is held with less and less enthusiasm, and becomes more of a burden than a positive asset. Indeed, it may well be that modified inerrancy will prove to be a temporary way-station on the road, not to apostasy as Lindsell darkly warns, but to a non-inerrancy position on biblical inspiration. It serves at present as a momentary shelter for critically honest but cautious evangelicals who want to scrutinize the terrain just ahead before moving into it.[8]

Pinnock then challenged the non-inerrancy camp to provide "a positive and compelling understanding of biblical authority . . . which can command the assent and appreciation of God's

---

the literary and historical judgments (so often controversial for the inerrancy issue) that prepare the way for theological thinking must also be carried out.

[6] *The Justification of Knowledge* (Phillipsburg: Presbyterian and Reformed, 1979) 116. We do well here to heed Martin Luther's advice ("Preface to the Wittenberg Edition of Luther's German Writings," trans. Robert R. Heitner, in *Luther's Works*, vol. 34 [Philadelphia: Fortress Press, 1960] 285f.), who warns us against presumptuousness as students of the Scriptures and bids us approach them in humility after the fashion of the psalmist in Psalm 119, who comes prayerfully and repeatedly to the text, wanting "to lay hold of the real teacher of the Scriptures himself, so that he may not seize upon them pell-mell with his reason and become his own teacher."

[7] "On Revelation and Biblical Authority," 72. Pinnock's recent book in this area, entitled *The Scripture Principle* (New York: Harper and Row, 1984), will be discussed below (see n 13). It came into my hands only after the present work was essentially completed.

[8] "The Ongoing Struggle Over Biblical Inerrancy," *JASA* 31 (1979) 70-71.

people, who are anxious to know where and how the Bible can be trusted if it cannot be followed everywhere, and what are the limits that prevent a dismantling of biblical teaching in the name of 'liberation from inerrancy'." He anticipated a new evangelical outlook that would include

> a greater emphasis upon the Bible's own stated purpose, to give knowledge of salvation through Jesus Christ, and resistance to substituting for that purpose such an extraneous ideal as factual precision. Stress will be placed on the competence of the Spirit to use Scripture in nourishing the Church and his dependability in keeping believers in the truth. . . . Validation of biblical authority will be sought, not in scholastic controversy, but in the effective preaching of the Word and in its proven relevance for decision making.[9]

Lest we suppose here a drift into a lop-sidedly subjective approach to Scripture, it must be noted that Pinnock later reaffirmed that he has never endorsed limited inerrancy in the sense of "a policy of pick and choose what Biblical teachings we intend to respect."[10] But when we recall the criticism made of Fuller and the unavoidably relevant question posed to non-inerrantists about limits to the deconstruction of the biblical word, are we not ourselves stuck for an answer if we take up such a position without at the same time explicitly repudiating the principle of autonomy in the approach of empirical/rationalism? Can we really do justice to the objectivity of the authoritative word of Christ—particularly if we are also going to be highlighting the weakness of the biblical spokesmen, as Pinnock allows[11]—unless we affirm very plainly that our openness to the signs of human weakness in the text is not born of a need or of a willingness to subject the text to our own determinations, but is altogether contained within our recognition of the entire trustworthiness of the address itself?[12] Otherwise,

---

[9] Ibid., 72-73.
[10] "A Response to Rex A. Koivisto," 153.
[11] "The Ongoing Struggle Over Biblical Inerrancy," 73.
[12] I.e., unless we recognize inerrancy *in its broader terms* as bound up in our Christian confession, the proper focus on biblical teachings rather than on biblical phenomena prepares the way for a departure from what the authors actually said to what we imagine they were getting at as best they could. That would not be respect for the word of Christ, and such slipperiness in addressing the inerrancy issue cannot provide a satisfactory solution. Indeed, none is possible while clinging to the old epistemology.

confession of the Lordship of Christ through the Scriptures does not touch down altogether on the level of our actual involvement with the Bible, which is one reason *why* "overshadowing our parochial disagreements there hangs a very real and not imaginary threat to biblical inspiration," as Pinnock is quick to point out. Fortunately, it is in the direction I am commending that he moves in his most recent work.[13]

Apart from this specific repudiation and affirmation, it seems to me that there is no sufficient response to the modern wave of scholars, churchmen and lay-people who would like to force on the Church a false distinction between κήρυγμα and διδαχή, relativizing a great deal even of what Pinnock touts as the evangelical's "respect for what we could call the didactic thought models of Holy Scripture as divinely given and inspired."[14] This growing crowd of "kerygmatic theologians" (if we may borrow the terminology sometimes applied to proponents of the new hermeneutic), having already accepted the validity of much modern criticism of the Bible but remaining unwilling to part with the essentials of orthodox dogma, utilizes a focus on the gospel itself (not on the act of proclamation) to

---

[13] In *The Scripture Principle* Pinnock does, to some extent, repudiate the principle of autonomy behind empirical/rationalism, and moves toward a dynamic confessional approach to the authority of Scripture (cf. p. 228, n 30). This book deserves high marks both for tone and substance, and for its very practical orientation. Pinnock reaffirms here—now in a more organic way—the crucial bond between revelation and Scripture, and develops the role of the Holy Spirit in establishing the Church's testimony to the canonical service of every passage of Scripture. Despite a genuine frankness about the problems evident in Scripture, he suggests (p. 62) that the battle line over biblical authority is indeed to be drawn in connection with the question whether everything in Scripture is God's Word, so long as it is understood in terms of what God *teaches* his people in and through the biblical texts. He encourages "a moderately phrased category of inerrancy" as possibly "the best operating principle" in the current theological atmosphere, while making inerrancy "relative to the intention of the text" in a manner that at least approaches a hermeneutical solution to the debate (pp. 60, 78; cf. chap. 6 below). Unfortunately—and this is not a complaint against the frankness just mentioned, which certainly prevents one from thinking that Pinnock is returning to anything like his earlier conservatism—the slipperiness I have been attempting to guard against is not yet eliminated in *The Scripture Principle*. In my judgment, at least, Pinnock does not attain to a full appreciation of the concept of *canon* (or of the confessional approach) and still leaves the reader a little uncertain as to how to apply his "moderately phrased" commitment to infallibility.

[14] Ibid. Note: I do not think that Pinnock intended this somewhat vague terminology to bear the full weight of an evangelical doctrine of inspiration; in my judgment, it would not be able to.

break with the traditional respect for the Scriptures. These folk acknowledge no outright authority mediated in and through the teachings of Scripture per se, that is, they do not regard what every passage has to say to the Church as carrying the authority of God's own instruction and correction. Their authority lies in the gospel which they glean from the Scriptures, and the essentials of that gospel are the only supposed limits to the dismantling of biblical authority. Taking their cue from a very narrow understanding of 2 Tim 3:15 and from the critical results of certain schools of scholarly thought, the Bible is reduced to an infallible guide to salvation in Christ; "every passage" as theopneustic instruction and correction for the righteous man has slipped from view. Scripture is perceived simply as an historical interaction with God's redemptive program, providentially achieving its divine purpose of leading men and women to salvation. *Any* form of inerrancy (historical or theological) is an unacceptable doctrinal accretion incompatible with the historically conditioned documents, despite the overall certitude that remains about the basic message of the Bible and its proven relevance.

Why would there be no sufficient response to this serious encroachment on biblical authority, with its reductionist approach to biblical instruction? We might be quick to contend that the New Testament knows no such distinction between κήρυγμα and διδαχή.[15] We could point out that this view of Scripture is not that of the passages we examined in chap. 3. We could argue that this position is a rejection of any verbal objectivity to the authority of Christ, for the merely human word of Scripture (which is no longer Christ's word as such) intervenes between Christ and his gospel. We could insist that on this view one could not speak of the Christ-of-the-gospel in the same sense that we have been speaking of the Christ-of-the-Scriptures. We might even say very gravely that this has never been the view of the Church. But for all that, in the *practical* forum the distinction between the two positions continually breaks down. For if we ourselves are willing to submit Scripture's teachings to contrary judgments which our own comprehension of reality suggests to us, rather than to return constantly to the drawing board out of subjection to Scripture, then there is no uncondi-

---

[15] Cf., e.g., Rom 16:17 and 16:25; cf. also Acts 5:28, 2 John 9.

tional confession of the Lordship of Christ in recognizable
canonical terms, and no distinguishable area of respectful submission that is less than arbitrary. "Pick and choose" becomes
inevitable and there is no response within the Church to one
whose judgment on the viability of a biblical viewpoint should
happen to differ from our own. Would we not then be wiser
simply to accept this unshepherded pluralism and admit that we
were only giving lip-service to the Lordship of Christ in and
through the Scriptures? What else can we do if we have no desire
to return to the polar tensions of the inerrancy debate?

Of course, there are always more moderate approaches
which appear to provide an appropriate mediation of the difficulty. Richard J. Coleman's article "Another View: The Battle
for the Bible" has this look about it, for example.[16] Coleman, in
fact, does not reject the inerrancy doctrine altogether; he simply
argues (not unlike Pinnock) from the kerygmatic context and
character of Scripture's composition that it should not be judged
according to the formal requirements of dogmatic truth. He is
justifiably concerned about those who have conceived the inerrancy issue as a black and white choice between full and
limited inerrancy. He dismisses unqualified inerrancy as obscurantism and suggests that we need an open, flexible concept of
inerrancy that does not rigidly limit qualifications to the doctrine. Nevertheless, for Coleman

> a concept of qualified inerrancy does not mean a restriction of
> inspiration to certain kinds of subject matter. Infallibility is
> limited only by the intention of the author and the kerygmatic
> nature of the biblical message. As a Christian I trust Scripture as
> it faithfully presents the good news of God's grace and judgment.
> As a Christian historian, I see the Bible as *the* remarkable account
> of the historical acting out of God's love and man's response.
> The tensions, difficulties, and possible contradictions we encoun-
> ter are not the blemishes of a system of doctrine and practice, but
> the natural results of writers who were compelled to preach the
> Gospel in the language and forms of their contemporaries.[17]

Coleman's approach has much to commend it, but in this
form, at least, it will not stand up to close examination. Mediation cannot be achieved merely by generalization. Coleman

[16] *JASA* 31 (1979) 74–79.
[17] Ibid., 78.

rather glibly assimilates the intentions of the biblical authors in all their material to *the* biblical message and to essential kerygmatic truths. This generality does not meet the challenges of the questions being asked today and actually leaves room for the same gradual dismantling of the specific, practical biblical authority that concerns the Church on a daily basis. Vern Poythress, commenting on an earlier article by Coleman, criticizes a vagueness that could be interpreted *"either* as defending a traditional view *or* as making enormous concessions."[18] Notice how the question is put earlier on in the article from which I have already quoted:

> There appears to be a concensus among prominent evangelical scholars that the point of no return is over the word "intends." Is Scripture inerrant in all that it communicates or only inerrant in what it intends to teach as essential?[19]

The "intends . . . *as essential"* really neglects, rather than highlights, the important territory between exhaustive inerrancy, on the one hand, and an "infallibility" based on 2 Tim 3:15 that ignores v 16 ("every passage"!), on the other. Such slippery terminology is naturally a temptation when no effort is made to face the issue before us. But the ground of which I speak must not be passed over so readily if any solid *pou sto* is to remain at all; it is the ground of *Christ's own authority in and through the word,* an authority which demands that both the essential and the peripheral concerns of his spokesmen take precedence over human judgment.

Without losing the historical sensitivity and dynamic hermeneutical focus of the kerygmatic perspective, we ought in fact to object to the increasingly common question, "dogmatic or kerygmatic?," wherever that question arises as an invitation to adduce a distinction between the gospel and its biblical expression. Certainly we ought to refuse any disjunction between the speech of the human author and the word of God in connection with Christ, such that the objective significance of inspiration is detached from the actual witness itself and located somewhere *within* what the author has communicated. That would mean a return to the form-content dualism and a denial of the objective

---

[18] "Problems for Limited Inerrancy," *JETS* 18 (1975) 93f.
[19] "Another View: The Battle for the Bible," 75.

and identifiable verbal form taken by the divine Speech-Acts of the Lord of the Church.[20] Scripture would then confront us only as a long historical sermon in which essential truth is thought to be perceived, but in which the problem of subjectivity in the task of interpreting and applying the human testimony is magnified beyond all proportion. The teacher of Scripture, on this view, must not only be prepared to comprehend carefully just what has been said in preparation for the further task of bringing the modern listener into intelligible relation to it, he must also decide what is authoritative and reliable by virtue of being essential. Of course, it might be protested that evaluation of what is essential is an important part of the hermeneutical process, and so it is. But now the interpreter may be allowed, or even expected, to draw lines in Scripture around that to which the hearer must be brought or to which he ought to respond! This is no longer an exegetical judgment, a question of contextual significance, of semantic role and relations or emphasis and balance; it passes over into another sort of value judgment, into a truth judgment. But who will determine what is essential kerygmatic truth, or what pertains to godliness today and to the renewal of the modern mind? And how, as Poythress inquires, will we avoid the presumptuous application of an arbitrary filter to Scripture in order to screen out its impurities?[21]

On the principle of human autonomy represented by empirical/rationalism, a variety of filters are inevitable. For if Scripture is not regarded in immediate connection with Christ our Lord at every point, it passes from being his Scripture to

---

[20] Or to use terminology employed by Nicholas Wolterstorff ("On God Speaking," *RJ* 3 [July–August 1969] 11), God's speech-*acts* must not be cut loose from the speech-*objects* of his speaking, i.e., the words of his spokesmen. We are called "to a concentrated attention to the very words," says Berkouwer, who warns us that the dualism of which we speak "can easily mask itself by adducing the distinction between kernel (center) and periphery"—though that does not mean we must reject the whole idea of the centralization of Scripture and the notion that the information it contains is governed throughout by God's revelatory purpose (*Holy Scripture*, 178f.). Berkouwer demonstrates balance here that Coleman seems to lack. He rejects the idea that any sifting of Scripture is necessary or appropriate, and reminds us "that one should never be guided by an antithesis between *words* and the *gospel*" (ibid., 166; cf. "Another View," 76–78).

[21] "Problems for Limited Inerrancy," 96f. Poythress has carried the argument a bit far, however, by failing to consider the matters of which I have been treating.

being our Scripture. We will not behold Christ in Scripture, but examine Scripture to see where it fits with our own restricted vision of Christ and his world. Description of the character and value of Scripture in its various parts, then, will no longer serve a genuine responsiveness to the Christ who reveals himself in and through all of Scripture in a variety of ways. It will be loosed to an arbitrariness that may include actual rejection of various Scriptures under the dictates of a methodology that shuts out the sound of his Lordship by its formal and reserved approach to Scripture. It is this that has led not only to the weakening of confidence in the full scope of biblical teaching, but also to the advances of the more radical attempts to silence the Word of God.

Once again, the real battle here is not over the question of errors in the Bible, but over the manner in which we approach the Bible. Indeed, it is certainly *not* incumbent upon us to indicate "where and how far the Bible can be followed," but to indicate simply and conclusively that we come to the Bible in *order* to follow it wherever it leads us. At the same time, we are not obligated to uphold exhaustive inerrancy, making the length of Pekah's reign a matter of much greater concern than Paul's theology, as it were. Certainly the proverbial fear of the loosened tent-flap which permits the camel to worm its way in is not entirely unjustified, but in the case of Scripture this fear is only generated by a pre-commitment to the principles of empirical/rationalism, which ought to be repudiated consequent to confrontation with Christ. There is the real battle. The sloping platform of much modern biblical scholarship is indeed a serious problem, but exhaustive inerrancy is not the solution. We should not wish to share the same shaky footing at all, clinging tenaciously to the very upper end of that platform; at best we could only turn this slide into a sort of teeter-totter, with obscurantism on one end and unbelief on the other. Only a complete and resounding reaffirmation of the Church's commitment to work under the Word in every way and at all times can restore equilibrium to the work of its scholars and theologians. The solution is a return to focusing on the living Christ in all our regard for Scripture, with due respect for the fact that Scripture not only speaks about him, but with his own self-authenticating Voice. The battle for the Bible ought to be nothing more or less than a persistent invitation to *listen* to our Lord.

Rethinking Inspiration

With this in view, perhaps the area most deserving of our attention is the doctrine of inspiration itself, which ought to be reconstructed in a more Christocentric fashion. A great many inadequate ideas concerning general inspiration are still current today—speculative ideas which can only be read *into* the biblical testimony. Of these, some are of the sort I have already criticized in chap. 3, that is, ideas implicit in a rigid view of inerrancy which identify the whole of Scripture word for word with a static revelation of the mind of God, however the actual process of inspiration might be conceived. Such views are at least as old as Philo, but are not deserving of the veneration of their age; they are governed by fanciful pneumatology apart from incarnational Christology, and lack the vitality of a focus on Scripture's participation in Christ's living revelation.[22] With the recent insurgence of alternative views of inspiration, however, many have turned to describe the relationship between Christ and the Scriptures (and hence, the question of biblical reliability) in ways quite inadequate to the faithful teaching ministry of the Spirit who bears witness to Christ, that ministry which both produced Scripture and today employs it in Christ's service. In yet more blatant ways the Scriptures are being distanced from the divine Lordship in discussions about their origin.[23] Against

[22] Von Balthasar (*Word and Revelation*, 12f.) is helpful here. Christ's life is a fulfilling of the OT Scriptures and the opening of the possibility of the NT Scriptures, the living gospel that proceeds from him: "If then the incarnate son merges all scripture in himself so as to make it fully what it is, namely the word of God the father in the son, he also sends it forth from himself so as to make it fully what it is, namely the word of the Spirit whom he sends out at the end of his earthly course, upon his return to the father." This is the context in which inspiration needs to be discussed, but generally is not. The dryness of most conservative formulations—i.e, that conservatism which regards the doctrine of inspiration as little more than justification for the existence of an inerrant book-revelation—is epitomized by the way one of conservatism's most vocal critics accounts for it: "Nowhere is the *rationalism* of fundamentalist argument more clear than in the doctrine of the inspiration and infallibility of the Bible itself," says James Barr (*The Scope and Authority of the Bible*, Explorations in Theology 7 [London: SCM Press, 1980] 70; emphasis mine).

[23] This latter problem is not unconnected with the former. Some time ago G. W. Bromiley ("The Church Doctrine of Inspiration," in *Revelation and the*

these it is also necessary to speak up, only in the context of constructive discussion—however brief and inadequate this discussion may be in such a broadly stimulating subject.

Inspiration may be understood as the verbal breath of the Incarnation; it involves, in the intellectual and linguistic sphere, both the "inhaling" of God's identification with man and the "exhaling" of his loving Lordship among men.[24] It is therefore as communal and public a fact as the womb of Israel in which Christ was incarnated and as the body of which he is the Head, while often at the same time as distinctly personal a phenomenon as the communion with Christ that is at the heart of each believer's own experience with Scripture. In both testaments (if in differing ways) it belongs to the work of God the Holy Spirit in his determination and ability to include men and women in the fellowship of the Father and the Son which is made open to them by the Son's Incarnation. The Scriptures generated in the Spirit's work of patiently making Christ known belong to Christ as the instrument of his leadership in the worship of the community; he speaks through them by the same Spirit in order to instruct men about their participation in the fellowship he himself enjoys. Biblical inspiration is therefore but one moment in the work of revelation accomplished by the Incarnation and realized in the Spirit. According to the sovereign will of God it transpires in the context of revelation with a view to a special consequence: a word that will serve future revelation in a

---

Bible, ed. Carl F. H. Henry [Grand Rapids: Baker, 1958] 216) insightfully inquired: "Why is it that for all the tenacity displayed and scholarship deployed, orthodoxy has proved so feeble and ineffective in face of this upsurge of the human spirit with its claiming of the Bible and its inspiration for itself? The answer to this question is undoubtedly to be found in the approximation of orthodoxy itself to an abstract, schematized and basically Judaistic understanding of inspiration. . . . [O]rthodoxy was already finding in the Bible a mere textbook of dogmatic truth rather than a concrete and living attestation of Jesus Christ."

[24] A two-way movement was involved in the provision for human knowledge of God, writes Torrance (*The Mediation of Christ,* 17): "an adaptation of divine revelation to the human mind and an adaptation of articulate forms of human understanding and language to divine revelation. That is surely how we are to regard God's long historical dialogue with Israel: the penetration of the Word of God into the depths of Israel's being and soul in such a way that it took human shape and yet in such a way that the human response it called forth was so locked into the Word in God that it was used as the vehicle of further address on the part of that Word to Israel."

canonical fashion. It has as its long-term frame of reference the cultivation of men and women in the mind of Christ, and in his ability to "speak spiritually about spiritual matters." It is comprised of a divine teaching ministry that is consummated not in the authors of Scripture but in its audience, and thus the interpretation of this inspiration should not be attempted without reference to the greater purposes which controlled it.[25]

The Scriptures themselves, then, must be understood to bear on the community of faith both as the address of God to man in Christ and as the pattern for man's proper response to God in the community which Christ set out to establish around himself. This is what the Spirit has achieved. But there are two temptations here we need to recognize and avoid: isolation of the biblical documents from the realities of the community of faith in which and for which this response was cultivated, and isolation of the writers and editors of the Bible from the personal oversight of the divine Author who chose (and still chooses) to address the community through them. The former temptation is often successful with those of a strictly conservative bent and the latter with those of a more liberal persuasion;[26] the real difficulty in both cases is a failure to take seriously the determining impact of the Incarnation on the doctrine of Scripture and its inspiration. When we fail to hold Christ and the Scriptures together in our own thinking, we are unable to hold God and man together in the process and results of inspiration. The inspired text (by which I mean Scripture as it reflects and embodies and serves the teaching ministry of the Spirit) is either absorbed upward into the realm of pure oracular speech as the

---

[25] "Concerning this salvation, the prophets, who spoke of the grace that was to come to you, searched intently and with the greatest care, trying to find out the time and circumstances to which the Spirit of Christ in them was pointing. . . . It was revealed to them that they were not serving themselves but you . . ." (1 Pet 1:10–12). Barth, more than anyone perhaps, realized the importance of understanding biblical inspiration only within, and not apart from, "the circle of the mystery which proceeds without a break from the revelation of the triune God to the present illumination of our hearts" (*Church Dogmatics* 1/2. 519); thus he decried the degeneration of the idea of verbal inspiration into that of mere "verbal inspiredness." Cf. also Berkouwer, *Holy Scripture*, 161f., who draws on Bavinck to make a similar point from another perspective.

[26] "If the liberal view tends to lose the Bible in the larger cultural context, the conservative view suffers from the necessity of isolating the Bible from that context," says Paul Achtemeier (*The Inspiration of Scripture*, 49–50).

word of God to man, or downward into the realm of mere human response to largely silent acts of divine revelation. Nothing more than lipservice is given to inspiration as incorporating a genuinely cooperative process in which there is a meeting of God and man on man's own ground for the realization and communication of Christian truth. But that is exactly what the incarnate Christ reveals to us as the necessary and appropriate nature of the inspiration his Spirit brings. For when we hear Christ we hear one who is in himself "the Word spoken from the loftiest, most luminous transcendence and likewise the Word heard [and answered] in the deepest, darkest immanence," as Barth puts it.[27] If Scripture speaks to us with the Voice of Christ, then it speaks to us with divine authority from out of the depths of human relativity, and this bidirectional movement in Christ of God to man and man to God will be understood to have shaped the text at one and the same time without contradiction, as it reached out to embrace and include the biblical spokesmen for the sake of those who would hear them.

What emerges from sustained consciousness of these things is a down-to-earth approach to Scripture that refuses to pervert the doctrine of inspiration by using it to hide from the human frailty of the text, but is nonetheless reverently committed to beholding Christ even in that frailty and to recognizing his right of disposal over it. The doctrine of inspiration espoused here respects Scripture as the verbal exhaling of his Lordship to the very same extent that it is the inhaling of human frailty. Of course, that necessarily means something of a transformation of that which is inhaled, according to the redemptive power of the humanity of Christ, who is always entirely in tune with the truth on our behalf.[28] This respect therefore regards the wooing

---

[27] *The Humanity of God*, 46–47. In *Church Dogmatics* 1/2. 505f., he describes biblical *theopneustia* both as "the act of revelation in which the prophets and apostles in their humanity became what they were," and as "the special attitude of obedience in those who are elected and called to this obviously special service."

[28] This transformation is an ongoing event rather than one that is complete at the point of inscripturation of the human word. Torrance remarks in a footnote (*Reality and Evangelical Theology*, 162–63) that "a full account of the actualization of God's self-revelation in Jesus Christ . . . must reckon with the fact that this is achieved within our estranged and impaired existence, and, therefore, only through atoning reconciliation and sanctifying re-creation. This

and instruction of the Holy Spirit (who presents Christ to us) as
entirely successful with regard to the authors of Scripture, in
order that it may also become so with respect to the readers of
Scripture. The Church, in fact, is only able to make progress in
truth and understanding as it recognizes that in the Book which
lies open before it the Spirit invites it ever onward, and never
backward or astray, in its knowledge of things pertaining to
Christ. And all Scripture pertains to Christ if it truly bears
denomination as theopneustic.[29]

Unfortunately, these essentials stand in stark contrast to
much that passes for a doctrine of inspiration today. For many
the great divorce between the ἄνθρωποι ἐλάλησαν and the ἀπὸ
θεοῦ continues.[30] And if the battle for the Bible ironically
requires confrontation with conservativism and its tendency to
bypass the challenging communal and evolutionary *humanity*

---

is why it would not be theologically proper to offer an account of the inspiration
of the Holy Scriptures apart from a doctrine of atoning mediation between the
Word of God and the word of man." He elaborates on this notion in *Theology
in Reconstruction* (Grand Rapids: Eerdmans, 1966), 138ff., where it becomes
clear that although "Holy Scripture is assumed by Christ to be his instrument in
conveying revelation and reconciliation," it nonetheless continues to belong "to
the sphere where redemption is necessary." The Word of God, he says, "comes to
us in the midst of our sin and darkness, at once revealing and reconciling, but it
comes with strong crying and tears, pressing its way through the speech of our
fallen flesh, graciously assuming it in spite of all its inadequacy and faultiness
and imperfection, and giving it a holy perfection in the Word of God." For this
reason, Torrance prefers not to speak of infallibility/inerrancy, but does acknowledge that "the Word has so imprinted its own image upon the human
word as to make it a faithful reflection of its own revelation." In all this he is
more or less at one with Barth in both christology and bibliology, but has
achieved a better balance. In fundamentals I can agree with this construction in
large part (a proper christology demands it), but I do not think it improper
nonetheless to speak of infallibility in terms of the functional inerrancy set out
in the present volume.

[29] Without question, we must allow here for the deep contours of Scripture
in its witness to Christ; for its contributions are nothing like uniform in the
directness of their proximity to Christ. Many biblical statements have no
canonical relevance whatever apart from the touch of color (including the gray
shading to be found here and there) they add to the setting of some larger thing.
Paul, we discover in 2 Tim 4:13, once left a cloak at Troas with one, Carpus;
such touches speak loudly and clearly of the humanity of Scripture and render a
formal view of inspiration absurd, though I do not doubt that even this verse is
able in God's providence to serve larger purposes (bringing down to earth our
perception of Paul and his sufferings, for example).

[30] Perhaps we may invest the Greek word-order with the significance of a
symbolic warning against any such divorce: ἐλάλησαν ἀπὸ θεοῦ ἄνθρωποι.

of Scripture, it just as certainly requires a rebuttal of the various and sundry attempts to distance the text from the effective guidance, instruction and correction of that humanity by the reclaiming and transforming power of the Spirit of Christ, who establishes the human word as his own. When, for example, we are reminded that to err is human, with the added implication that humans *must* err and so must Scripture, does it not begin to look as if we are led in precisely the opposite direction from that in which the doctrine of inspiration would lead us?[31] Or when it is proposed that we ought not to understand inspiration and inspired texts in terms of divine speaking at all, making irrelevant any discussion of infallibility, of course, can this be treated as a serious attempt to grapple with biblical inspiration? Yet such suggestions are cropping up even within evangelical circles.

William J. Abraham attempts to sustain such a proposal by drawing a clear distinction between the divine acts and speech-acts of special revelation and the inspiration which took place in and with them. Inspiration is not divine speaking, he says, but an accompanying stimulation that admits of degrees and does not eradicate human fallibility. Nor is inspiration per se to be confined to biblical times and biblical writers, though the authoritative revelation in and through which their inspiration occurred, and of which their writings spoke, is indeed a unique foundation which lends an authority for faith and practice to the biblical documents.[32] But this point of view falls far short of doing justice to the larger doctrine of canonical Scripture. The Scriptures are not canonical merely because they are the result and embodiment of the inspiration most immediately attached to the special foundational events of revelation. The Scriptures are canonical because they have been uniquely bound to Christ and sanctified by God as the instrument of his ongoing self-revelation to men and Lordship over the Church, and because

[31] Cf. Dewey Beegle, *Scripture, Tradition, and Infallibility*, 302 (he quotes Bruce Vawter approvingly to this effect). On one level we cannot disagree with this contention, but in *practical* terms—where the idea that we should stand over against the Bible with our own corrections begins to come into view—we must disagree. Cf. Kenneth Kantzer's struggle with this issue in "Biblical Authority: Where Both Fundamentalists and Neoevangelicals are Right," *Christianity Today* 27 (October 7, 1983) 10ff.

[32] *Divine Inspiration of Holy Scripture* (Oxford: Oxford University, 1981) 58ff.

they are thus employed by God in a manner that has called forth the recognition of the Church.

Biblical inspiration cannot be comprehended or expounded in neglect of this situation. The ultimate consequence of biblical inspiration, for the Church and in the Spirit, is precisely divine speaking. Inspiration itself belongs to the *circle* of revelation (as Barth and Bavinck and Berkouwer, e.g., have surely made clear to us in a variety of ways) and the resulting texts are not merely a fallible human link which can be split off from the divine speaking that is the very essence of revelation. It is exactly this fundamental point over which so much teaching on inspiration stumbles, failing to grasp the essential involvement of Scripture with the Presence of the incarnate Word who reveals God.[33] On the liberal side this takes the form of a failure to recognize the genuine verbal objectivity of his Word as it comes to us in the form of the biblical witness; there is a failure to grasp the uniqueness of τὰ ἱερὰ γράμματα, and hence of biblical inspiration. This presumably explains the ability to treat so lightly the biblical testimony itself, which is far from inconclusive on this matter despite the fact that, as we saw, it offers no justification for the efforts of some conservatives to tie Christ to the very words of Scripture apart from the message they convey.[34]

---

[33] Barth's whole discussion of the Word of God in its threefold form, as he has it, makes plain how fundamental he considered this involvement to be. Berkouwer, too, who with different concerns than Barth stresses from the Church's confession simply that the Bible *as human witness* is the word of God, also argues along with Bavinck that this is so precisely "because the Holy Spirit witnesses in it of Christ" (*Holy Scripture*, 162). The doctrine of Scripture and its inspiration has no relevance, in fact, apart from the greater Christological Reality of divine *speaking*—past and present—and the speaking of this particular content. This greater Reality, despite its greatness, refuses to allow Scripture to be divorced from it but rather compels Scripture to just this holy service. We should note that Barth, his unsatisfactory handling of the infallibility issue notwithstanding, was not slow to admit that biblical inspiration is coordinated into the circle of God's manifestation by the Spirit as the verbal link between God and us, and that "God Himself says what His witnesses say" (*Church Dogmatics* 1/2. 518). But W. J. Abraham drifts away from this indispensable point.

[34] Abraham is correct in stating: "It has never been shown that God spoke or dictated every word of the Bible" (*Divine Inspiration of Holy Scripture*, 71). But his own account of inspiration—also very light exegetically—is inadequate because he thinks it helpful to pry apart revelation, inspiration, and divine speaking, giving no heed to the interdependence of these concepts in spite of the legitimate distinctions between them. The circle of revelation is thus broken and the link of biblical inspiration left dangling uselessly. This appears to be the

What generally takes place with this failure nowadays is a lopsided shift toward seeing Scripture as essentially a document of the Church, rather than of its Lord first and of the Church second. The locus of inspiration is discussed in terms of the community of faith as opposed to the authors or the texts themselves, specifically in terms of the intersection of its traditions, its present struggles, and its creative minds. Inspiration is a simple corollary of the divine Presence in the community, rather than the calling forth of a specific word appointed by God to and for the community. The Scriptures are the special, fundamental embodiment of that inspiration and its "authority"; they stand over against the community to query the authenticity of later developments in its thinking and behavior, but they do not stand above the community as the actual expression of divine Lordship. This is the sort of thing argued for by James Barr, for example, and in one fashion or another by a variety of other scholars. Such views often touch on genuine weaknesses in conservative doctrine and methodology, but cannot really satisfy legitimate questions as to how God's *own* Word rules the Church and causes it to stand in the truth.[35]

---

consequence of working under the illusion that θεόπνευστος may simply be equated with "inspired" and understood largely in terms of human analogies (ibid., 62f.). But Berkouwer (*Holy Scripture*, 161) warns us that "the nature of the God-breathed character of Scripture cannot be deduced by means of various analogies to the inspiration" precisely because of its place in this circle.

[35] Cf. *The Scope and Authority of the Bible*, esp. chap. 4. There are in any case a number of helpful elements in Barr's approach, among which are his recognition that acceptance of biblical authority belongs to a larger faith-attitude, that Christian faith is not faith in the Bible primarily, but in the Lord whom we meet there, that the Bible is not in essence a record as much as it is a forward-looking book with an eschatological function, and that it is (and has been from the beginning) a book by very nature bound up in dialogue with the community of faith. To this list we might add the point that biblical authority does not function on a simple, inductive basis; rather Christian doctrinal and ethical positions "have as their point of origin a total vision, a conception of what Christian, life, action and society should be like" (p. 62) that is queried and tested for continuity by the biblical vision. Yet throughout Barr's discussions one discerns that now hidden, now brazen, folly which churchmen of greatest faith and understanding have always sought to overcome, namely, the identification of the will and expression of the Church with the will and expression of the Spirit *to the point that the Lordship of the latter no longer stands over against the former* and cannot be distinguished from the Church's own self-will and self-understanding. The renewal of the Scripture-principle in the Church at the time of the Reformation was clearly only a single step (and a still painful one, at that) along a path from which Catholic and Protestant alike are constantly

Paul J. Achtemeier incorporates some of the insights and concerns of this perspective in a more balanced fashion, however, in *The Inspiration of Scripture: Problems and Proposals*. He admits in the early going that whatever authority Scripture has depends on its relationship to God, though he firmly rejects the temptation to attach inspiration exclusively to the individuals who penned or gave final shape to the biblical materials. He sees the Spirit of God and his inspiration of Scripture in the dynamic confluence of tradition, situation, and respondent (to use his own terms) within the people of God.

> Inspiration thus describes more the process out of which our Scriptures grew than simply the final result in canonical form. This of course is not to disparage in any way that canonical form. It is the only form we have of Sacred Scripture, and is surely to be understood as coming into being in accordance with the will of God, i.e., as inspired. It is to say, however, that we cannot, on the model of the prophetic understanding of inspiration, assume that such inspiration occurred only at the point that some author set down the canonical form we have. Rather, the final form is the culmination of a process of the growth of Scripture which began

---

tempted to wander. Barr, failing to heed even the contemporary warnings of a Barth or a von Balthasar, betrays an apparent uncertainty that the Word of God stands *above*—to make it perfectly clear—as well as both in and over against the Church in a concretely verbal fashion, identifiable as Holy Scripture. "Scripture certainly does not have a place antecedent to the church," says Barr (p. 60), meaning to include in "church" ancient Israel, of course. In fact, Scripture emerged from the tradition of the people of God, so that we must work on a model that looks like this: God > people > tradition > scripture; not God > revelation > scripture > church. Inspiration, then, ought to be understood only in the general sense "that God in his Spirit was in and with his people in the formation, transmission, writing down and completion of their tradition, and . . . its fixation as scripture" (p. 63). Note well that in this process "the final stage was the least important rather than the most important"; for authority, as Barr understands it, resides in the people of God as well as in the Scripture "which they formed and passed on to later generations as their own communication, as the voice which they wanted to be heard as their own voice" (p. 64). For all that is of value even here, there is a devastating failure to recognize the *independence* of Scripture from the community of faith as the expression of the Word that called—and still calls—that community into existence. This failure is, of course, inextricably bound up with Barr's critical assumptions about the Pentateuch; he has difficulty both hearing and accepting the message that the community of Israel was formed in *consequence* of the laying of the canonical cornerstone at Sinai. Consequently, he has difficulty with the entire concept of canon, not merely with inspiration.

with the primal event that shaped the community of faith, and has continued through the process of forming and reforming the tradition on the part of faithful respondents to new situations confronting that community.[36]

Achtemeier thinks we should respect what critical scholarship has taught us about the growth and formation of the canon, and take account of it in our doctrine of inspiration. He rejects both the extreme liberal view and the conservative view, which focus (in very different ways) on the inspiration of individual writers.[37] The centrality of inerrancy, which is bound up with such a focus in the conservative doctrine, is both inconsistent with the known character of the Scriptures and betrays a faulty approach to revelation and to the certainty of the faith; inspiration and the Bible itself are wrongly *equated* with revelation, and authority is therefore thought to hinge on inerrant Scripture. Achtemeier locates authority not in Scripture as a phenomenon, but in the content of the material as it points away to the revelation of God in Christ. It is from the Reality of God and what he does that Scripture's true authority, and the unity of its diverse traditions, derive. Through the Spirit who remains with the community to the present time, the Word himself continues to communicate God's Word to us for our situation. It is the intent of the doctrine of inspiration, he says,

> to affirm that in the experience of the Church that is exactly what happens when the message of the Biblical witness is proclaimed within the community of faith. The Spirit which vivifies the community of faith is also the Spirit which has summoned forth the words of Scripture from various junctures within the life of that community, both before and after the historical event of Jesus of Nazareth. The proclamation by that community of faith,

---

[36] *The Inspiration of Scripture*, 134-35. Achtemeier attempts to strike a balance here: "To be sure, communities as such do not write books, individuals do. But to put the total weight of inspiration on that final individual . . . is to make a mockery of the intimate relationship between Scripture and community and to deny to key individuals—Jesus, the prophets, apostles—their true role in the production of inspired Scripture" (p. 133).

[37] Ibid., 74-75. Conservatives are inclined to emphasize the authority of prophetic spokesmen and thus the inspiration of the actual texts they produce, whereas liberals focus somewhat enigmatically on the impulse and stimulation of the authors to write (on the dangers of both approaches, cf. Berkouwer, *Holy Scripture*, 156f.).

its witness to its living Lord, can therefore be the Word of God in all its timely relevance for the historic juncture at which we live. . . . Revivified individually and corporately by the witness of Scripture, the community of faith confesses in the doctrine of the inspiration of Scripture that the risen Christ continues to be heard, admonishing and comforting, challenging and directing the life of the community of faith as it seeks to be faithful in history to the will of the Lord of history.[38]

For the most part, this seems very commendable. Nonetheless, Achtemeier is left with a document and a proclamation that are related to the Word in a rather vague and unclear fashion. The Scriptures are a Christ-centered work of the Spirit in and through the community and its spokesmen, and they are the word which Christ today employs in speaking to the community, but yet they are still not quite Christ's *own* word. Achtemeier apparently does not want us to relate Christ and the Scriptures *too* intimately,[39] but that raises again the question of how, and how far, Christ communicates to us when Scripture is read and taught. How then will we come together over what Christ wishes to say in interpreting his salvation for us in our present time? If, as it might seem, the word which the Spirit calls forth from the community is to be understood essentially as a series of (sometimes conflicting) attempts to come to grips with the relationship between God and man, that word ceases to function plainly as a mediator of Christ and his authority.[40] Its relationship to God is, in the end, uncertain.

Now this complaint does not mean a return to handling inspiration primarily as a justification for inerrancy within a rationalistic approach to revelation and the certainty of the faith. It is indeed the purpose of the doctrine of inspiration simply to attest to and to elaborate the fact that the Word himself is heard in the proclamation of Scripture, and thus in continuity with the testimony of the community he has formed. Discussion of inspiration, whether in Scripture or in Church doctrine, arises out of hearing that divine Speech; the doctrine of inspiration explicates that fact in terms of the intimate (if inscrutable) involvement of the Spirit in the shaping of the

[38] *The Inspiration of Scripture*, 164.
[39] Cf. ibid., 54.
[40] Cf. ibid., 134f., 154f.

scriptural word. It is an explanation based on the ministry of the Spirit in binding individual men and the community itself together with Christ in a manner that finds faithful literary expression, in order that this same ministry may increasingly come to employ literary (i.e., canonical) means. What the doctrine most naturally refuses to do is to leave room for separation of the specific, biblical word in and through which Christ is known to speak from what he himself has actually determined to say in his self-communication. To do so is to negate the very grounds on which a doctrine of inspiration is called for. That is why the doctrine of inspiration cannot help but come down on the conservative side with respect to infallibility. It "comes down" there very simply because that is where it begins, with Christ speaking the biblical word.

Yet it is not thereby a conservative doctrine, and offers no actual support for exhaustive inerrancy or the restrictive hermeneutics which a narrow focus on pure inspired penmanship generates. It has no need of this, it is not confined to this, for the roots of the doctrine of inspiration are not in the demands of a strict syllogistic argument defending the faith, but in the call of the Word himself through the words of Scripture. There is room here for recognition of the Bible as a document which to a significant extent reflects the fact that it grew out of the community of faith and its traditions as his Spirit worked among them. Though for the Church Scripture really is God preaching,[41] that does not require us to suppose that the literary installments of his sermon have arisen in a purely oracular fashion; such was not the manner of his choosing. We are only obligated not to identify Scripture with the shortcomings of the community in any manner detrimental to its identification with the sure and sound leadership of Christ. In view of his Lordship in and through them, the inspired Scriptures cannot be treated merely as documents which reflect the highest reaches of the community in its regard for special events thought to belong to revelation, documents thus remaining entirely on the same level as the

---

[41] See J. I. Packer, *God Has Spoken* (London: Hodder and Stoughton, 1965) 66–67. This way of putting the matter, particularly with the stress he places on the present continuative aspect of this expression, answers well to the shortcoming in Barr's view indicated above; I am not altogether comfortable with his elaboration of inspiration in that location, however.

community, replete with inevitable and irreconcilable tensions. They stand above the community as a sure word and guide precisely because they have been lifted to that position by a special teaching ministry belonging to revelation—the ministry of inspiration and illumination accomplished by the Spirit of Christ working within the community and through those chosen to be servants of the Word. In other words, the suitability of these documents to serve as the address of the *Lord* of the community must not be limited by recognition of their origin within the relativities of the community itself, for it was the work of the Spirit in inspiration to make up the difference between community and Lord precisely at this point, even as it is his work today in and through the documents so produced to make up the difference between our perspectives and responses and those of Christ himself. That is why the Church must remain subject to Scripture, and why its hermeneutics must also reflect that respect and subjection.

Now if, as Achtemeier maintains, the liberal view of Scripture characteristically moves from the phenomena of Scripture to a doctrine of inspiration and the conservative view moves in the reverse direction,[42] it is evident why neither of these has really come to grips with inspiration. The doctrine of Scripture's inspiration arises out of exposure to Scripture neither as a collection of historic texts nor as a pre-formed plank in a doctrinal platform, but as a living instrument of the divine Lordship over the Church. It is formulated out of the real experience of instruction in the mind of Christ. It is a retracing of Christ's involvement with the origin and/or evolution of the documents in view of his involvement with them in the present for teaching, rebuking, correcting, and training in righteousness.[43] It guards against a subtle erosion of sensitivity to his

---

[42] *The Inspiration of Scripture,* 50.

[43] Timothy himself is a type, or rather a representative, of the Church, which continues in those things of which it has become convinced (namely, that which is taught by the Spirit in the Scriptures), knowing from whom it has learned them, even from the apostles and prophets Christ gave to the Church for its instruction. That is, we might say that as and because the Scriptures *continue* to be God-breathed, it becomes evident that they *were* God-breathed, and the Church attests this in its doctrine of inspiration. Cf. Calvin, *Institutes* I.ix.3, who tells us that God "sent down the same Spirit by whose power he had dispensed the Word, to complete his work by the efficacious confirmation of the

Lordship by making explicit the fact that these documents are truly his from beginning to end. The doctrine of inspiration is an inevitable consequence of the Word heard by the Church in Holy Scripture, and the criterion of this doctrine is the *practical* ability and authority of Christ to address men as Lord from within the community and to lay down a pattern for their response. Any watering down of the doctrine of inspiration, any supposition or conclusion about the genesis or character of the biblical texts that distracts the Church from hearing them as *Christ's* word called forth from his own people through chosen spokesmen and other participants, is rightly rejected. The power of the Spirit to call forth such a word, and to speak it again in our hearing, is an essential pledge of the success of the mission of the Incarnation.

For all that we are still in a position to heed the warning from many quarters against exclusive reliance on the so-called prophetic model of inspiration, which is one of the primary criticisms brought against the conservative view and a valid caution for those who would develop a sound and hermeneutically sensitive doctrine of inspiration.[44] Conclusions about the general nature of inspiration must not be drawn from a single mode of biblical speech or built on a single testimony like that of 2 Pet 1:21, for the power of Christ to shape a word suitable to himself scarcely requires such direct means in every case. What we can say, without relying exclusively on the prophetic model itself, is that both process and participants in the actual composition of canonical Scripture were endowed in one fashion or another with the prophetic spirit, that is, that the Spirit of God

---

Word"; and Barth, *Church Dogmatics* 1/2. 521f.: "We cannot speak of the inspiration of the Bible without that royal act of the original inspiration in which the risen Christ gave His own a part in His own divine Spirit. But no more can we speak of it without that other royal act—which is only a continuation of the first—in which the inspiration is imparted to us, in which here and now we are forced out of our position as spectators of the word and work of the biblical writers, in which the calling of the prophets and apostles becomes an event to us by the ministry of their word and work."

[44] Clark Pinnock ("A Response to Rex A. Koivisto," 155), for example, charges that "the strict inerrancy position is built on *one* (incorrect) assumption: that all Scripture is inspired by God in the sense of prophetic inspiration ("I have put my words in your mouth") which amounts to *de facto* dictation. . . ." This charge may be largely valid, though the biblically prominent prophetic model admits of a broader understanding than that suggested by Pinnock here, and its importance must not be downplayed in reactionary fashion.

was invariably involved for the *successful* accomplishment of a prophetic goal, even where specific material shows not the least characteristic of oracular speech. Prophetic speech is, after all, a much broader phenomenon than the first-person speech of divine oracles. That the entire community should speak prophetically as a way of life is one of the stated goals and potentials of the new covenant, a matter which finds expression on several occasions. At heart it is simply participation in the Spirit of wisdom who sets forth Christ in the context of the human situation of the people of God.

It is with this balance in view that decisions can be made about the use of such heavily-debated terminology as "verbal-plenary inspiration."[45] Many who are not at all shy of acknowledging the supernatural in connection with the formation of Scripture (precisely because they are not ashamed to acknowledge Scripture as the word of Christ) nonetheless shy away from speaking of inspiration as both plenary and verbal. In view of the frequent abuses of these terms in a manner linking inspiration with exhaustive inerrancy, such reticence ought not to be a point of division. That inspiration is verbal in the sense that it results in canonical *torah* (i.e., in authoritative written works for the instruction of all posterity) will not be denied. That inspiration is plenary, that is, pertaining to "every passage of Scripture," will also be admitted. What ought not to be taken from the two terms when they are put together is the implication that every word or detail owes its presence to the Spirit of God and bears the divine imprimatur, or that inspiration is something which does not admit of process or variation.[46] It is the shaping of true and worthy *torah* with which inspiration is concerned, not the making of a cabalistic playground, and when that instruction is understood to be centered on Christ the many contours of its participation, the high points and the low points of its insights and contributions, are visibly established. The recognition of varying levels, as well as varying means, of instruction and guidance in theopneustic wisdom is demanded

---

[45] "Verbal or plenary inspiration," writes Carl Henry (*God, Revelation, and Authority*, 4. 145), "has not infrequently been viewed as the issue separating nonevangelical and evangelical views of the Bible." The distinction between the two he considers largely semantic, since both terms rule out partial inspiration, but this opinion is not shared by all, nor is the construction of the issue itself.

[46] Henry (ibid., 145, 160) appears to reach just such conclusions.

by the varying roles of biblical passages in setting forth Christ, and in no way belittles our proper confidence in them.[47] This confidence should be equally shared by every passage and can indeed be realized only in connection with the words of each passage. As Barth says:

> If God really speaks to man, He really speaks the language of this concrete human word of man. That is the right and necessary truth in the concept of verbal inspiration.[48]

In fact, it is only the distortion these two terms bring to each other that holds back a hearty affirmation of inspiration as verbal and plenary. When they are brought together as mutual modifiers, suggesting that the essence of inspiration is wrapped up in the selection of a precise group of words, the dynamic focus of the doctrine on the instruction of God's people by the Spirit of Christ is replaced with a concentration on the static mystery of a sacred text.[49]

---

[47] Dewey Beegle (*Scripture, Tradition, and Infallibility*, 209) draws on Bruce Vawter (*Biblical Inspiration* [Philadelphia: Westminster Press, 1972] 163f.) for help in clarifying the question of variations in biblical inspiration: "'In the concrete,'" he quotes Vawter as saying, "'scriptural inspiration must have been as diverse as the human efforts that conspired to produce the Scripture.' But in recognizing these various expressions of inspiration he [Vawter] shies away from using the term 'degrees' to designate the difference: 'To think of one Biblical work as less inspired than another, and less the word of God, is to engage in a false problematic: it is to assume what we have just insisted can hardly be, namely that inspiration is something univocal that admits only of degrees. Rather, we must learn to think of one book as inspired differently from another, as therefore being, or mediating, the word of God in its own proper fashion.' Vawter is attempting to get away from qualitative, hierarchical judgments that are demeaning to parts of Scripture. . . . The semantic problem still exists, but perhaps he is correct that it is preferable to speak of different 'kinds' rather than different 'degrees' of inspiration."

[48] *Church Dogmatics* I/2. 532. Though Barth obviously did not accept the idea of a plenary inspiration signifying that every word of Scripture was Spirit-given, he does give the proper gist of plenary inspiration in a comment I referred to elsewhere: "If in their concrete speaking and writing the witnesses of revelation belong to revelation, if they spoke by the Spirit what they knew by the Spirit, and if we really have to hear them and therefore their words—then self-evidently we have to hear all their words with the same measure of respect. It would be arbitrary to relate their inspiration only to such parts of their witness as perhaps appear important to us, or not to their words as such but only to the views and thoughts which evoke them" (ibid., 517–18).

[49] "Believing Scripture does not mean staring at a holy and mysterious book," says Berkouwer (*Holy Scripture*, 166), "but hearing the witness concerning Christ. The respect for the concrete words is related precisely to this. . . ."

The pressing need in the battle for the Bible is never anything other than a renewal of our faith and our willingness to be addressed by Scripture as by the Lord, and no one escapes from this need whatever his doctrinal confession. The battle, as others have said, is really a battle for men and women, not for the Bible. So far as the doctrine of inspiration is concerned, however, its greatest assistance to the Church will surely be found in recognizing its service and obligation to the larger doctrine of the living Word himself. This was Barth's point, and it must be reckoned with even if we cannot agree with his conclusions about infallibility.[50] Barth complained about the *secularization* of the doctrine of verbal inspiration through its removal from the circle of revelation in the Spirit and from the mystery of the free grace of God. The growing stress in post-Reformation orthodoxy on the static "verbal-inspiredness" of the biblical text in and of itself, and hence the reduction of the Word of God to a phenomenon that can be grasped by man and subjected to his scrutiny, he considered to be more than a little responsible for the growing apostasy which accompanied it.[51]

[50] According to Barth (*Church Dogmatics* 1/2. 533): "Verbal inspiration does not mean the infallibility of the biblical word in its linguistic, historical and theological character as a human word. It means that the fallible and faulty human word is as such used by God and has to be received and heard in spite of its human fallibility." "That the lame walk, that the blind see, that the dead are raised, that sinful and erring men as such speak the Word of God: that is the miracle of which we speak when we say that the Bible is the Word of God" (ibid., 529). This miracle is not the miracle of an infallible text, a miracle which can thus be put on display, but the miracle of the event of the divine Word being heard in and through the witnesses of that Word, whose fallible humanity has not been "crowded out" in their call to service.

[51] See ibid., 514-26. Barth's emphasis was ever on the free decision of the grace of God, and therefore on the closing of the circle here and now; it was mainly to protect the truth of the Church's constant position of absolute dependence upon God—particularly in the face of rationalistic abuses of the doctrine of inspiration and the drive for a humanly-manageable security—that Barth argued against an infallible Bible. He wished to secure the point that "the door of the Bible texts can be opened only from within" (ibid., 533), that the Word of God always remains a matter of grace. It seems to me entirely unnecessary, however, to suppose that the actually invisible and unprovable "miracle" of an inspiration that, without crowding out the weak humanity of the biblical authors, nonetheless successfully incorporated that humanity into an entirely faithful witness, rules out or hopelessly obscures any further or greater miracle, namely: the event of that witness once again standing *for us* in actual relation to its content, just because it is breathed anew in our hearing by the Spirit of Christ as we attend to it (cf. p. 529). It would appear, in fact, that we must always speak of this *double* miracle in this double inspiration, if you

The solution to today's difficulties over inspiration and inerrancy unquestionably requires a return to focusing on Scripture in its present employment by the Spirit of Christ in the Church. That is where the doctrine begins, and that is where it must end also. Inspiration must be interpreted by *revelation*—the actual revelation of Christ in the power of his Holy Spirit. Only when the doctrine of verbal inspiration is understood in these *Christocentrically* objective, and therefore dynamic, terms, that is, only when inspiration in the past is directly related to illumination in the present (with the text as mediator between the two), will the temptation to manipulate the doctrine around to a justification of human control over Scripture be overcome.[52] This desire for control, of course, generally finds expression either in justifying the Church's right to differ with Scripture—in effect, to choose what it will be taught by the Spirit—or in hallowing, not the Lord of Scripture and the Spirit himself, but what actually lies within its own grasp, namely, the words of Scripture.[53] In either case it is not really revelation which has the decisive impact.

To recognize Christ at the center of any valid doctrine of Scripture and to regard Scripture as the instrument of the Spirit who reveals the living Word to the Church, *that* will lead to a sound perspective on inspiration and authority. Inspiration will not be attached to the Bible simply in and of itself, but will serve to express the attachment of the Bible to Christ. This attachment will be recognized of the Bible in its entirety, for the knowledge

---

please, for we ought to grant Barth's primary point, while still insisting that the text of Scripture either points faithfully to Christ or it does not. We cannot call on the sort of miracle that enables us to have it both ways.

[52] Calvin, while guarding against attack from a different direction, nonetheless makes the importance of these Christocentric and dynamic terms crystal clear in the *Institutes*, I.ix.3. It is also worth noting that Klaas Runia's useful discussion of inspiration and illumination in *Karl Barth's Doctrine of Holy Scripture* (see chap. 6) would be much more helpful were it not marred by his failure consistently to regard revelation in dynamic terms.

[53] Runia (ibid., 164) notes this comment made by John A. Mackay: "Loyalty to ideas about Christ can become a subtle substitute for loyalty to Christ himself. Ideas can become idols." The same might be said with respect to the very written word of Christ. There is a temptation to seek a false security in that which we can hold up and say of it: "Here! I have it!" (cf. Exod 32:4—"These are your gods, O Israel!"), but that is the essence of idolatry. It is possible, and sometimes attractive, to do this with the Bible and/or a set of doctrines. With Christ it is quite otherwise, of course; we can only repose humbly in faith that *he* has us.

of Christ is a corporate affair that is capable of canonical dimensions and is actually mediated by this canonical reality. Those who pick and choose what they will attend to in the Scriptures will continue to be an affront to the community for that very reason—certainly no less so than those who distract the Church from its focus on the Christ of the Scriptures by unnecessary disputes over the words of Scripture. The commitment to Scripture as the unchanging audible edge of *theopneustia*, of an inspiration belonging by grace to the community of faith, but finding appropriate expression by individual servants of the Lord in order that others might be faithfully instructed "in the presence of many witnesses,"[54] is the commitment which the inspiring Spirit elicits from the Church as he presents Jesus Christ therein.

Reclaiming the Human Context

Beyond any doubt, the malady leading to a loss of confidence in Scripture runs much deeper than an overweening confidence in autonomous critical processes and the lopsided emphasis on an evolutionary "inspiration" only asymptotically related to revelation. The Church must realize that at the heart of the matter lies a widespread failure to be openly determined by the Lordship of Christ in its attention to Scripture. To that extent, our attention has been false and we have been left to the inadequate resources on which unbelievers choose to rely. Alongside the aforementioned problems, therefore, the loss of confidence has in fact been influenced by a growing secular skepticism regarding the very potential of the human context to serve anything like an authoritative Scripture. This has led in some circles to a radical relativization of Scripture in whole and in part and requires a radical solution addressing the entire human context and the fundamental attitude toward the Bible that it engenders. Fortunately, the foundation for this solution is already laid.

To say that the Scriptures are attached to Christ is to say immediately that they are eminently human exactly in their theopneustic character. Their essential humanness, of course, is

[54] 2 Tim 2:2.

no longer doubted by most moderns, but it has been seriously misunderstood at the cost of the unfailing profitability of Scripture to which Paul testified. Awareness of the human character of Scripture has focused primarily on the humanity of the *writers* of Scripture, taking on in consequence a partially negative connotation, when in fact its focus belongs in a very positive way on the humanity of the One *witnessed to* in Scripture. In the broadest sense, the battle for the Bible—indeed, for the Church itself and the world as well—should be seen as a struggle to set the power and profundity of the *genuine humanity of Christ* to which the Scriptures have been assimilated in inspiration against the distorted expressions of humanity all around. It therefore amounts to a persistent staking of the claim that redemptive divine Lordship has entered personally into humanity and the human experience, and in that humanity taken precisely this way, the way of the Scriptures, in a reconciling self-communication to Church and world. That is the earthy, practical forum apart from which the question of biblical authority and reliability has no real significance or intelligibility.

What then should be our response when men expound the nature of the human situation—notably difficult questions of language and culture, of finitude and *Weltanschaaung* and *Geschichtlichkeit*—in a manner that turns out badly for a book that is supposed to be suited for that sort of verbally specific Lordship? What shall we say to the tiresome complaints, and almost equally tiresome responses, about the shortcomings and final inadequacy of human language for the purposes of such a revelation? More seriously, how shall we respond to those who wish in any event to shed the cultural and intellectual forms of the biblical witness, given that it comes to us in the humanity of prophets and apostles belonging to ancient and foreign communities, in writings determined by perspectives thought to be of only relative or restricted value in today's world? These challenges are no longer confined to secularizing schools of thought, or even to the works of liberal and existentialist theologians. They are being bandied about in a variety of versions and perversions throughout the Church, often in the attractive garb of a quest for renewed relevance or (in the latter case) an ironic celebration of diverse human potential. Alongside the simple insistence that Scripture is often flatly mistaken in the manner of all human documents, such challenges serve perhaps the most pervasive and effective assault on Scripture so far as its bearing on the immediacy of Christian life and witness is concerned.[55] Certainly the discussion of Scripture as an *infallible* authority is nowhere rendered more obviously irrelevant than in a context where the humanity of Scripture is approached on terms other than those determined by the unveiling therein of the humanity of God!

What solution is there to such seemingly fundamental objections to our confession of Scripture? When it is realized that they are actually objections not simply to the idea of a *bona fide* Bible, but to the very possibility of a genuinely human Messiah-Lord, it will be more readily grasped that there can be only one solution: to allow the incarnate Word of God to reclaim the human context for himself in our own hearing and for our own sakes. But what does this mean? It means that the Church requires a view of Scripture that is related to a soundly *Christological* anthropology, that it must look to Christ to properly interpret Adam as a hermeneutical creature of language and culture and literary capabilities. It means that it cannot criticize, expound, or celebrate its own humanity without its eyes firmly fixed on Christ's humanity. It means that the Church cannot reflect on words and verbal communication, nor on Scripture as an example of such, apart from its dialogue with the *living* Word. It means that the historical nature of man and his speech must be understood in light of the unique history of Christ; it means that here again the Presence of Christ must be taken seriously, that here as everywhere we must *begin* with the Christ of the Scriptures if we are to stay on the path of understanding.[56] Of course, all this presupposes an operational

---

[55] The unforeseen extent to which this assault has been effective even within the Church itself can be illustrated by the current dispute over the ordination of practicing homosexuals, a matter that has demanded and received attention (though not approval) from one or two major Protestant denominations in North America. The arguments in favor of such a travesty are not put forward without exegetical and theological justifications, of course; such exegesis and theology are thoroughly rooted in brave suppositions about cultural relativism and "the real meaning" behind what the biblical authors actually said—if not in the right to challenge directly the abiding authority of what this or that author may have said. The fact that these arguments have achieved a hearing at all speaks volumes to believers and non-believers alike.

[56] See Dietrich Bonhoeffer's little work, *Christ the Center*, and note what Barth says in his programmatic essay, "The Humanity of God" (p. 47): "We do

recognition of the fact that Christ causes Scripture, for all its own "historicalness" in language, culture, and intellectual forms, to stand out ever and again as a word for the present, as the word of him who is the same yesterday, today, and forever, and who sums up all humanity in himself as Head over all things for the Church.

Let us then reflect briefly on these two very basic matters of language and culture, in the light of Christ. If we are going to let the Word of God reclaim the human context so that we are free to hear further and more plainly God's reconciling Word, we must be willing to do that.[57] The failure to attempt this at all is exactly what is lacking in many discussions which in effect downplay the authority of Scripture as written. Many are mistakenly granting methodological priority to some trend or other in *non*-theological analysis of these fundamentals, thereby creating unnecessary problems which need to be pointed out as such.

To be sure, it is commendable in itself if one finds it difficult to think comfortably about inspiration without so much as a nod in the direction of those whose thinking has concentrated not only on Scripture per se, but on the medium of human language and its essential matrix in communal living. Certainly

---

not need to engage in a free-ranging investigation to seek out and construct who and what God truly is, and who and what man truly is, but only to read the truth about both where it resides, namely, in the fullness of their togetherness, their covenant which proclaims itself in Jesus Christ." Christ, in Bonhoeffer's words, is the center of human existence. What we therefore need if we are to answer fundamental questions about the humanness of Scripture is a theological anthropology that, in considering Christ, comes to comprehend the true order of humanity and the nature of its disruption through sin, as well as the process of its reintegration into harmony with God (see Ray Anderson, *On Being Human*, 15f.). In such a context we are able to explicate Scripture as a *human* document in its service to divine revelation, precisely because in his Incarnation the Word of God "assimilated the hearing and speaking of man to himself as constitutive ingredients of divine revelation," as Torrance puts it (*Reality and Evangelical Theology*, 88; cf. 84f.).

[57] Many, of course, are very skeptical of the goals we have in view here. Dennis Nineham (*New Testament Interpretation in an Historical Age* [London: Athlone, 1976] 14) is one who thinks that "Jesus has no answer to the question, 'Tell us Thy name in our speech and for our day.'" But this is not compatible with the confession, *Immanuel*. Nor is the hermeneutical skepticism behind it convincing in any case; see Anthony Thiselton, *The Two Horizons*, 52–60; also J. I. Packer, "Infallible Scripture and the Role of Hermeneutics," in *Scripture and Truth*, ed. D. A. Carson and John D. Woodbridge (Grand Rapids: Zondervan, 1983) 331f.

the study of language (not to mention anthropology in general) has burgeoned into a very complex field, offering much of value along with a good deal of self-indulgent obfuscation. Bernard Ramm once testified that

> modern studies of linguistics inspired by the growth of modern anthropology, modern studies in the philosophy of language, modern philosophical developments in linguistic philosophy, and modern development of communications theory calls for a rethinking by evangelicals of the twin doctrines of revelation and inspiration.[58]

Undoubtedly, that is a fair claim. Betraying something of a fascination with the modern, however, he went on to admonish that "evangelicals must be prepared for what is now being called 'future shock.'"

> Evangelicals will be forced to rethink the entire problem of the authority of Scripture (the power of Scripture as a written document to function as the Word of God). Evangelicals who do not anticipate what computers will solve in the future with reference to all the literary documents of antiquity are very nearsighted. They need to be doing some pioneering ("proleptic") thinking now on the possible solutions to the new problems.[59]

What damaging mysteries of literary criticism computers will unveil still remains to be seen, but the evangelical view of Scripture has certainly been challenged already by a variety of linguistic philosophies and literary theories.

What does not seem to be clearly in view here, though, is that the Church should not be on the defensive (however proleptically), but on the offensive. It should be establishing its *own* ground—that is, exploring the ground on which Christ sets it—for research and evaluation in linguistics, literary criticism, hermeneutics, cross-cultural proclamation, and the like. Because we heed the living Word and not a mere collection of documents, we must not be afraid to speak first when entering into dialogue even with the linguistic philosopher, for example. Exactly because of the primordial nature of his subject, it is he who is in need of guidance. At the same time, of course, we will

[58] *The Evangelical Heritage* (Waco: Word, 1973) 163.
[59] Ibid., 166–67.

not be ashamed to admit that we are more than ready to seek help ourselves in responding to the potential of human language and to the literary subtleties of so broad and deep a document as Holy Scripture.

Now when we set out as believers to reflect on language in light of the divine Word we have heard in the biblical witness, we cannot avoid reckoning with the inseparable relationship between words and reality when Christ speaks. "The words I have spoken to you are spirit and they are life," said Jesus.[60] God is able indeed to take to himself human speech in the Incarnation, without disrupting his own divine integrity of Word, Act, and Being in that accommodation; to suppose otherwise is to take a docetic view of Christ. Not that the words or sentences themselves have become divine, of course, which would amount in a perverse sort of way to a "docetic" view of the Scriptures. They are human words, disrupted from their usual profane purposes under the impact of Christ in order to conform to the Truth of God incarnate in time and space, so that they are able to become for us spirit and life by leading us to participation in the divine Word who speaks them. But the shocking effect of this disruption from the *merely* creaturely orientation of secular language (an orientation only thinly disguised in idolatrous— i.e., non-Christocentric—religious language) reveals the fact that elsewhere a serious breach has arisen between language and reality in man's deliberate forgetfulness of God.[61] It reveals that human speech has developed a deceptive independence from reality in order to survive its self-imposed exile from the truth and harmony of Eden. Fortunately, it also generates confidence in a thoroughgoing reattachment of human speech to reality, in view of the fact that the Creator has come in the flesh to turn creation back to himself from the inside out. The very character of language as constructive *witness* to reality is in fact reaffirmed in the mission of Christ, who is sent to speak out of his unique knowledge of the divine Reality in order to lead men to the Father. It should hardly be necessary to add that no greater, and no other, justification of the service of human language in directing us even to things divine is possible than the fact of the

---

[60] John 6:63.

[61] Cf., for example, Paul's speech in Acts 17 (noting his redirection of Stoic and Epicurean language) and its consequences.

Incarnation itself. Certainly that one fact renders it absurd to perpetuate the aforementioned breach at its most crucial point by stubbornly continuing to insist on the inadequacy of human words for such a role.[62]

The great rock of stumbling in theologically uninformed views of language, however, remains this incipient tendency to divorce words from their true, responsive subservience to reality, an inherited tendency springing originally from union with the Father of Lies in the Garden. Language is increasingly supposed either to contain its own meaning, or to create its own meaning.[63] At any rate, as the inability of secular or idolatrous language to properly penetrate and open up the true context of man's existence catches up with him, there begins to be a shift of focus from a broad and progressive engagement with reality itself to an introspective engagement with man's own speech.

---

[62] Cf. John 3:31ff. It is obvious, I trust, that to speak of language as witness in no way confines consideration of language primarily to literal, declarative statements, though it maintains the importance of such statements. The witness that arises from genuine involvement with reality can take many creative forms. Scripture, as A. F. Holmes says in *Faith Seeks Understanding* (Grand Rapids: Eerdmans, 1971) 132, is a richly diversified literature, conveying knowledge of God also "by stories and symbols and paradoxes and engaging dialog, by imperatives, rhetorical questions and pleas."

[63] That is, language is no longer consistently perceived as that which derives its meaning directly from a reality that stands behind it and shows through it, to which it is therefore immediately responsible with respect to the particularities of its content and approach. It is seen by structuralists, e.g., to have its significance primarily in its own internal relations and substructures, which may (or may not) be understood as abstract reflections of the overall structure of reality. "For structuralism," writes Paul Ricoeur (*The Rule of Metaphor*, trans. Robert Czerny [Toronto and Buffalo: University of Toronto, 1975] 319), "language does not refer to anything outside of itself, it constitutes a world for itself." Existentialists, on the other hand, understand language to have its significance in what it sets in motion in and for the individual; they operate on the personalist and phenomenalist level of abstraction, in which language constitutes a world for its listener. Or, at the shallowest point of intersection between these two perspectives the significance of language is understood by pragmatists to be determined by its involvement with an evolving human behavioral environment, which generates a complex of external codes for language use. While each of these approaches to language offers legitimate insights, they are ultimately self-destructive by reason of their attempt to understand speech and written texts *independently of their service to the actual realities of which they allege to speak*. At both the structuralist and existentialist poles language is treated very much as if it differed little from sheet-music: i.e, noteworthy texts are largely dehistoricized into self-contained meaning-structures or into mere potentialities. Of course, these more philosophical approaches are unable to account for a great deal of common language use; at

What takes place to a most surprising degree, in one fashion or another, is the substitution of language for reality itself, even to the eventual deification of Language. This is a charge one is especially inclined to lay at the feet of Martin Heidegger and his followers, of course, including his theological heirs in the school of the new hermeneutic.[64] Unfortunately, the general failure here is so widespread as to have affected even more orthodox views of language, wherever the implications of the realist mode of thought demanded by the Incarnation have not been grasped. Torrance roundly criticizes fundamentalists, too, for getting so far off track as to confuse truth of statement with

the much more accommodating center between them, however, one hears only a sort of "muzak" in which language lacks the highs and lows produced by a vital relationship to the contours of reality itself. Such a view also depends on an observationalist abstraction (of an operationalist sort) in which language and community are co-determined with little concern for the rootedness of both in larger realities.

[64] Gerhard Ebeling and Ernst Fuchs, the post-Bultmannian "theologians of the word," are the names most prominently attached to the new hermeneutic; they and those who have followed them have been critiqued often and adequately. Yet naturally we must look back much further even than Heidegger in order to understand the development of the difficulty in which they have become embroiled. Walter Thorson ("Science as the Natural Philosophy of a Christian," 68f.) points out that Descartes indirectly became the father of existentialism "by introducing self-consciousness into rational discussion as the primary fact of direct, conscious knowledge." Descartes almost single-handedly entrenched a severe subject-object tension into the thinking of modern philosophy, making explicit in his famous *cogito* the absolute, isolated centrality of the human subject in his very attempt to *eliminate* the subjective element from human knowledge (a need which, after all, was nothing more than a by-product of the unmanageable principle of autonomy on which he was already working). Kant was not able to escape the growing tensions of this enterprise and only contributed to the eventual emergence of a radical dualism which reached its futile extremes in positivism on the one hand, and reactionary existentialism on the other. Whether in the transformation of Descartes' strict rationalism into a rationalistic empiricism or in the violent attempt to overcome the subject-object distinction altogether, *language has in consequence lost its appropriate inconspicuousness.* As Kenneth Hamilton points out in *Words and the Word,* the empiricist tradition has come to regard language with suspicion as that which distorts genuine objectivity, while the idealist tradition, in which Hamilton includes existentialism, has come to venerate language as the very "temple of Being" (Heidegger)—or at least begun to employ language as a sort of "surrogate absolute" (Robert Detweiler; cf. Vern Poythress, "Philosophical Roots of Phenomenological and Structuralist Literary Criticism," *WTJ* 41 [1978] 170) in place of an objective footing in reality and its Creator. One way or another, attention that belongs to the realities signified by language is gradually being transferred to the linguistic signs themselves, whether negatively or positively, for the subject-object dilemma in the anthropocentric perspective inevitably

truth of being, which also suggests a breakdown in the proper relationship of language to reality and again (if by different means and for different purposes) allows language to assume an exalted place not its own. In both cases language gets in the way of reality by attracting improper attention to itself.[65]

Torrance indicates that language is properly related to reality when words and statements are understood to point away from themselves to the objective realities which they help to disclose. The realities thus "show through" the statements about them, as he puts it, and the statements themselves do not pretend to take their place or to usurp the ontological primacy of these realities over what is said about them. The adequacy of language (both semantically and syntactically) is thus in its ability to serve genuine involvement with reality; its truth and "adequacy" are not its own, as if by a sort of direct equivalence to reality.[66] Wherever language is cut loose from reality, then, allowing a blurring of the distinction between the two and a loss of primacy or control to the latter, might we not expect this to be signaled by regressive and addictive linguistic difficulties (as

---

casts the linguisticality of human existence into a position of impossible stress. One may grant that in the case of Heidegger and the new hermeneutic, at least, this tension has in some small way helped to revitalize certain fading dimensions of the sanctity and power of human speech, yet every attempt to reconstruct philosophy and theology on a linguistic basis is finally only an indication of the emptiness and poverty of introspective modern thought. Everywhere we hear of "the new status of language," even of "the revelatory potential of language itself," but this is only an empty response to the cold and fragmented thinking of narrow empiricism. In fact, the literature and lecturing touting these very ideas by and large displays this fact most plainly, in that it is generally among the most opaque and unintelligible speech that can be found. In modern linguistic philosophy one often has the distinct impression that one is viewing a corpse.

[65] See *Reality and Evangelical Theology*, 16ff., 65f., 130. Sadly, there are Christian versions, both liberal and conservative, of almost all the perversions of linguistic philosophy ever proposed or assumed. That the Word of God is not mere Scripture, however, but incarnate personal Truth, answers to the harmful tendencies on both sides. It refuses to release even so-called symbolic or religious language from its service to actual space-time realities, as liberalism would have it, but at the same time rejects the notion that linguistic truth has any adequacy in and of itself, particularly with respect to the Word of God. On the contrary, says Torrance (ibid., 96), the Scriptures direct our understanding to the Word of God in a self-effacing manner, inasmuch as their adequacy comes from beyond themselves from Christ, in connection with whom they are actually made to indicate more than they can naturally express (p. 108).

[66] Ibid., 65–66.

opposed to the productive challenges of language that is continually being adapted to the rationality of the realities coming
into view)? This is just the sort of thing that characterizes
skeptical debates about the viability of biblical speech as mediator of an authoritative revelation in Christ. What began as
valid, content-oriented discussion about the possibilities and
limitations of language, about metaphor and genre, about the
personal-social nature of speech and the entire matrix of associations with which and in which language functions, has
frequently been overwhelmed by a flood of philosophical or
psychological jargon bent on extracting from the very attempt
to speak a substance and value that belongs to what is spoken
about. There has been a gradual submergence of the demands of
specific objects of human thought and expression in a sea of
speculation about language, speech, and hermeneutic. Language
and the speaking subject are more and more being turned
inward and away from objective reality. Many are trying to
answer the foolish and impossible question of exactly *how* (vs.
when) language bears on reality,[67] having despaired of previous
attempts to sustain any such actual bearing in a comprehensive
and satisfactory manner.

This inward-looking approach to meaning has thrown up
a variety of challenges to those who look to the Bible for
direction, but contrary to appearances is not really foundational
in the process of rejecting an authoritative Bible; rather it is
already the product of distinctly post-biblical thinking. Nor can
the challenges set forth in this context attain any real coherence
for a retrospective attack on the traditional Christian approach
to Scripture, for they are themselves torn apart by the ancient-
modern tension between the spirit of freedom and autonomy
and a rationalistic inclination toward determinism, now commonly reflected methodologically in terms of the tension between
phenomenology and structuralism.[68] Whatever real opposition

---

[67] Torrance (ibid., 73) warns against the fallacy of trying to state in statements how statements bear on being; the situation is analogous, as he says, to
our inability to picture how a picture pictures a landscape.

[68] Langdon Gilkey, in *Naming the Whirlwind: The Renewal of God-
Language* (Indianapolis and New York: Bobbs-Merrill, 1969) 59, speaks of this
tension as belonging especially to the modern outlook—though in one form or
another it is as old as pre-socratic Greek philosophy, and older no doubt, for it is
inherent in human thought and experience apart from a right and true knowledge of God. I might add that despite the differing sentiments and tendencies

is left to the Christian approach—apart from a blank stare or a sad shake of the head—owes its tenacity to the vain hope on the side of the phenomenologist that in this very autonomy or inwardness lies the only promise for man as such. Any vestige of a truly binding authority is seen as an impossible anachronism impeding the one path for progress left open to modern man. Language and culture belong to man as creator of his own meaning; they cannot and must not be stolen from him as the *open* possibility defining his very existence.[69] Ancient texts such as the Scriptures may have a significant role to play in man's discovery of authentic selfhood or of authentic Being (the latter could also be turned to a structuralist interpretation), but no such specific developments of ancient thought or culture-bound embodiment thereof can be considered binding today. This inward-looking relativism coexists with a simple and somewhat contradictory empiricism in a variety of spheres, and it is in this total atmosphere that specific arguments pertaining to matters of language and culture come and go.[70] The status of language thus remains up for grabs, but one thing is certain: confidence in any authoritative Scripture is long gone.

How can the Church keep itself on an even keel through all this? Very simply, by looking to the one Man who is in fact the source of his own meaning (i.e., as the Word of his Father) and whose speech is therefore inextricably bound to reality. An examination of the central function of his speech will reveal the

---

expressed in phenomenology and structuralism, the essential criticism of *both* methodologies remains their dualistic abstraction of form from being, whether on the level of appearances (oriented to the individual) or on the level of pre-conscious semantic substructures (oriented to societies).

[69] See Gilkey's concise and moving account of this conviction under the rubric "Autonomy" (ibid., 57f.), which face or aspect of secular man he describes as "the source of whatever optimism and courage the modern spirit possesses" in the midst of its contingency, relativism, and temporality. In this connection it may be noted that even the structuralist approach has been explicitly overlaid "with a heavy layer of twentieth-century relativism," as Poythress puts it ("Philosophical Roots of Phenomenological and Structuralist Literary Criticism," 169–70).

[70] They do indeed come and go!—"Whorf, meet Chomsky; Chomsky, meet Ian Robinson" (whose controversial volume, *The New Grammarians' Funeral* [Cambridge: Cambridge University, 1975], at least makes rare interesting reading) . . . etc., etc. Of course, related theological fashions are no less unstable. At any rate, it should be recognized that views on matters of language, culture, and history seldom, if ever, admit of rigid classification in terms of methodology, philosophy, or theology.

deepest nature of all human speech and make plain both the
possibility and the importance of canonical Scripture for the
realization of authentic human speech and culture. Perhaps
the most obvious way in which Christ serves as a paradigm of
homo loquens can be expressed in terms of the call and response
motif that is so prominent in Scripture, especially in the
prophets, and finds its culmination in the *Abba* prayers of Jesus.
To understand this we must begin at the beginning.

The creation narrative (understood in the light of the New
Testament) allows us to speak of a divine Speech that is in-
wardly a matter of fellowship in the Godhead, and outwardly
the creative Word in Christ that calls into existence that which
was not, addressing the newly-created man on his own level
with blessing, guidance, and promise—that is, with affirmation
and invitation.[71] Human speech was once clearly reciprocative
within this context and intimately tied to divine Address and the
privilege of image-bearing; as such it was intended to serve
fellowship with God and harmony in creation, as a response
both to the call of God and to the inarticulate voice of created
reality.[72] It made possible the priestly, prophetic, and kingly role
ordained for man. With the rejection of this proper reciprocity,
however, human speech was no longer recognized as creative
response to the divine Word, but became rather the vehicle of an
independent interpretation of reality which resulted only in
alienation. At this point, God reintroduced a narrow stream of

[71] Arthur Custance (*Genesis and Early Man* [The Doorway Papers; Grand
Rapids: Zondervan, 1975] 268) notes that divine *conversation* enters the creation
narrative when God comes to the creation of man (Gen 1:26); this sudden break
in the simple divine *fiat* is a literary device pointing not only to the fact of man's
uniqueness in creation, but also, perhaps, to the nature of his uniqueness as a
linguistically *responsive* creature. Von Balthasar (*Word and Revelation*, 25)
writes that "a human being means one to whom God has spoken in the word,
one who is so made as to be able to hear and respond to the word." Ray
Anderson (*On Being Human*, 35) likewise, building largely on Karl Barth,
defines human being as "differentiated creatureliness, experienced as response to
the creative divine Word." Human subjectivity, he says (p. 56), is posited as a
response to the determination of this creative Word, which has addressed and
continues to address the human creature; human being can best be understood
in terms of "response-ability"—made visible in the further fact that man exists
materially as such in the co-relatedness of male and female (thus reflecting the
differentiation in the Being of God himself; cf. Gen 1:27).
[72] Vern Poythress ("Science as Allegory," *JASA* 35 [1983] 65f.) describes all
of creation as a response to God's Word, under the metaphor of a choral poem,
of which man is the interpreter and narrator in word and deed.

true prophetic interpretation into the midst of the false for the purposes of salvation, culminating in the perfect response of his own incarnate Word.[73] "I called, but you did not answer," nonetheless remained the constant lament until that momentous event, when finally a servant appeared with this testimony:

> The Sovereign LORD has given me an instructed tongue,
>   to know the word that sustains the weary.
> He wakens me morning by morning,
>   wakens my ear to listen like one being taught.
> The Sovereign LORD has opened my ears,
>   and I have not been rebellious; I have not drawn back.[74]

This is the One who by coming into the world reminded us that the very potential for human speech and human existence rests on God's gift of his own Light to every man. This is the One who speaks out of a listening posture and discloses the primary context of human speech as that of response to God the Creator. This is the One in whose Incarnation we come to realize that the Word of God is indeed spoken on our own level and in our hearing, and that response is possible; who even makes it possible for man to preface his response with *"Abba*, Father!"[75]

What we are faced with in Christ is the actual reality of dialogue between man and God, a dialogue grounding his Scriptures in an unbreakable living relationship at their own center. What we are consequently faced with in Scripture itself, as I pointed out in the previous section, is the word of God's Address and the word of man's appropriate witness–response. By virtue of the fact that the Scriptures are thus grounded from both sides in one abiding Mediator, we are confronted therein by an abiding word that belongs at the core of any true dialogue with God. Though the grass withers and the flowers fade, God's Word and his words stand firm. Thus a special assurance to God's people has become possible: " 'As for me, this is my covenant with them,' says the LORD. 'My Spirit, who is on you,

---

[73] Cf. Cornelius Van Til, *An Introduction to Systematic Theology* (Phillipsburg, NJ: Presbyterian and Reformed, 1978) 125.

[74] Isa 50:4–5. The call and response motif is very prominent in Isaiah 40–66 and contributes a great deal to the holding together of these materials, as well as to the highlighting of the so-called servant songs.

[75] John 1:1–18, Gal 4:4–7.

and my words that I have put in your mouth will not depart
from your mouth, or from the mouths of your children, or from
the mouths of their descendents from this time on and forever,'
says the LORD."[76] With this in view, what possible disparage-
ment of an authoritative scriptural deposit remains, despite its
specificity of language and culture, so long as it is not separated
from that same Spirit of God and the living Christ?

The viability of a canonical version of the dialogue between
man and God—something much more definite than a mere
exemplary authority *for* dialogue, which is all that some wish to
find in Jesus and the Scriptures—is already implicit in the fact
that Christ is not only the source and interpreter of his own
meaning, but of ours as well. The simple truth of the matter,
which must shape Christian response to every argument about
the restrictions that language and culture place on the biblical
word and the biblical view of reality, is that the Church knows
of but one place where dialogue with God actually takes place,
that is, in Jesus Christ. Mankind is altogether summed up in
Christ, locked into him, insofar as it is restored to genuine
humanity and reciprocity with the Word of God. It is locked
into *that* man Jesus, in the womb of *that* nation Israel and its
historical situation in the language, culture, and circumstances
of the ancient Near East.[77] And it certainly cannot be allowed
that Christ is in any fashion less communicable for the complete
particularity of the Incarnation. It must be affirmed instead that

---

[76] Isa 59:21 (cf. 40:8). The thrust of this passage in its wider context is that
the word of God, by virtue of the Spirit who acts in conjunction with the faithful
Servant, would eventually hold fast to God the formerly unfaithful and unbelieving community—i.e., that the God-given word would indeed fulfill its
canonical function.

[77] "This relation established between God and man in Jesus Christ constitutes Him as *the place* in all space and time where God meets with man in the
actualities of his human existence, and man meets with God and knows Him in
His own divine Being," writes Torrance (*Space, Time and Incarnation* [London:
Oxford University, 1969] 75). In *The Mediation of Christ* (p. 28) he adds: "I
believe that the inextricable interrelation between God's self-revelation in Jesus
and his self-revelation through Israel, and thus the permanent authoritative
patterns of understanding which God has forged for us in Israel, require to be
re-assessed and appreciated by us today in a much deeper way than ever before.
We have tried to understand Jesus within the patterns of our own various
cultures so that in the West and the East we have steadily gentilised our image of
Jesus. We have tended to abstract Jesus from his setting in the context of Israel
and its vicarious mission in regard to divine revelation."

the particularities of language and culture involved with the historical Jesus and the community of faith attached to him are indeed able to serve as bearers of the revelation that is offered in and through him, for the revelation of the living Christ we know today comes to us in no other way. In fact, it cannot be denied that the actual concreteness of the Incarnation rules out any other avenue for the knowledge of God and relativizes all other possible expressions of the dialogue between God and man to itself, to this man Jesus. Nevertheless, we must be careful to insist that it is exactly as the One who sums up *all* humanity in himself that he has been revealed. While we cannot know him apart from a ready embrace of the cultural and linguistic forms in which he arrives, we must readily confess that the content of Christ establishes and determines these forms in such a way that they open out to an infinite breadth.[78] That is how the Word of God reclaims the entire human context.

The Scriptures which lead us to Christ therefore comprise a unique book which "never bolts any doors but opens all locks," as von Balthasar puts it.[79] Yet they alone, in all their earthy particularity of thought and culture, provide access to the place where the Truth of God resides. If one would enter there, one must humbly accept the unconditional precedence of the biblical word which points the way. There are, in fact, no insurmountable barriers to the survival of this historical word as the word which must be spoken again today, as is, with the utmost authority. The biblical word is, after all, a word which throughout bears witness to him who is the Lord of history. Certainly it partakes of the limitations characteristic of all historical human speech. This word, like other words, can be accused of shrinking and freezing living reality into linguistic preserves and of doing so largely from within a given (and limited) worldview with its conventional ways of seeing reality and putting it to words. Likewise, the words to which its vision is put admit of the same degree of fuzziness and indeterminacy plaguing any composition. But can these difficulties be considered barriers to confession of the infallible authority of Scripture? Surely they can again steer us away from misguided interest in a technical or

---

[78] Cf. Torrance, *Space, Time and Incarnation*, 78–79.
[79] *Word and Revelation*, 28.

exhaustive inerrancy, but do they mitigate against the sort of confidence we have in mind when we speak of Scripture's complete reliability, of its functional inerrancy?[80] On the contrary, if our reading, as the biblical authors' writing, is truly governed by the ultimate Object coming into view in Scripture, then the necessary perspective on whatever realities may be

---

[80] Richard K. Curtis took note of several such difficulties some years ago in a controversial series of articles in the *Gordon Review* (Sept. 1955, 97-108; Dec. 1956, 149-51; Feb. 1957, 13-23) entitled "Language and Theology: Some Basic Considerations," observing toward the end that communication is "a social act, in which adequacy, rather than infallibility is the rule" (pp. 20-21). What he really meant to imply by this statement—not altogether a disagreeable one—was left unclear, but his handling of the linguistic issues involved was seriously marred in any case by a tendency to focus exclusively on the subjective pole of language and, indeed, of semantics. Such an approach is often characterized by references to something along the lines of the Whorfian hypothesis and to the idea that "meanings are in people," and by the faulty supposition that the immediate referent of language is a set of ideas, not reality itself. Mature linguists with a broad basis in actual fieldwork, however, have helped to make clear and explicit that when this set of drums is beat too loudly it is sheer nuisance, not scholarship. B. Siertsema's "Language and World View: Semantics for Theologians" (*The Bible Translator* 20 [1969] 3-21), Eugene Nida's "Implications of Contemporary Linguistics for Biblical Scholarship" (*JBL* 91 [1972] 73-89), and Kenneth Pike's "The Linguist and Axioms Concerning the Language of Scripture," e.g., make better reading here. Their findings uphold what a realist orientation in linguistic philosophy would expect. Thought and communication of thought, in the effort to grow and to share in genuine knowledge of reality, is not seriously hobbled—though it is often profoundly challenged—by the shortcomings and idiosyncrasies of language. At least, there is nothing of substance in applied linguistics to turn us back from a responsible pursuit of speech that is *determined by what is spoken about* and *able to communicate its concerns effectively,* if somewhat laboriously on occasion. Pike makes plain that with respect to ordinary (i.e., non-scientific) language like that of the Bible, even transculturally effective communication is certainly possible, though he admits that we must distinguish in this enterprise, as in interpretation, between *linguistically* relevant features and *functionally* relevant features (I have taken this terminology from J. C. Catford, *A Linguistic Theory of Translation* [London: Oxford University, 1965] 94). We can therefore speak meaningfully about the truth of biblical statements, and even about biblical infallibility, despite the relativity of the linguistic and perspectival incidentals that color all speech, despite the many obstructions to perfect communication cast up by language, and despite the impossibility of anything like a complete or perfect reproduction of knowledge in words. And what criterion of truth "will work for a natural-language statement which is neither complete nor unambiguous in its detail," asks Pike (ibid., 48)? "Here, as Edward J. Carnell said once (in *An Introduction to Christian Apologetics* [Grand Rapids: Eerdmans, 1956] 45), 'The true is the quality of that judgment or proposition which, when followed out into the total witness of facts in our experience, does not disappoint our expectations.' That is, the true statement leads us to act so that we will not be upset by finding out further details of a situation; we will not have been misled by false information."

involved will be genuinely attained, and the shrunken letter referring to these realities will successfully achieve its purpose as it is filled out in accordance with the Reality of Christ himself. Of course Scripture does not and cannot do full justice to reality; no speech can. But Scripture is entirely *just* in its relation to reality, for it consistently submits to reality as it directs us toward it. It is this that can and should be asked of all human speech, though its actual achievement in the case of inspired Scripture reflects a very special measure—to accompany the very special purposes—of the grace of God.[81]

But while many have in fact partially recovered from the modern wave of linguistic uncertainty in a prevailing of common sense and for obvious pragmatic reasons, there has been an unfortunate spillover into general anthropology which has led to adoption of a markedly relativistic cultural hermeneutic. This, above all, cannot pass without notice. One of the greatest challenges presently facing evangelical scholarship is to contain and correct an approach that outwardly acknowledges biblical authority, but regularly tends to "render to Caesar" what belongs to God. Here as well there are several arguments ready-to-hand against allowing to Scripture the binding authority of its actual verbal direction. Working on a model inspired by translation theory, it is proposed that a sort of cultural dynamic equivalence is required in order properly to respect and apply the Bible outside its original context. The culture-bound perspectives of the biblical authors embody (however well or poorly) trans-cultural principles and ideas which may require radical trans-formation of actual biblical statements if their truth is to be preserved. Such transformation may even involve reversal. For example, "Elders shall be husbands of one wife" may become

---

[81] Scripture more than any other book, in fact, is a "shrunken letter," because of what Barth (*Church Dogmatics* 1/2. 468) calls "the unusual pre-ponderance of what is said in it over the word as such." But then Scripture is met and fulfilled by what is said in it in a way that can only be the envy of every other word spoken by men. When by the Spirit the reader is brought into that same special attitude of obedience to revelation in which Scripture was written, i.e., when the Church "looks only in the direction indicated by the witness which speaks to it in Scripture, with no glances aside in any other direction" (*Church Dogmatics* 4/1, 722), there is, in von Balthasar's words (*Word and Revelation*, 30), an "outpouring of the infinite riches of scripture into the church; . . . and the more we probe it the more do its divine dimensions broaden and impose themselves."

"Elders shall be husbands of more than one wife," in the case of a society that affords greater respectability of reputation to men who can manage large households.[82]

The issues involved here—and there is much of real value to interest us—would carry us far beyond the reasonable scope of our discussion if allowed to do so, but it must be observed that biblical authority is often rendered just as meaningless by this sort of approach, whatever the lip-service offered that authority, as by the linguistic subjectivism dealt with above. In the one case, through an unnatural entanglement of speech with the supposed isolation of historical moments and of individual speakers (an entanglement accompanying its divorce from reality itself), there results a denial that any recorded speech-act can survive the actual circumstances of its own origin with complete integrity. In the other, through an unnatural entanglement of the biblical messages with changing cultural forms of human existence (an entanglement accompanying their divorce from the specific, concrete grid of the Incarnation and the womb God prepared for it), there is a denial that the messages of Scripture can survive without constant revision by the cultures to which they are brought.[83] Here too we find a form/content dualism at work divesting Scripture of its immediate participation in Jesus Christ and his authority, generating its own process of de-

---

[82] David J. Hesselgrave notes this example in the ICBI syllabus on hermeneutics for the conference held in Chicago, Nov. 1982 ("Contextualization and Revelational Epistemology," 33); it is taken from Charles H. Kraft, perhaps the leading exponent of the cultural dynamic-equivalence approach. Kraft (*Christianity in Culture* [Maryknoll, NY: Orbis, 1979] 178ff.) argues from a dynamic view of revelation that the Bible, rather than being perceived as a mere deposit of revelation, should be understood as a yardstick for the comprehension and experience of present revelation, which has a context all its own. He wants us to see the Bible as "God's inspired casebook," to view its instruction as casuistic rather than strictly apodictic, and to allow for an acceptable range of variation in interpretation. But problems arise here in connection with his central tenet that "revelation is receptor-oriented." See n 84 below.

[83] Certainly there is a profound *involvement* of human speech, including the biblical messages, with the individuality of the speaking subject and with the culture to which he belongs and with which he undoubtedly shares certain aspects of his worldview. But contemplation of this involvement has become a jungle of relativism, under the heat and pressure of our own worldview; involvement is being seen as an overpowering *entanglement*, because of an unbalanced focus on subjectivity. Those who set off into the jungle in this direction must realize that they are following a path which intersects with that of Bultmann and the new hermeneutic.

mythologizing and remythologizing. This same problem might also be expressed in terms of a nature/grace dualism that ironically weakens what is ostensibly being upheld—namely, the affirmation of humanity in the Incarnation—in that the Christ of Christian proclamation is detached from the historical, human Jesus and from Israel as his chosen parent, prophet, and servant.[84] Perhaps we cannot avoid observing as well that this very serious error naturally tends toward an open disrespect for certain "unfortunate" intrusions of cultural bias into the biblical testimony—which most often indicates nothing other than a bias in favor of one's own culture and its limited (if fervently held) perceptions of certain thorny issues requiring concrete direction.[85]

In conclusion, the Church must contend for the fact that of the multitude of problems for the authority of Scripture, whether raised in the present field of discussion or any other, none is without solution if Christ himself is seen to be at the center of

---

[84] On Israel itself as *the* prophet of God, see Torrance, *The Mediation of Christ*, 22ff., who warns us against the fatal error of trying "to peel away from divine revelation what we tend to regard as its transient physical clothing" (p. 25). As I see it, the major flaw in the approach taken by the often helpful Charles Kraft is the supposition that we should work primarily from a basis in general principles *abstracted* from "God's inspired casebook," in order to remain free to the interests of revelation as a present event which takes to itself new forms in all sorts of differing cultural contexts. In his approach it appears at times that revelation (which is rightly distinguished from the Bible, per se) is being posited *alongside* the Bible—while tethered to it, in his metaphor—and that proclamation, adjusted culture by culture, can therefore in some sense stand in place of Scripture rather than in the immediate service of Scripture. The real essence of the phenomenon of canon and canonical authority, namely, the verbal mediation of revelation by virtue of Scripture's intimate, spiritual attachment to Jesus as its unifying *scopus*, is entirely overlooked in the "inspired casebook" approach. It is the Christ-of-Scripture to whom we must be brought if we are to know God's revelation—to this Jewish Christ and his Jewish Scriptures. The proper request of Greeks and heathen alike arises in connection with the pilgrimage to Jerusalem: "Sir, we would see Jesus" (John 12:21, *KJV*). In that sense, we cannot say simplistically that "revelation is receptor-oriented." Revelation means our reorientation to God in Christ; it is confrontation with Jesus, an experience which may be as demanding with regard to our culture as it is in other aspects of our personal existence. Culturally-*sensitive* translations, exegesis, and theology are obviously of paramount importance for the Church and its witness, but this does not and cannot mean culturally-*shaped* translations or culturally-*determined* exegesis and theology. That sort of dualism only leads to syncretism.

[85] See n 5 above.

the doctrine of Scripture and the Church's experience with it. As incarnate Word he is able to command both language and culture, and even man himself, to the ends of his own revelation. It is precisely that revelation, granted to us in and through Scripture in connection with the work of inspiration, which reveals to us the proper nature of the crucial aspects of human existence on which we have touched. The potential of the individual person to speak and participate meaningfully in communal habitation of God's creation both within and across temporal, cultural, and linguistic barriers, is guaranteed in him. The precedence of the Christ of the Scriptures from beginning to end, as the paradigm for humanity in all things, is the proper confession of the Church. Any other approach winds up with man usurping for himself what belongs to him only in Christ and finding himself entirely unable to handle it.[86] That is also why man, when he tries to judge Scripture's capacity to speak a fully authoritative word by looking at himself rather than at Christ, is left only with doubt. But the comprehensive authority of Scripture (along with the relative values of its parts) is firmly established by its attachment to Christ and given a truly primordial and abiding character. No matter in what connection the claim is made, then, we should always be ready to deny that Scripture somehow fails to provide us with adequate direction, or points us in one direction while the truth for us, at least, lies in another. For he who speaks *as* man and *to* man out of his own sovereign Truth has found Scripture entirely speakable. In Scripture we therefore face nothing less than the abiding Word of Truth.

[86] This will surely prove to be the practical (and possibly disastrous) outcome of liberation theology, for example, not to mention less Christian social ventures, just as it has been in the intellectual collapse and radical fragmentation of the more speculative, academic approaches to human potential.

6 | The Hermeneutical Challenge

In the opening chapter I noted (with Dr. Packer) that the controversy to which the inerrancy debate belongs is at bottom the question of the authority of God, speaking through the Bible, to rule his Church. This fact makes the relationship of the debate to hermeneutical endeavor of the highest possible significance, since it is nothing less than obedient *hearing* of the Word that is ultimately at stake in a faithful confession of Scripture. "To recognize the interrelationship between authority and hermeneutics is precisely to give authority cash-value and a cutting edge," says Anthony Thiselton.[1] Any answer to the inerrancy question that fails to indicate its bearing on the hermeneutical task—indeed, to clarify and establish the integrity of that task—can hardly be considered adequate or even relevant. But it is all the more important to be clear on the *mutual* bearing which these subjects sustain, and it is this that will guide the considerations of the present chapter.

Certainly the broader terms of the debate and the resolution upheld here (namely, that every biblical message is trustworthy) do involve a hermeneutical commitment and direction. Packer spells out in a couple of places his view of what the evangelical doctrine of Scripture requires of the hermeneutical endeavor—three things in particular: a continuing commitment to the grammatico-historical method in exegesis, characterized by a well-rounded canonical perspective; a commitment to the principle of harmony in theological synthesis of these exegetical results; and a commitment to the principle of universalizing in application, such that biblical knowledge of God resolves into

---

[1] *The Two Horizons*, 436. As he says, "the actual experience of the authority of the biblical text is something which occurs in concrete and dynamic terms," i.e., only in the impact of Scripture within the stream of human thought and activity.

187

authoritative proclamation (for biblical hermeneutics is concerned both with the fact that God *has* spoken and with God
speaking).[2] On the other hand, he is also clear on the fact that
the evangelical doctrine of Scripture is itself subject to revision
from within the hermeneutical circle. Exegesis, necessarily
approached on the basis of preunderstandings, produces a doctrine of Scripture which in turn yields hermeneutical principles
and a hermeneutical outlook, thus guiding our return to the text
in greater precision of exegesis, and so forth. This one-way
circle is traveled many times in a spiral of successive approximation, as Packer puts it, meaning that the doctrine of Scripture
must constantly come under review in light of contributions
made at every level of our involvement with Scripture.[3] Clearly
the basic dynamics at work here must not be neglected if our
doctrine is to be protected from hardening into a barrier between
us and the truth, and if genuine balance is to be achieved in our
examination of the interrelationship between authority and
hermeneutics.

What ought to be noticed as well, however, is the significance of understanding the inerrancy commitment, as Packer
and others do, essentially in terms of an affirmation (taking
shape early in this process) that one is committed in advance
"to receive as God's instruction and obey as God's command
whatever Scripture is already known to teach and may in the
future be shown to teach."[4] This understanding of inerrancy

[2] Cf. "Hermeneutics and Biblical Authority," 6f.; "Infallible Scripture and
the Role of Hermeneutics," 349f. The third of these commitments, along with
an elaboration of *invalid* approaches to the hermeneutical endeavor, is added in
the latter article; here Packer also deals with the flip side of the coin, namely,
conceptions of Scripture which are hermeneutically invalid (pp. 353–54). The
commitment to infallibility and the hermeneutics with which it is bound up
(particularly the continued devotion to grammatico-historico-canonical exegesis) flows from the conviction of both Scripture and Church that God has
effected an identity between his own speaking and the words of his spokesmen,
such that these men are worthy of our utmost attention in whatever they set out
to say—it entails no other *a priori* commitments of any sort, in his judgment.

[3] Packer ("Hermeneutics and Biblical Authority," 7) cautions evangelicals
against over-simplifications of their commitment, the most basic of which
"consists simply of forgetting that, as our concept of biblical authority determines our hermeneutic in the manner described, so that concept itself is always,
and necessarily, open to challenge from the biblical texts on which we bring our
hermeneutics to bear."

[4] "Infallible Scripture and the Role of Hermeneutics," 351; similar language may be found in ICBI literature, though it is often questionable how

brings to light the fact that there is a practical intervention of textually-responsive hermeneutical endeavor between the *doctrine* of inerrancy and any substantial *application* of the inerrancy commitment. Plainly stated, it relates inerrancy not to the text simply as such, and therefore to all its phenomena, but to the text in its communicative function as God's message-bearer.[5] It therefore renders inerrancy ultimately a *post-hermeneutical* concern, and its boundaries become, in fact, a hermeneutical judgment. Though governed by the principles mentioned above, hermeneutico-exegetical questions about the scope of a passage, its literary genre, the range and content and character of the actual assertions made, etc., are seen to precede and determine any direct invocation of inerrancy. Packer himself notes that answers to these questions

> must be determined entirely inductively, by grammatico-historical exegesis. It is necessary to insist constantly that the concept of inerrancy gives no direct help in determining such questions as these. It is *not*—repeat, *not*—an exegetical shortcut.[6]

If we follow through on this line of thinking, the true mutuality of the relationship between the doctrine of biblical infallibility and hermeneutics begins to come clear as the process of interpretation takes place. Interpretation, as the bringing forward of the text, is also the setting forth of that to which infallibility pertains, for the trustworthiness of Scripture has no significance except in terms of the actual hearing of a biblical word. It is therefore in a hermeneutical context that lines are drawn between the broader and narrower terms of the inerrancy debate, and that questions about possible errors in Scripture are finally answered according to their bearing, or lack of bearing, on the actual messages of Scripture. Though the Church's recognition that God has spoken through historical men,

---

exactly we are to take such statements in their qualification of the inerrancy commitment. Packer himself leaves the impression of some ambiguity here.

[5] We cannot afford to lose sight of the fact that Scripture is (or can be) God communicating with us, and that God's communication is something that terminates on man in a purposeful manner, as Packer says ("Hermeneutics and Biblical Authority," 11); cf. 2 Tim 3:15-17. When we deal with Scripture in terms other than those of its message-bearing function, both our doctrine of biblical authority and our hermeneutics inevitably go astray.

[6] Ibid., 12.

effecting an identity between their speaking and his, leads to testimony about an "advance" commitment to Scripture, this (as I emphasized earlier) is not a formal commitment, but one that is realized only in and because of actual involvement with Scripture. From this the very important conclusion follows, to which I have been pointing all along, that *the immediate scope of inerrancy is a fluctuating matter tailored to each individual passage, and its parameters are determined in appropriate exegesis of a passage in light of its greater context.*

The practical challenge of the inerrancy issue, then—short of our active obedience to the Word we hear in Scripture and which we allow to instruct us there—is the hermeneutical task of careful regard for the text, and attainment to its own perspective and communicative design as witness to Christ. Inerrancy and its relevance is wrapped up in the results of discussions about genre and style and tone and intention, about context and purpose and canonical role, about exegetical clarity and the fusion of horizons. It is exactly this work of respect for the service of the text that enables clear affirmation of inerrancy in the broader terms of the debate and occasional negation in the narrower terms to stand together with a practical, workable integrity, for the final application of inerrancy pertains to the *results* of exegesis, despite the fact that our exegesis is hardly infallible. But perhaps this still requires some elaboration.

Recovering the Hermeneutical Factor

The doctrine of inerrancy commonly runs into trouble where the preunderstanding that a very mechanical sort of identity exists between the speech (and mind) of the human and divine authors refuses to subject itself to modification in the hermeneutical circle. It is this that has led to the loss of the hermeneutical factor in discussions of inerrancy in certain quarters, and indeed, to a decreasing sensitivity to the whole mystery "that the Word of God does not draw us away from the human but involves us with the human," as Berkouwer says.[7] Moreover,

---

[7] "It comes to us in the midst of an overwhelming multiformity of human witnesses, of human questions and answers, of skepticism and trust, of faith and unbelief, of lamentation and jubilation, of tenseness and rest finally granted. The charge to understand this is immense; it encircles the ages" (*Holy Scripture*, 167).

the hermeneutical task itself is often brought to the brink of suffocation in this atmosphere. Those who attach to the theopneustic nature of Scripture a divine activity invariably determinative of each and every word do so at considerable risk. They not only encumber themselves with an awkward doctrinal accretion and trammel themselves with a defense of Scripture in matters irrelevant to its own purposes, they also incline themselves toward an unnatural, word-study oriented exegesis. A sentiment once expressed in the theory of holy languages thus continues to survive in terms of a "holy hermeneutic." Matters of historical, theological, and literary context are quite regularly ignored, along with the contributions of various literary devices, when the proper focus on message and communicative design is traded for a fascination with precision of individual "divine words." Such an approach naturally tends as well toward an unusual defensiveness about the supposed literal sense of these words, which is often carefully guarded in ways that tend to embellish, if not to contaminate and obscure, what the text is actually saying. Further, textual detail is not judged primarily according to its contribution in context, but in the name of verbal inspiration and inerrancy is superficially upheld as being important in its own right.[8]

Perhaps a few examples of the sort of thing one encounters in this strange atmosphere would be helpful. A somewhat bizarre illustration can be found in the proposal that out of faithfulness to Scripture we should even dogmatize so mysterious a matter as the location of Sheol-Hades, the place of the

---

[8] Contemporary exegesis of a very conservative bent still shows pockets of resistance to the well-placed criticisms of observers like James Barr, Eugene Nida, and a host of others. Nida comments that it is only within its context "that the semantic structure of any word or semantic unit can and must be defined" ("Implications of Contemporary Linguistics for Biblical Scholarship," 77). And of course a great deal goes into the making of a context: basic theses and a variety of supportive ideas, each bearing on the others; literary genre, and a variety of psychological factors and indicators; selection of words and syntactical relations out of a particular set of options, etc.; along with a host of background factors. Over-emphasis on the word-by-word analytical approach to Scripture reflects the outdated assumption that words are the basic units or carriers of meaning, says Anthony Thiselton, an approach which "may seem to be connected with a theory of 'verbal' inspiration, but is in reality based, rather, on ignorance about the nature of language" ("Semantics and New Testament Interpretation," in *New Testament Interpretation*, ed. I. Howard Marshall [Grand Rapids: Eerdmans, 1977] 78). Whatever its origin, however, it persists partly because of unwarranted theories of inspiration.

dead. After all, the biblical text speaks of the nether parts of the earth, and consistently of going *down* to Sheol—and "from any position on the face of the earth, the heart of the earth is down," says one writer; therefore Sheol "must be located in the heart of the earth."[9] But this is a very patent abuse of Scripture, not faithful respect for it, and to follow the operative principle of this proposal would certainly drum up a host of unnecessary problems for inerrancy. When the passages in view are allowed to control our exposition, it is readily apparent that the location of Sheol is nowhere under consideration; only the condition of the men and women referred to is a matter of genuine interest. Because the grave was both a symbol of and the gateway to the nether world, it was entirely natural to speak of "going down" to Sheol (which often, so far as the primary thought goes, signifies nothing more than 'grave' anyway). We should take note, however, that rejection of any such handling of Scripture is not a denial that the ancients may well have believed something of that sort, though they would not have conceived of it in terms of "the heart of the earth." Quite openly, it is an assertion that faithfulness to biblical instruction does not require us to follow them in that belief or any modification of it, though it does suggest that we allow their expression of the matter to have the intended impact on us in graphically presenting the fate of man as he "goes down" to Sheol under the burden of sin and the mortality it has brought.[10]

Such examples can easily be multiplied, of course, to illustrate from a variety of angles a very legitimate hermeneutical problem connected with the direction in which some have tried to take the doctrines of inspiration and inerrancy. It is with good reason that inerrantists have often been reminded of statements like that in Qoh 1:5: "The sun rises and the sun sets, and hurries back to where it rises." Of course, everyone now recognizes in this the language of appearance and its complete legitimacy (the truth of the matter having proved much more accessible to us than in the case of the previous example!). Old literalist herme-

---

[9] Herman A. Hoyt, *The End Times* (Chicago: Moody, 1969) 44.

[10] Of course, there are those who would question the reality of Sheol/Hades in terms anything like the ancient conception of it, and there is room here within the biblical teaching for some difference of opinion, but no justification for the pseudo-scientific skepticism characterizing the modern perspective.

neutical failures have been corrected and no real dispute about biblical error remains. But there is still a lesson to be learned, for again, who will deny that the Teacher believed the sun actually to return to its place? We do not require Scripture to be literally true in this expression and it is *not* because we suppose its author to have aimed at a purely poetic description, but because nothing scientific is at issue in what he himself is saying; he is concerned only with the impression of endless cycles. But then it is sense and interpretation which are seen to govern our concern about inerrancy, not the reverse. Might not the same approach also be taken with regard to other passages, then, and to a variety of problematic details, whether they involve expressions, numbers, names, or any other "scenery" in the setting created by a text, the quality or accuracy of which is not intrinsic to the communicative design of that text? (This we can pursue in a moment, though it is worthwhile at present to remain with the point that exegetical and hermeneutical integrity must in every case be upheld in remaining faithful to Scripture, for it is precisely at that level that something concrete begins to be at stake.)

A very *practical* example of the distorting impact of an insensitive inspiration/inerrancy doctrine with restrictive hermeneutical tendencies might be apropos as well. Prov 22:6 tells us: "Train a child in the way he should go, and when he is old he will not turn from it." It is not difficult to find interpretations of this passage, influenced by the simplistic "divine words" approach we have in view, which appear to undermine the validity of the proverbial form (that is, of instruction and encouragement by means of the typical example) altogether! A simple proverb is quite thoughtlessly transformed from an encouraging observation into a mathematical equation, with the consequence that a defense of Scripture's integrity allows us, indeed, requires us, to assume hidden faults in the parenting if a seemingly well-trained child does in fact go astray in later years. Though it can be inferred from the proverb that faults of upbringing are *generally* involved where children go astray, this is not always the case and the supposition is not necessarily justified. The proverbial form of this "promise" will not support such inflexible inferences and requires no such commitment in defense of its integrity. Only a narrow, overzealous approach to inspiration and inerrancy could produce such an interpretation. Sadly, deviations like this are not rare occurrences in fundamentalist circles.

The kind of inerrancy that is rigidly concerned with the integrity of so-called divine words is clearly not well-equipped to cope with the variety of challenges facing the interpreter of Scripture, or even to highlight this activity at all. It is stuck with an innate inclination toward bare, absolutizing logic that often leaves the real world behind, or rather, that never attains to the real world.[11] One way to convey the character of the resistance faced here is simply to contrast it with the attitude toward words and their function in context gained by reflection on the most potent literary form of all, namely, poetry (which accounts for a very considerable portion of the Old Testament and some highly significant passages in the New). Thinking about poetry turns our thoughts to poetic license, to heightened contributions of metaphor and tone, and to a host of other elements hinging on human creativity and responsive judgment. Sympathetic comprehension here must even take into account that for which Owen Barfield coins the word "tarning" (from the German *Tarnung*) to express the function of poetic diction to say one thing in order to mean another, that is, in order to enhance its communication of this other. We might say, suggests Barfield, that "the metaphorical proposition contains a judgment, but a judgment pronounced with a wink at the Court."[12] This is an especially important factor in any attempt to say something new—a very common feature in Scripture—but exhaustive inerrantists are known to frown rather heavily on those who wink at the court! It would be interesting to speculate on the significance of the general discomfort of fundamentalist inerrancy in such matters for interpretive difficulties on a much larger scale than the simple illustrations I have used. I am thinking of the propensity to embrace extreme dispensationalist viewpoints and the like; that is a discussion belonging to another place, however.

---

[11] Thiselton ("Semantics and New Testament Interpretation," 79) warns us that "a persistent preoccupation with descriptive assertions or 'propositions' tends to flatten out the distinctive contributions of biblical poetry, metaphor, parable, and apocalyptic, reducing it all to the level of discursive 'units of information.'"

[12] "Poetic Diction and Legal Fiction," in *Essays Presented to Charles Williams*, ed. C. S. Lewis (Grand Rapids: Eerdmans, 1966) 111f., 123-24.

The present discussion is simply meant to reinforce the message that there is something awry in any view of Scripture that does not take the hermeneutical task with the utmost seriousness and reflect itself in interpretive practices well-tuned to the primacy of context as arbiter of meaning and judge of the kind of relevance and adequacy belonging to its own statements or details. A focus on God-given words apart from their actual literary service to Christ unfortunately results in restrictive hermeneutics and a subsequent inattention to the hermeneutical factor as a meaningful contributor to solution of the inerrancy debate. Instead, it aggravates the debate. This very serious situation can receive some initial correctives from common communication theory, of course, which (without regarding words as merely arbitrary) explains how context is indeed the constructor of meaning and the necessary avenue of approach to what any writer or speaker says. This will loosen up the approach to Scripture and to inerrancy to a certain degree. At bottom, however, it is thoughtful reflection on the Lordship of Christ which Scripture mediates and knowledge of the bond between Christ and Scripture—it is the liberating *realism* of Christian thinking and the simple, corresponding conviction of Scripture's suitability and vitality as *witness to* (not substitution for) reality—which restores the hermeneutical factor and a responsible relationship between inerrancy and hermeneutics. A dynamic focus on the Bible as bearer of messages which command our attention only to divert it away from themselves to that (and to him) of which they speak, is the consequence of such reflection. This focus liberates both inerrancy and hermeneutics from a merely mechanical fixation on the text and frees them to the truth of what is being said in the text, as we come to recognize that believing Scripture "does not mean staring at a holy and mysterious book, but hearing the witness concerning Christ."[13]

At the same time it leaves no doubt that the hermeneutical task is the process of opening oneself to determination *by* the

---

[13] Berkouwer, *Holy Scripture*, 166; see also Torrance, *Reality and Evangelical Theology*, 113ff. C. S. Lewis's comment on Scripture in *Reflections on the Psalms* (New York: Harcourt, Brace, Jovanovich, 1958) is worth noting in this connection as well, for the Scriptures, he says, "proceed not by the conversion of God's word into a literature but by the taking up of a literature to be the vehicle of God's word" (p. 116).

text, or rather, through the text by the divine and worldly realities of which it speaks. It guards against any form of independence from the text, which always wreaks havoc with the very idea of hermeneutics and renders inerrancy meaningless. On the contrary, the bond between Christ and Scripture makes plain the rootedness of both the biblical messages and the hermeneutical task in reality itself, and thus establishes a meaningful context for the assertion of inerrancy. This special relationship leaves no room for external criteria to be applied to the text as part of a self-directed hermeneutic—that is, external canons of knowledge or epistemology which have the function of controlling meaning or delineating truth. It is understood that meaning and truth are determined once and for all in Christ, and that the responsibility of biblical hermeneutics is responsiveness to the messages of Christ as to Christ himself. This responsiveness may be enhanced by many outside contributions (whether historical, cultural, scientific or philosophical, etc.), but we are oriented fundamentally to the internal criteria of the meaning structure of the biblical passages themselves, in their own responsiveness to the realities in view, as determining the word which lays claim to our commitment and submission.[14]

Yet these last remarks, important though they be, put us at constant risk of returning inadvertently to a merely formal view of Scripture, unless the one "internal criterion" that really counts in our hermeneutics is determination by the Word himself. At the very heart of all that can and should be said against a self-directed hermeneutic lies the admission that in the bond between Christ and Scripture we are oriented to Christ as the interpreter of his own word. I have already hinted at the importance of this fact once or twice, but if we are to speak with complete seriousness about recovering the hermeneutical factor we must attend directly to two very significant implications.

First, if all Scripture partakes in divine revelation precisely because it participates in the Word which God has spoken in human terms for human eyes and ears, then *ipso facto* the incarnate Christ must determine its meaning according to the revelation contained in his own Person. This not only speaks to the entire character of biblical hermeneutics as profoundly tuned to the living Jesus, but contains an important qualifica-

---

[14] Cf. Nicholas Wolterstorff, "Canon and Criterion," *RJ* 3 (October, 1969) 14.

tion for the much-maligned principle of harmony. The harmony of interpretation to which the Church is committed in its attestation of biblical infallibility is not a shallow and artificial harmony in which passage is set beside passage and coerced into agreement. It is a harmony that flows from recognition of one and the same Christ in every passage. In other words, it is the harmony produced by Christ as he deepens our vision of himself and his kingdom to the point of intersection between the differing visions of the passages before us. This sort of harmony, of course, does not flinch at the fully human character of the Word's own participation in worldly existence; nor then does it look to his biblical word in the naïve terms of "absolute truth," which may be found only in his Person. One of the very things which makes the book of Qoheleth so valuable, for example, is its deliberately relative way of expressing things:

> Do not be overrighteous, neither be overwise—why destroy yourself?
> Do not be overwicked, and do not be a fool—why die before your time?
> It is good to grasp the one and not let go of the other. The man who fears God will avoid all extremes.[15]

Doubtless it is this very device that renders Qoheleth suspect in the view of many conservatives, who malign the Spirit of Christ and Jesus himself—the Teacher of wisdom in whom the tensions of the wisdom literature do indeed find resolution—by putting down Qoheleth to the will of God to include in Scripture a sample of "the best man can offer on his own," which is tantamount to denying its theopneustic character. But unless we recognize the relativization of all of Scripture's statements by the Person of Christ and admit what T. F. Torrance presses us to admit in *Reality and Evangelical Theology*, namely, that we must look through Scripture to Christ himself if we are to speak meaningfully and respectfully about him, we cannot hope for hermeneutical integrity, nor can we expect any easing of tensions in the debate over infallibility.

Secondly, however, it is just as important to say that, if Christ really does determine the meaning of Scripture, then objective hermeneutics remains a genuine possibility for the Church and formalism need not give way to an even more

---

[15] Qoh 7:16–18.

damaging functionalism. We must not allow ourselves to surreptitiously reassume control over Scripture by paying heed to
those who are fond of stressing the inevitable individuality and
partiality of all our hermeneutical efforts, however well-tuned.
For there are some who seem to be of the opinion that the very
fact of our hermeneutical activity seriously relativizes any sure
and common footing in the objectivities of the text, and hence,
presumably, in the objectivities about which the text has led us
to dare to speak. They suggest that our discussions of biblical
hermeneutics and authority would benefit from a more descriptive (less prescriptive) approach, relative to what is actually
happening in the Church's use of Scripture. They do not want
us to speak so boldly of a book in which the Church of every
time and place faces a common obligation to the Word of Truth.
But this should not be construed as real respect for the depth and
breadth and freedom of the Word of God in connection with the
ever-present Holy Spirit, as they would have us think. It is
rather a backhanded justification of the *Church's* freedom to
employ the biblical word as it sees fit. Those who are inclined
toward this view have failed to reckon with the impact of the
self-interpreting Christ on the role and function of Scripture in
the Church. When it is understood that the one incarnate Lord
continually presents himself, and no other, in and through the
canonical Scriptures he has raised up for an abiding witness, it
will be seen that in so doing he provides an indissoluble link
between the biblical messages and the Church's comprehension
of them. Christ is able to govern the inadequacy of our hermeneutical endeavor just because God has determined that one
Word, and only one Word, should be spoken in the biblical
testimony, yet spoken again and again. Exactly in returning
time after time to listen do we truly benefit from the living
authority of the Word over our own fallible efforts to come to
grips with what is being said. Thus we are able, in fact, to regard
our own inadequacy while still believing in our mutual obligation before the Christ of the Scriptures, and without falling prey
to the relativism arising from phenomenalist observation of
human efforts to interpret the Bible.[16]

---

[16] See, e.g., David H. Kelsey, *The Uses of Scripture in Recent Theology*
(Philadelphia: Fortress, 1975) 205ff. Kelsey is altogether mistaken in thinking
that an entirely formal concept of theology, or a purely functional (operationalist) understanding of "scripture" and "authority," is in any sense tenable

The hermeneutical factor is thus restored to every consideration of biblical inerrancy, yet without being turned around and
made over into a denial of the possibility or relevance of such a
commitment. The hermeneutical factor asks that the inerrancy
doctrine accept no other challenge than the challenges that
come from being genuinely attuned to the biblical word as it is
spoken for and by and about Christ. Why *shouldn't* we be
attuned to what the Bible is attempting to say as a message-
bearing vehicle, as well as to that about which it is speaking,
rather than to the distractions of the vehicle as such? After all,
our doctrines about inspiration and infallibility are only designed to focus us on the canonical *service* of Scripture as the
word of Christ and on our pressing need to *hear* that word—to
remain free to our precommitment to receive what the text has to
say in order that we may also receive that which it promises. The
hermeneutical factor is the link between our actual response to
the biblical word and the doctrinal reminders of our obligation
to it. As such, it is co-extensive with, and inexpendable to, any
legitimate concern with the infallibility of Scripture or with
biblical inerrancy. If the overall shape of evangelical hermeneutics to some extent reflects the inerrancy commitment, so indeed

---

(p. 207). From the side of the Christian Church, one could only fall into this
dualist trap by losing sight of the fixed character of the bond between Christ and
Scripture, neatly balanced in the Reformation principle of the indivisibility of
Spirit and word. Christ himself is the content of Scripture and the proper
content of theology, for which reason it is a very serious fault to approach either
of these apart from immediate involvement in the concrete "Who?" question
answered again and again in and through Scripture by the once-for-all revelation of God in Jesus Christ. One cannot begin merely with the hermeneutical
activity and theologizing of the Church, then go on to determine the "morals for
doctrines about scripture" that Kelsey attempts. Nor can one adequately determine the most fruitful questions "to put to the intellectual structures Christians
build" (p. 9) from a formal, disinterested standpoint; no depth perspective is
possible as a mere spectator, whatever the value of one's surface observations.
Kelsey works from a phenomenalist stance in which it is impossible to distinguish between the Word of God and the creative response of the community,
though the distinction itself be allowed. But as Torrance (*Reality and Evangelical Theology*, 156) rightly says, "we do not operate with a criterion of truth
lodged in the subjects of the interpreters or theologians (whether as individuals
or the church)—for we are thrown back objectively upon the Truth and Word of
God himself, who forces us to call in question all our preconceptions and
prejudgments as he declares himself to us in the present." Kelsey's position is
one in which the significance of revelation, and therefore of canon, have not
been and cannot be grasped, and in which the theological positions and
proposals determined by such a grasp are therefore not susceptible of genuine
analysis in any case.

does the inerrancy commitment properly reflect a high view of the hermeneutical endeavor and assert itself only *after* leaving room for that endeavor. To recognize that is to recover the hermeneutical factor.

A Hermeneutical Solution to the Inerrancy Debate

To involve oneself with Scripture is always to involve oneself in a search for meaning; we are not amiss in saying that it is a hermeneutical activity through and through. Scripture itself has no lesser ambition than the interpretation of salvation history and the Christ who stands in the midst of it. By the power and providence of God that interpretation has been shaped in such a way that it pleased God to offer it to the Church in Christ as his own instruction. Thus it is that Scripture stands before us as a series of diverse, but organically related, messages which God himself wills to speak in our hearing; our attempt to stand before the text in such a way that we may hear clearly we call hermeneutics.[17] Inerrancy is wrapped up in the results of hermeneutical labor because we do not have to do with facts for facts' sake, but with messages from Christ for the digestion of the Church. But if, in that case, we can hardly avoid asking the inerrancy question hermeneutically (if we wish to ask it with meaning and integrity, that is), then it has become

---

[17] "Hermeneutics" is a word appropriately derived from the name of the one who delivered the messages of the gods, placing these messages before men, or—which is the same thing—placing men before the gods. This was also the function of poets, according to Plato; in Christian thinking, it is first a function of inspired prophets and apostles, then of the Church itself, which listens to those who heard from God and bore witness, in order that in their hearing it too might hear and bear witness. But that means, as Richard Gaffin ("Contemporary Hermeneutics and the Study of the New Testament," *WTJ* 31 [1968] 141ff.) points out, that the hermeneutics of the Church is "interpretation of interpretation," in view of the fact that both Christ's own spokesmen and the Church itself "share a common interpretive interest" relative to the God who speaks and acts in history. Biblical hermeneutics is therefore both a profoundly spiritual and a profoundly scientific activity; in fact, it is spiritual insofar as it is scientific and scientific insofar as it is spiritual. Note that all this again implies a realist rather than a rationalist approach in dealing with the original and canonical interpretation, an approach not concerned with the perfection of the biblical spectacles but only with the true focus they provide on all that God has done, and is doing, in connection with his time-space revelation in Christ (it is the time-space nature of Christian revelation which allows us to make use of the visual metaphor).

clear that the final focus of the debate must be adjusted to the immediate concerns of any given text's service in conveying its messages. Thus far we have come, and in exploring this matter we have a very healthy freedom, as I intimated earlier, for the bond of which we have been speaking establishes full confidence in the messages we have received (so that we are not faced with the frustrating and impossible task of second-guessing Scripture), while at the same time delivering us from any inclination toward a doctrine or a hermeneutic that suffers under the stringent conditions imposed by flight to a self-made "see-no-error" safety.

I have already indicated that each passage functions by means of an internal and an external semantic hierarchy, within which the significance of lesser units is determined by their greater context. When we affirm inerrancy within the broader terms of the debate, that is, when we speak of Scripture's infallibility as God's instruction, we are committed to embracing the whole of each biblical text as constructed by its author and illuminated by its canonical context. We are therefore certainly responsible to every aspect of the text, yet only as determined by the communicative design displayed therein. With Christ, we are convinced that the Scriptures cannot lose their force or be regarded as unfit for their task; they are adequate guides to reality, adequate expressions of the truth in whatever manner they choose to convey it.[18]

---

[18] Here a word must be said about the fact that a hermeneutical orientation in the debate about Scripture brings to light the polymorphous nature of the "truth" question out of respect for the polymorphous nature of human speech, and underlines the need for sensitivity in expounding the claim that the Bible is always "true." To begin with, it should be noted that a realist approach to language allows us to escape narrow and inadequate theories of truth and to avoid what Torrance (*Reality and Evangelical Theology*, 60) calls "the oscillating dialectic" between coherence and correspondence theories, which is the inevitable legacy of the dualist framework. This in turn allows us to escape narrow or inadequate approaches to inerrancy built around such theories. For when Scripture is examined in the confusion of this stroboscopic light—when it is made to stand still by the unnatural demands produced by the dominance of either of these theories—no happy assessment of the inerrancy issue is possible; a severe headache is the only consequence. (For a broad overview of truth theories see A. Thiselton, "Truth," in *NIDNTT* 3, 894ff.; cf. Torrance, ibid., chap. 2, and *Theological Science*, chap. 4.) The realist view makes clear that all speech—and to begin this way is not necessarily to neglect the later Wittgenstein's warning about abstractions and generalities, but is in this case rather to *establish* the importance of the particular case and the variety of contexts in which language

But when we come to the narrower terms of the debate with the hermeneutical factor in view and a growing appreciation for how written texts function, it is not so difficult to show how the biblical texts, which are not *in* error, may in fact *contain* errors without jeopardizing or diminishing their ability to mediate Christ's authority over the Church. Recognition of the varying roles played by various bits of biblical detail according to the manifest purposes of the author allows us to discern the differing demands placed on those bits of detail. This is a natural and necessary interpretive process in the first place, but may be extended to address the matter of *inconsequential error.* (That there can be such a thing in biblical material, as in virtually any other material, is self-evident once the requirement for a Maginot Line defense has been disposed of, along with misconceptions in the area of verbal inspiration.) If in the course of normal hermeneutical activity it becomes evident that the function of a particular detail does not hinge on its correctness, why should the matter not rest there, whatever the case may be? Deliverance from a slavish fuss over the inviolability of extraneous detail is one of the happy consequences of recovering the hermeneutical factor, and it is this which shows promise of a satisfactory solution to the inerrancy debate among evangelicals.

Earlier I tried to illustrate from the crucifixion story the sort of thing I have in view here, but the principle itself deserves elaboration. Some facts are incidentally incorporated into any

---

functions—has the proper function of pointing away to a larger, independent reality with which it is concerned. This is true even of performative speech, though such language lays claim to an immediate and integral involvement in the reality at hand; it is likewise true of myth and parable, for example, though in a manner quite different from that of simple assertive or descriptive speech. Human speech is true when it fulfills its obligation to reality, i.e., when it is so constructed and employed as to assist us in recognizing, penetrating, and in some manner involving ourselves with various realities or aspects of reality. But language does indeed serve the disclosure of reality in a great variety of ways and on several levels, and this variety means that there is also a variety in what specific sense a given utterance may be regarded as true or false, particularly when we allow for various combinations of purpose in and behind that utterance (cf. G. B. Caird, *Language and Imagery of the Bible*, 8). To claim that biblical speech is always true, therefore, is not yet to say precisely in what sense a particular example serves our engagement with reality; it is to say nothing yet about *how it is to be construed* or *what expectations it invites.* That is an intuitive, contextual judgment which can only be made in a sympathetic following of the text as it directs us through its own selected devices to the realities which gave rise to it.

account (even into some didactic materials) as background, as what I have called "scenery" or what might be called color. But one color may serve as well as another in certain places. It is not improper to ask how various details relate to the governing meaning-function of their context, only to discover that they serve no purpose *directly* dependent on their specific constituent information. (This was Beekman's point in the reference to Matt 3:17 and parallels, and many such illustrations come quickly to mind—the trivial differences between Stephen's account of the patriarchs in Acts 7 and that of the Genesis records, for example.[19]) The presence of such detail contributes only to the overall "feel" of the story or text. This is so whether we are dealing with something as mundane as genealogical records or with the high drama of the resurrection story. Attempts to paint the context, as it were, need not necessarily be factually flawless in order to achieve their goal without distortion.[20] Various aspects are often of a truly incidental nature so far as the actual intentions of the text are concerned, and where this becomes apparent we may show a corresponding lack of concern about inerrancy, for we are dealing with nothing relevant to the central idea of *infallibility*—accurate or inaccurate we are no better or worse off, we have gained or lost nothing of genuine import. When we take a dynamic and practical view of Scripture, and thus allow to the hermeneutical process its appropriate priority over any reassertion of our intellectual obligations, inerrancy takes on this textually-determined freedom from obscurantist scholarship and its provocative ways.

[19] What possible gain is there in troubling oneself to maintain that any mistake here belongs to Stephen alone, not to Luke and his readers? It is interesting to note that Carnell and others offered a hedge for inerrancy in the fact that the Bible often quotes non-canonical sources, whose errors, argues Feinberg ("The Meaning of Inerrancy," 302), should there be any, might well be accurately transmitted, "since Scripture's intention is not to approve those errors as true." But only exegetical labor can tell us what Scripture meant to assert in its use of a source—i.e., what actually matters in the material quoted—and the fact remains that we often cannot tell whether a specific source is being used or not. Actually, then, we can speak no differently of quoted portions than of original ones: both must be received as accurate so far as the purposes of the text demand, with no further obligation. Likewise, both may contain errors in inconsequential points of detail.

[20] Matt 8:5ff. will illustrate the point (cf. Luke 7:6f.). It should not be supposed, by the way, that to draw on analogies of pictures and painting is to revert to a "picture theory" of language; these analogies are useful for certain

The New Testament, in its employment of the Old, helps to make clear what sort of respectful attention is called for by the biblical texts. Frequent appeal to the sometimes loose (but well-known) renderings of the Septuagint, along with a freely interpretive handling of canonical quotations on other occasions, demonstrates a certain degree of flexibility and an undeniable concern for meaning and impact over a literal jot and tittle conformity.[21] Likewise, recent works on the shape and service of canonical literature have emphasized in a variety of ways that, while the actual form of the biblical materials must be allowed much greater respect than past critical studies have afforded if any real penetration of the text is to take place, when this is granted it is increasingly apparent that the primary concern is always religious and didactic.[22] Even historical passages have not got the flavor of simple reportage, but have emerged out of serious theological reflection functionally related to the community of faith. That is, all these materials appear to be shaped by deliberate canonical and kerygmatic goals rather than by simple, backward-looking historical interests, and the inerrancy criteria applied to them must be determined with that in mind.

---

language-functions and certain genres of literature unless and until language is inflated by allowing for a sort of formal equivalence between language and reality. Quite obviously, that is not my intention.

[21] The ability to quote Scripture as much and as well as the early Christians did, given the impracticality of constant reference to the scrolls themselves, demonstrates a very high respect for Scripture. But it does not resolve the tension sometimes created by the deliberate NT employment of *divergent* LXX translations (cf. Berkouwer, *Holy Scripture*, 221ff.). While this tension, which is part of a very complex matter, can easily be abused in favor of a predisposition to regard somewhat lightly the sanctity of the written word of God, it nonetheless supports the qualified assertion made earlier in raising the whole question of the LXX, that the theopneustic character of Scripture is not altogether concerned with a rigid expression—indeed, with a rigid set of data—respecting the matters it has in view. Obviously, theopneustic wisdom is confined to an *adequate* expression, but all this still militates against the indiscriminate, "unhermeneutical" strictness with which those of Warfield's persuasion approach the text.

[22] Brevard S. Childs' *Introduction to the Old Testament as Scripture* (Philadelphia: Fortress, 1979) will serve as a notable, if somewhat atypical, example; of course, Childs' view and treatment of Scripture can hardly satisfy most evangelicals, but his rejection of certain speculative critical excesses and his refocusing of attention on the designs of the text has helped to win a more sympathetic hearing among them than among his own colleagues. As a matter of fact, innovative studies on several sides, involving both testaments, are serving to refocus evangelical perspectives and revitalize its exegesis (but see below and n 23).

Once again, we must not give way in all this openness and flexibility to the subtle temptation to lose track of our commitment to receive as from God *all* that Scripture chooses to say to us. We may ponder the form and feel of a text, and examine the thrust of a passage as it stands both in and out from the *Sitz im Leben* and perspectives common to its author and the community for which he wrote. We may contemplate the developing themes and religious concerns which shaped the biblical materials. We may learn to make very sophisticated historical and theological judgments. But even in pursuing such hermeneutical sensitivity, we must not tolerate the inclination to replace a hermeneutical or textually-determined view of what is "irrelevant overtone" (as Torrance puts it) with a premature exercise of our own judgment on the matter. That is, we must not stop short of *full* exegetical faithfulness to the text.

To allow this to happen would be to set ourselves above the sacred writings through which Christ gives us understanding. This illegitimate rise to power over the disposal of Scripture often begins without fanfare. We may quietly buy into the distorted procedures of that common phenomenalist methodology which subtly separates canonical texts and the theological reflection they contain from the actual events and realities to which they refer. Unfortunately, this divorce in the name of untrammeled literary or even theological criticism only ensures that the communicative design of the text itself suffers disruption.[23] The very idea of infallibility may seem happily to become less and less relevant, but that is a sure sign that hermeneutics is

[23] There is a real risk in the coming-of-age of evangelical hermeneutics of simply falling unawares into the same mistakes made by less vital approaches to Scripture. It should be obvious, but perhaps is not, that *mere* attention to literary form and theological shaping cannot serve as a sort of pass-key for evaluation and interpretation of biblical documents if it is the realities of which they themselves speak that ought to concern us. Defending redaction criticism in the Synoptics, e.g., has become popular of late in evangelical circles, with some rewarding results; but Torrance (*Reality and Evangelical Theology*, 80ff.) warns us that "form criticism and redaction criticism alike work with the discarded assumptions of observationalism and phenomenalism." They assume, he says, "that theoretical elements can only have a later origin and have to be put down to the creative spirituality of the early Christian community rather than to Jesus himself. Thus they disrupt the way in which the empirical and theological elements . . . are already coordinated in the evangelical tradition, but since this takes away from the Gospel presentation of Christ its underlying coherence, different conceptual patterns have to be brought in . . . to tie what remains of the

moving away from the actual time-space interests of our very earthy Bible and that the most significant aspects of the inerrancy debate are being ignored.

Less subtly, and therefore less seriously, while avoiding this error we may decide that rather than struggle with the principle of harmony over some relatively insignificant difficulty (e.g., who provoked David's census of Israel—God or Satan?) we will simply regard problematic statements as local color, so to speak, and no part of the actual word of God to us. But then even this apparently harmless approach can be pressed quite a long way. Soon it will deliver us from having to contend with the vindictive materials in the Psalms or the "indiscriminate" judgment on the Canaanites, for example, then from seemingly inconsistent statements in anthropology, applied theology, and so forth. But already it can be seen that what we have to say about the text has come to override what the text itself has to say. And this, we must be clear, violates the very principle we are working on, which is thoroughly hermeneutical in its judgments *from the text up*; wittingly or otherwise such a stance reopens the entire question as to Scripture's power to serve as Christ's authoritative word to the Church. In the hermeneutical circle as described above—and this lies at the heart of even the faintest concern about inerrancy—it is plain that it is *via* the texts themselves that Christ roots the thinking of the Church in his own authority. That is why the circle is indeed a circle, and the traveling of that circle a perpetual journey. That is also why the hermeneutical factor must never be cut loose from what each passage actually has to say, or be used as an excuse to stand above the text on any subject germane to the text's own interests, even the least of them.

Not that genuine labor in and around the text has everywhere succeeded in explaining perplexing problems in what the

---

material together. A similar problem arises when literary forms, phenomenologically detached from the event-situations in which they are embedded in the Gospels, are conceptualized through assimilation to the alleged patterns of consciousness in the Christian community, and then new event-situations have to be thought up for them in the community in order to make the reconstruction seem plausible." The temptation to get caught up in such remodeling of the Scriptures, it seems to me, is all the more dangerous because it sneaks up on the interpreter almost unawares, and leads him down a very long garden path indeed.

Bible appears to have said about this or that! The principle of harmony and the factual clarity of Scripture have by no means been fully vindicated, at least not among those who are unwilling to trade hermeneutical integrity for harmony. Nonetheless, remarkably productive insights are constantly surfacing in difficult areas, which are very much in the minority to begin with (despite the charges of self-confident skeptics, who by reason of their little interest have difficulty penetrating such matters at all). At any rate, commitment to inerrancy, even in its broader terms, doubtless requires faith in the *future* resolution of a number of problems in Scripture, through a deeper penetration of the text itself and of the realities to which it refers. This expectation is not unscientific, though it certainly is unique in its regard for a written canon which asks of us "advance" commitment to its teachings.[24]

In the meantime, the great majority of so-called errors thrown up like a siege ramp against the confession of biblical infallibility fall into one of four categories: (a) apparent theological inconsistencies susceptible of solution by greater depth perception in theological thinking;[25] (b) any variety of

[24] Every genuine scientific vision creates a climate of expectation concerning its power to supply answers yet unseen; the uniqueness of theological science is such that this confidence can embrace the unthinkable confession of *canon*. Again, however, we must keep in mind that this "advance" commitment does not signify something prior to our being directed to Christ in and through Scripture (whether considered as an entire experience or in connection with our regard for specific portions of his word). It only means that, while we bring our doubts with us when we come to Scripture, we also come prepared by God for subjection to the Lordship we have already met there, which has created in the Church and in us an abiding and ultimately irreversible expectation. In the context of this unshakable conviction and commitment—unshakable because there is, after all, no competing Lordship to that which grips us here—there remains nonetheless a progressive intellectual and experiential verification, if you please, and a growing certitude, in consequence of the ongoing process of exposure to the Word of God in and through the word of Scripture. And to this the multitude of problems already resolved through advances in archaeology, history, geography, and other sciences may be allowed to contribute, though they form no essential part of its foundation.

[25] Contradictions frequently appear in Scripture as elsewhere (indeed, in Scripture especially) when natural depth dimensions are ignored in a purely formal thinking that flattens out the multiple levels of reference in reality, i.e., in thinking that has lost its ontological connection. See Torrance's many discussions of this fundamental point; care taken in this area, as he indicates in another context, "will go far toward clarifying the semantic focus of the biblical documents" (ibid., 74).

misconceptions arising from a failure to interpret properly the context of the statement(s) or the stylistic devices of the author;[26] (c) apparent historical inconsistencies arising from an author's liberty to make minor modifications in his source materials for the sake of a more cogent presentation of the points he wishes to emphasize;[27] (d) matters of incidental "scenery" or "color," that is, trivialities lying outside any direct concern of the author. In other words, many challenges to Scripture's veracity will admit of a genuine hermeneutical solution. Beyond any doubt, the inerrancy debate would cool down a great deal if there were widespread acceptance of the fourth category in particular. I have already made clear what stands in the way and how ill-founded it is.

The challenge that remains is for those who hold to the infallibility of Scripture to continue to probe the hermeneutical procedures currently employed in various problem passages with a view to bettering their ability to distinguish between triviality and essential detail. This may seem at first an un-welcome burden, and one which offers its bearer no easy grip, but in the final analysis it is an essentially positive labor pertaining to any careful exposition; certainly it also curtails any tendency to focus only on that which naturally grips and persuades the reader. Whatever principles might be developed here, it is eminently clear that the difference between details intrinsic to the communicative design of the text and trivialities (extrinsic detail, if you like) cannot be mechanically established, but must be discerned through *comprehension* of each biblical passage and the complex of messages it contains. If asked what

---

[26] On a level integrating with the previous category, Thiselton is helpful in chap. 15 of *The Two Horizons*, particularly in the application of his observations to the differences between James and Paul on justification (pp. 415ff.); this example would serve just as well as an illustration of either category. Alleged contradictions in the creation accounts of Genesis 1 and 2 might also serve as an illustration here. Of course, on a more mundane level this category embraces simpler interpretive blunders as well, which are largely the result of misconstruing the proper referent(s) or failing to recognize the mode of speech being used or ignoring implicit cultural factors, etc.

[27] This is particularly relevant for the study of the gospels, of course, but applies elsewhere as well. There is another warning here for inerrantists with regard to the principle of harmony—R. T. France ("Inerrancy and New Testament Exegesis," *Themelios* 1 [1975] 17) advises that a "too hasty, mechanical harmonization" runs the risk of missing the whole point of an individual author's treatment of the incident in view.

is meant by "message," perhaps the best answer is the most flexible: that which one person wishes another to know and, to some degree, reflect upon. Ultimately, we are able—in view of Christ—to speak of *the* biblical message, but only by way of "every passage of Scripture" as part of a great series of contributing messages, comprised in turn by any number of smaller constituent messages within a given pericope. This reminds us once more that comprehension of Scripture must take into account the profoundly contextual nature of everything the Bible has to say and strengthens our conviction that the value and sanctity of biblical statements must not be construed after the manner in which a Muslim views statements in the Koran.[28]

What the one holding to biblical infallibility is clearly committed to is examination of every passage with a view to allowing the author to direct his thoughts with entire freedom. Every constituent message (which may or may not correspond to a simple statement of some kind) must be obediently received with that end in view, that is, *according to the service it was intended to have in the development of the passage itself.*[29] This is the central qualification I have been emphasizing as the hermeneutical answer to much of the difficulty in the inerrancy debate. Perhaps by returning to the problem of David's census and to the earlier question about the thief(s) who mocked Christ, I can illustrate the two-way implications of this qualification: "Again the anger of the LORD burned against Israel, and he incited David against them . . ." contains two related messages for the information and reflection of the reader as he approaches the story to follow. So does the following statement, which introduces the parallel account: "Satan rose up against Israel and incited David to take a census of Israel." This apparent conflict cannot be ignored, for it cannot be maintained that the

---

[28] Even the word "pericope" contains a warning for the exegete; περικοπή meant "a cutting all round, mutilation" (Liddell and Scott).

[29] The proposition may be the basic unit of communication, but the context in which each such unit occurs determines its significance, multiplying the relational factors to the point where it is impossible to correlate "messages" simply and directly with assertions contained in the text in one form or another. Any analysis attempting to do so will indicate many peripheral and some central or important messages plainly, while at the same time adding, distorting, obscuring, or entirely misplacing others (particularly if it is not carried out with an intuitive grasp of the subject matter). Yet it would be disastrous to abandon

element of conflict here is incidental to the purpose of the statements.[30] On the other hand, the problem noted in my illustration from the Synoptics, arising in connection with Matthew and Mark's statement that "those crucified with him also heaped insults on him," *can* be ignored. Though this message clearly contains information (conflicting with Luke's account) that two criminals mocked Christ, examination of the passage does not support the contention that this information is offered as a distinct message—on the definition offered above— to the effect that there were not one, but two, who mocked. That information makes no recognizable contribution to the substance and value of the account, and the significance of the statement itself is not lost in questioning its accuracy, for the

---

the qualification in view here by charging it with the so-called "intentional fallacy," which moves from a focus on the public affair of textual meaning—i.e., from what is actually said—to the inaccessible ruminations and aspirations of the author. Genuine interpretation is indeed based on what the author *meant* (a common sense notion defended by E. D. Hirsch, Jr. in *Validity in Interpretation* [New Haven and London: Yale University, 1967]), though this can only be discovered in what he said. Again the point is simply that what he said cannot be taken piecemeal; the contribution of every portion must be determined by the whole text, and by the context in which and for which it was written. It is a misunderstanding of this qualification to think that it justifies the biblical exegete in dismissing any part of the author's meaning as communicated in the text by appealing exclusively to the main point of a passage, or to essential existential considerations, or to what the text is supposed to accomplish for its audience, etc. To speak of service or function *according to authorial design* guards against both *misunderstanding* of the significance of certain comments in the text, and *misappropriation* of the text itself by those who would take it away from the prophets and apostles and deliver it into the hands of un-authorized surgeons. Twice over, then, it has implications for the inerrancy debate.

[30] Cf. 2 Sam 24:1 and 1 Chr 21:1. Those who jump quickly to the conclusion that these statements are simply contradictory—and relatively unimportant— introductions to duplicate accounts of the incident show the same sort of hermeneutical insensitivity as the inerrantists they criticize. By examining other differences as well, the two narratives (beginning with their introductions) will be seen to offer deliberately different, but complementary, perspectives, in keeping with the different themes that gave both books a position in the canon despite the repetitious nature of the Chronicles. Where 2 Samuel is concerned with the relevance of this incident to the dialectic of judgment and forgiveness, blessing and curse, all taking place within the providential purposes of God, 1 Chronicles shows more attention to the evil character of the act itself, perhaps in keeping with the chronicler's interest in documenting the relationship between action and effect. In any event, this certainly is not the only place where the activities of God and Satan are shown to have intersected—no small point for the penetration of theological thought into the nature of reality in "this present evil age"—and both points of view are indeed significant.

element of conflict is indeed incidental. That is why the passage, while it may well contain an error, is still not *in* error; it has not failed its readers by falling short of reality so far as the author's purpose is concerned, as I demonstrated in chap. 4.[31]

In the first case, then, the principle of harmony sets out a theological task we ought not to avoid as we compare and contrast the two passages; the difference must be satisfactorily resolved. In the second case, however, a comparison of the statement quoted with that in Luke's more detailed account simply points us back to a greater hermeneutical sensitivity in reading both, while the conflict between the two may be allowed to stand. The key to all this, quite obviously, is exegetical acumen in discerning in each biblical statement the desired direction for our thoughts. This is by no means a purely scholarly activity; such discernment is at heart a very common intuitive process (in the Spirit) as involvement with the text's own interests grows. That is, as we seek to look through the text at Christ and the worldly contexts he has chosen for his self-revelation, we gradually come to appreciate the manner in which the text focuses on the objects of its concern and how each statement made contributes to the vision there achieved. This must be our goal if the freedom of the biblical word is to be honored.

Now there are several elements of context which help to qualify the role a given statement is intended to play, and to keep the focus of biblical authority where it belongs; some of these have already been named. Certainly the most fundamental is that of the argument itself and the greater vision of reality which gives rise to it. Nothing more can be demanded of a

---

[31] Cf. Matt 27:44, Mark 15:32 and Luke 23:39-40; all three accounts make clear that Christ was mocked by the criminal element as well as the upper crust of society. Clark Pinnock ("The Inerrancy Debate Among the Evangelicals," *Theology, News and Notes*, Special Issue [1976] 12) commented on the Lausanne Covenant's confession that Scripture is inerrant *in all that it affirms* this way: "I doubt whether the upholders of inerrancy have reflected sufficiently on the implications of this qualification, according to which one could fairly say that the Bible *contains* errors but *teaches* none, or that inerrancy refers to the *subjects* rather than all the *terms* of Scripture or to the *teaching* rather than to all the components utilized in its formulation. It is important to notice that, when we qualify inerrancy hermeneutically and place it into relation to the authorial intention, we shift the emphasis from *errors as such* and place it instead on the *nature* and *purpose* of each biblical passage." Taken in the framework and with the cautions I have been laying out, this is a useful way of putting the matter.

biblical statement than what it offers out of its own character as called forth by the movement of thought of which it is a part (though this fact must never be abused so as to deny any statement the right to add whatever it is, however peripheral, that it sets out to add). Of course, we will quickly recognize that "argument" is much too narrow a concept to indicate properly the dynamics of a great deal of biblical literature, which is often comprised of narrative, legal, or liturgical documents, for example. The Scriptures develop our vision through a wide variety of materials in appropriate intellectual forms and literary vehicles. Consequently, if we are to deal effectively with the role of a statement in its material context, primary attention must likewise be given to the mode of speech being used, that is, to the matter of genre. That will allow the Bible itself to make clear the kind of authority it means to have in a given instance.[32]

This is the very sort of thing that landed Robert Gundry in trouble with some of his fellow-evangelicals, however, in his commentary on Matthew, where he contended that the evangelist consciously employed an editorial method for which "the adjectives 'midrashic' and 'haggadic' become appropriate."[33] According to Gundry, differences in descriptive detail between Matthew and the other Synoptics are in many cases neither incidental errors nor matters calling for harmonization, but rather acceptable and effective editorial liberties for legitimate theological purposes. Various thoughtful scholars have disagreed with Gundry's research, and thus with his conclusions as well, in a very healthy exercise of what biblical scholarship is all about. Unfortunately, there are those whose disagreement

---

[32] "In determining the intention of the sacred writers, attention must be paid, *inter alia*, to 'literary forms for the fact is that truth is differently presented and expressed in the various types of historical writing, in prophetical and poetical text,' and in other forms of literary expression. Hence the exegete must look for that meaning which the sacred writer, in a determined situation and given the circumstances of his time and culture, intended to express and did in fact express, through the medium of a contemporary literary form. Rightly to understand what the sacred author wanted to affirm in his work, due attention must be paid both to the customary and characteristic patterns of perception, speech and narrative which prevailed at the age of the sacred writer, and to the conventions which the people of his time followed in their dealings with one another" (Dogmatic Constitution on Divine Revelation, 12 [*Documents of Vatican II*, 757–58]).

[33] *Matthew: A Commentary on His Literary and Theological Art* (Grand Rapids: Eerdmans, 1982) 628.

appears to be founded in an unwillingness to grant any real place to the hermeneutical factor in the question of biblical authority, calling into question the validity of most of the categories mentioned above for dealing with apparent errors in Scripture. Gundry's own approach is much more enlightened at this point (whatever conclusions one might reach regarding his handling of the materials themselves): "In and of itself," he says, "the question whether midrash and haggadah are to be found in Matthew is a question of hermeneutics, not a question of biblical authority."[34] Inspiration does not guarantee historicity in his view, but relates rather to the soundness of what the author intends us to take from what he has written. Gundry thus calls for an enlargement of the room given to differences of literary genre, lest our high respect for Scripture suffer ship-wreck in today's increasingly close reading of the text, or in backing away from just such a practical evidence of our respect.[35]

Actually, where there is no humanistic paranoia over the defense of Scripture, there is already a good deal of room for such differences. Only one consideration governs this liberty, namely, the bearing of what is said, and of what is at stake in what is said, on the historically-grounded realities which give rise to the text. That these realities come to true, adequate, and honest expression in the text, whatever the means chosen, is the proper contention of a faithful confession of Scripture.[36] That

[34] Ibid., 637. "We must remind ourselves," he says, "that taking Matthew's intent to be solely historical is as much a critical judgment (conscious or unconscious) as taking it to be a mixture of the historical and unhistorical" (p. 633).

[35] Ibid., 639 (cf. p. 625). Speaking of shipwrecks, we might add here the example of the book of Jonah. Once recognized in terms of genre as a deliberate, well-constructed satire—a recognition entirely necessary to the impact of the book—the question of its actual historicity loses much, if not all, of its significance.

[36] The ICBI conference on hermeneutics (article 13) appropriately affirmed that "awareness of the literary categories . . . is essential for proper exegesis," while denying that "generic categories which negate historicity may rightly be imposed on biblical narratives which present themselves as factual." The next article, however, appears to rule out an approach like Gundry's *a priori*: "We affirm that the biblical record of events, discourses and sayings, though presented in a variety of appropriate literary forms, corresponds to historical fact. We deny that any such event, discourse or saying reported in Scripture was invented by the biblical writers or by the traditions they incorporated." While I believe this position to be essentially correct, it ought not to function as a hermeneutical

the documents themselves intend nothing else is not difficult to see; certainly we must never impose on Scripture generic categories contrary to its own self-understanding, whether replacing history with myth or imagination with literal history. In any case, the thoroughly historical underpinnings of what the Bible has to say are eminently clear, providing stimulation for various creative expressions of the truths there perceived, as well as a secure anchor for all such expressions.[37] Whether or not we are

---

a priori, which it is in danger of doing when ensconced in such a statement. It might also be asked what it means to say that an event, such as the cleansing of the temple in John's account, "corresponds to historical fact," or that "Genesis 1-11 is factual" (article 22). There is undoubtedly a true correspondence and factuality in these accounts, but it is very doubtful whether that factuality and correspondence includes the actual order of events, for example; it was not meant to. It can legitimately be asked, then, what other freedoms the authors of Scripture indicate to us that they are taking in order to communicate effectively the nature of the facts with which they are concerned. So far as Gundry's approach is concerned, in addition to the primary question about the adequacy of his exegetical results, one might be excused for asking whether the invention of events and dialogue is at all likely in a book like Matthew's or those of the other Gospel writers, who were already faced with a Man about whom, if everything were written down, "even the whole world would not have room for the books" (John 21:25)! Nor is it clear whether that sort of midrash was ever conceived or accepted in a manner that might allow it to achieve canonical status, as distinct from that of secondary (if hallowed) commmentary. A broader methodological caution has already been raised in n 23.

[37] The central fact of Jesus the Christ—God incarnate in the midst of history, especially the history of the people of God—renders it unintelligible for the faithful to deny the *profound historicity* of the OT as well as the NT. Erich Auerbach, though not writing from this perspective, uses just these words in the very stimulating opening chapter of his volume *Mimesis* (trans. Willard R. Trask [Princeton: Princeton University, 1953]) to describe the literary character and impact of the OT. But this does not mean that all that is contained therein is history in the modern sense of the word; in Auerbach's view, at least, the OT "ranges through all three domains: legend, historical reporting, and interpretative historical theology," often passing imperceptibly from one to the other (pp. 20-21). Naturally, the mention of legend, midrash, fiction, and myth raises some thorny problems and triggers all sorts of warning alarms, but strongly negative reactions are often conditioned by years of weariness from wars with the alien analytical frameworks of liberalism and existentialism. There is in fact a genuinely evangelical pursuit in view here, following the trail laid out by the presence in Scripture of parable, apocalyptic, poetic representation, and a great variety of other literary devices, such as that represented by the book of Job. From the poetic structure of Genesis 1 to the visionary strokes of Revelation 22 Scripture is fraught with creative color. Leland Ryken's *The Literature of the Bible* (Grand Rapids: Zondervan, 1974) is helpful along these lines, as is Northrop Frye in *The Great Code* (despite his fatal error in sailing with those who long ago weighed anchor and lost from view the true historicity of the Bible). Aid may be sought here from C. S. Lewis, who offers us a much healthier view of "myth" than Bultmann does, by the way, and who makes clear in several

expected to regard any particular as actual and precise historical information is made evident first by the nature of the text (How is the author approaching his subject and what literary genre is he employing? What kind of factual liberties, if any, may be allowed out of deference to his overall design?) and, second, by the functional significance attached to given bits of information (Assuming a literal mode, is this detail intrinsically or extrinsically related to what the author is trying to say?). To choose a very simple illustration, a detail in casuistic law is anything but extrinsic to the meaning and function of that passage, whereas a very similar detail in a narrative section might be altogether incidental and the exact fact of the matter open to some adjustment without damaging the integrity of the text and its purposes.

Without belaboring the matter further, can we not confidently say that the hermeneutical factor does indeed allow us to uphold biblical infallibility while accepting the presence of certain errors in the text—and to do so without subjecting Scripture to canons of our own determination, but rather within our very attempt to submit ourselves to Scripture's desire to determine us? As long as we remember that in arguing for flexibility in the narrower terms of the debate we have committed ourselves to shoulder gladly the burden of conscientious exegetical labor, we have integrity in this. And this is as it should be. In a helpful article entitled "Inerrancy and New Testament Exegesis," R. T. France rightly insists that one who holds to a high view of Scripture "has, if anything, a stronger incentive than anyone else to work hard and critically at his exegesis."[38] This kind of attention to the text can only deepen

---

of his works that to read the Bible broad-mindedly on its own literary terms is hardly to capitulate to the "shocking lack of perception" (*Christian Reflections*, ed. Walter Hooper [Grand Rapids: Eerdmans, 1967] 155) demonstrated by such learned, but skeptical, critics. It can be confessed very simply that the commitment to biblical infallibility lays down such claims to Scripture's literal historicity as the text itself lays down, i.e, *self-consciously* lays down; it stakes no lesser or greater claims. While the preponderance of biblical literature presents itself in plain historical terms, the excess of reality over what can be said in such a book (or anywhere for that matter) naturally suggests the inclusion of other forms of speech to aid the cause, for nowhere but in the living Christ is the intention of Scripture completely captured and expressed.

[38] France (p. 18) warns against the "blinkered critical procedures" that make biblical studies the laughing-stock of scholars working in related disciplines, while encouraging the use of all such critical tools as may be disengaged from faulty critical assumptions.

our involvement with Scripture—creating new problems, to be sure, but solving problems old and new. It will sometimes bring to the fore the fact that the flawed humanity of the biblical witnesses has not been crowded out (in Barth's expression), even if appropriated and redirected, by the Spirit of God. It will certainly face us with the frustration of our own weakness of vision. But as we strive to look through the text at that to which we are directed, by God's grace it becomes plain that Scripture's direction is indeed successful. To that direction we therefore attend with both eyes and both ears, undaunted and undisturbed by the petty concerns that distract the fearful and the doubting.

7 | Functional Inerrancy: The Infallible Word

It is time to gather the preceding reflections into full focus. Where have we been, and to what place have we come? I began by affirming the importance of the inerrancy debate, so long as we know it to belong to much larger discussions within the entire Church on the practical role of Scripture in God's self-revelation. I suggested that there has been an almost uncontrollable tendency toward polarization in the debate, however, owing to a dualistic and man-centered epistemology that inevitably sets up a tension between the fanciful integrity of human knowledge and the fear of complete erosion of the Christian faith. I argued that the true footing of the Church's confidence in Scripture rests in the active Lordship of Christ, and finds expression in a simple confession that Christ has bound the Scriptures to himself, and the Church with them. It then seemed plain enough that, in the absence of the fear generated by epistemological self-reliance, the affirmation of Scripture's infallibility need not be accompanied by any paranoic protectionism respecting every detail of "the original autographs," but only by a happy confidence in what this book has to say as the work of Christ's own messengers. After demonstrating exegetically that the Bible's self-awareness, so to speak, suggested nothing other than this (despite many claims to the contrary), I also tried to demonstrate briefly that there are no sound reasons for importing a stricter view into our doctrine of Scripture. This has only led to needless and very harmful disputes, as the Church at large and other onlookers have not failed to notice.

With these folk also in view, however, I devoted one chapter to very cursory discussions of the significance of the Lordship of the incarnate Christ to the much more relevant battlegrounds of epistemological methodology, the understanding of inspiration, and the suitability of human language and culture to serve the purposes of an abiding canonical communication. In the last

217

chapter I returned to the thought of Scripture as Christ's message-bearer, in order to develop the practical side of the only solution to the inerrancy issue that seems to me to hold real promise. This is one which accepts the priority of the exegetical task over invocation of the inerrancy commitment, such that biblical infallibility is not conceived in terms of exhaustive inerrancy, but in terms of the Church's confidence that God has everywhere seen to it that Scripture leads us into the truth and not away from it.[1]

What we have come to, then, is an understanding of Scripture as the unfailing Word of Truth, whose messages, whether the greater or the lesser, are entirely reliable in addressing the matters in which and by which the Holy Spirit wishes to instruct us. No one has satisfactorily explained how any lesser view of Scripture answers to the Lordship of Christ over the Church, which has continually revitalized the confidence of the faithful in the canonical documents down through the centuries— whether before, during, or after the so-called Enlightenment and the attacks of the period of skepticism that followed. But to speak of Scripture as the *unfailing* Word of Truth is to employ a thoroughly *functional* concept. The doctrine of infallibility and use of the word itself must not be allowed to continue its drift toward the stagnant pools surrounding the opposing (yet still rationalistic) fortress from which the "Battle for the Bible" troops are wont to issue. Nor can inerrancy be allowed to continue to divide the faithful over mere trivialities: "Warn them before God against quarrelling about words; it is of no value, and only ruins those who listen."[2] The genuine guidance

---

[1] In the *Evangelical Dictionary of Theology* (ed. Walter A. Elwell [Grand Rapids: Baker, 1984] 142) Paul Feinberg defines inerrancy as "the view that when all the facts become known, they will demonstrate that the Bible in its original autographs *and correctly interpreted* is entirely true and never false in all it affirms, whether that relates to doctrine or ethics or to the social, physical or life sciences" (emphasis mine). If the significance of the emphasized phrase were really considered, would it not call for a recasting of this definition along less technical and more practical lines?

[2] 2 Tim 2:14. Walter Thorson ("Science as the Natural Philosophy of a Christian," 72) expounds what he calls a "functional ontology" of truth, pointing out that belief in "truth" is at bottom a matter of commitment to the practical authority of reality, to the fact that truth—though mediated in the context of imperfect knowledge—*makes a difference*. Likewise, when we speak of the truthfulness of Scripture, we should have in view nothing about which no one can demonstrate that it "makes a difference."

everywhere received from Christ in Scripture is the confidence we guard in the confession of infallibility. Very simply, we are attesting (along with the Spirit) the fitness of Scripture to the living Word. Nothing else concerns us.

The fact that some find it difficult to distinguish between a practical, functional orientation of the doctrine of Scripture and a *functionalism* that refuses to grapple with certain very important questions of objective biblical truth is most unfortunate.[3] But this should not deter us from seizing happily on terminology like that offered by Beekman—namely, "functional inerrancy"—to show that we do not mean anything else by this affirmation except that we were serious when we said that Scripture does not fail to speak truly in addressing man on behalf of God. It should be clear by now that this is not at all the same as limiting inerrancy to "matters of faith and practice," an unhappy distinction hinging on an unacceptable form/content dualism. Rather, the Bible everywhere and in a variety of ways opens up its readers to the realities involved in the revelation of God in Christ, through human words appropriated by the Spirit for the service of that revelation. The word thus given us by God cannot be divided up any more than the Christ who presents himself to us in this nexus of worldly realities, for as Christ fulfills and unfolds the Scriptures, all of its messages become "spirit and life" in him.[4] To say "functional inerrancy" is to say that the Bible is invariably suited to its service, that it is invariably successful in grasping and conveying appropriately the truth about every matter to which it attends, within the

---

[3] Carl Henry (*God, Revelation and Authority* 4, 99f.), for one, gives this impression. Some of his criticisms of Barr's functionalism, or of Kelsey and others, are cogent. But it seems that he feels compelled to add a strict form of inerrancy to the doctrine of the practical infallibility of the biblical word because God *himself* is not, on his view, the justifier of Scripture's truthfulness; that justification depends on tightly demonstrable argumentation with no untidy details. In other words, Barr's criticisms also have some merit, and one might be grateful if one were not forced to choose between them at just this point.

[4] John 6:63. As von Balthasar (*Word and Revelation*, 24) says: "The primary content of scripture is always God himself. Whether it is narrating historical events, enunciating laws or relating parables, God is speaking and speaking about himself, telling us what he is and about the manner in which he surveys and judges the world. To penetrate into the spirit of scripture means to come to know the inner things of God and to make one's own God's way of seeing the world"—and God sees the world "in no other connection than in the son."

limitations of its own designs (not salvific designs in distinction from cognitive designs, but cognitive and communicative designs as such, which have been committed by God to the service of our salvation).[5] Likewise, to say "infallibility" is to say that Scripture is not given to failure in expressing the truth, but to this success; it is to say that Scripture cannot lose its force in interpreting reality or its bearing on the minds and hearts of men and women.

Success, however, does not mean perfection; it means entire profitability. And the standard of Scripture's profitability is set no higher and no lower than *its profitability to Christ*, who perfectly fulfilled the Old Testament Scriptures in his earthly life and laid the cornerstone for the New, on behalf of the Church. If Scripture cannot be broken, it is because it must be embodied and fulfilled![6] Do we now move back again in the direction of "matters of faith and practice"? Of course we do! What relevance has the inerrancy debate apart from Christian faith and practice, indeed, apart from Christ-likeness? But now we are not speaking of matters of faith and practice as arbitrarily distinguished from other matters that sneaked into the biblical fold over the wall, so to speak. We are only saying that if what Scripture sets out to convey is to be received as that which is profitable to Christ, and hence to the Christian, then however hard and long we may have to look in order to see the relevance of some passages and the messages they contain, we will do so; but we will certainly *not* say that it is a stumbling-block to

---

[5] I have phrased this so as to avoid two errors: when we speak of *function*, we must also speak of *semantic design*, in order to prevent (a) the removal of the meaning of the text from the author's control with a view to placing it at the independent disposal of the reader, (b) the spurning of the meaning of the text in favor of a direct appeal to what the author wanted to accomplish by it (what some have criticized as the so-called "intentionality view of truth").

[6] This is the message of Matt 5:17f., John 10:34f., etc. Von Balthasar (ibid., 12f.) remarks that Christ's life as Word made flesh is a fulfilling of Scripture, "fashioned, step by step, by all the forms of the word in the law and the prophets." The Christian's loyalty to Scripture, then, can only be loyalty to *Christ*, his regard for Scripture, regard for its *profitability* to Christ and the formation of Christ in himself. That is the message of 2 Tim 3:10ff.; Edward Goodrick ("Let's Put 2 Timothy 3:16 Back in the Bible," 486–87) is absolutely right when he insists that, despite the polarizing tensions of the inerrancy controversy, one cannot change the fact that the focus here is on "profitable." One should hardly enlist this passage to support "the pristine character of the autographs," he says, but rather *"exploit it to the full to demonstrate how valuable the God-breathed Scriptures are"* (emphasis mine).

Christ or his Church if we notice in passing that some trivial detail, not affecting these messages and their profitability, has strayed. Even a soundly constructed and perfectly useful sheepfold may have tiny chinks in the wall through which a blade of straw might pass. It is not faith, but fear, that peeps through these chinks and trembles at the wolves outside, deceiving and being deceived. Then again, it is not faith, but folly, to open the gate and allow even the smallest instruction which Christ found profitable enough to include in the fold to pass out because the wolves are howling for it.

By rejecting the polarization of the inerrancy issue and its atmosphere of fear, and by looking immediately to the hermeneutical task for a solution to the stand-off in the debate, functional inerrancy steers clear of the so-called "false in one, then false in all" arguments and counter-arguments, which some feel are so central to the debate. Functional inerrancy, when rooted in a confessional approach to the Scriptures, is not working from the defensive side of the field, so to speak, and therefore does not stake its claim in a manner that gives rise to this false dilemma. On the basis of its confidence in the God who speaks in Scripture it does refuse to stand in judgment of the word it has received, whether in this place or that. Instead, it is tuned to the instruction of the Spirit of God by full attention to the messages of Scripture. But consequently it is able to work with the possibility of error in trivialities, which are built into virtually all common communication and in other circumstances are generally dealt with almost unconsciously in the hermeneutical process.[7] To accept the presence in the text of

---

[7] "Trivial" does not mean altogether irrelevant, for every detail has its place. But we may nonetheless distinguish in any text certain cultural or historical elements which are not intrinsically involved in the semantic design of that text, the correctness of which is therefore unimportant because it is without direct bearing. To borrow from Thiselton ("Semantics and New Testament Interpretation," 82), who is borrowing for other purposes from Saussure's analogy between language and chess, we might say it like this: "The 'value' of a given piece depends on its place in the whole system. Depending on the state of the whole board when one piece is moved, resulting changes of value will be either nil, very serious, or of average importance." To apply: the "moving of a piece" in a text by correction of a factual discrepancy *may* result in no change of value, i.e., it may not disrupt the text or come into conflict with it; in that case it is a triviality. The biblical exegete may only adjust or leave aside the factuality of certain textual data where it is evident that they are trivialities, i.e., without genuine bearing on what the text is saying.

trivialities which may be in error without causing a breakdown of comprehension or a maladjustment of focus in either the author or the reader, while yet rejecting out of hand any deconstructions, reconstructions, deletions, or additions in handling the canonical word, is the strength of functional inerrancy. To take this position is to firmly expect true guidance from the words in which the Word of God speaks. To *follow* the words of the Word, which only lead us back to himself, that and no other is understood to be our proper commitment.

To be sure, it is the fate of such a position to be objected to on both sides. From beyond the inerrancy camp we will hear the call that we expect too much of Scripture. From within the camp many will say that holding to the broader terms of the inerrancy affirmation is not enough. But when all is said and done, the one who approaches Scripture as humbly as he can, to listen as intently as he can, and to take with him everything that is offered him there is simply holding to Scripture and to the Christ of the Scriptures. Anything "more" is actually less by virtue of the distractions it offers, and anything less is more respect for one's own thoughts than for Christ.

Is this mediating position sound? In attempting to relate inerrancy to the messages of every passage of Scripture, without thereby precluding all possibility of trivial human error, I have sought to avoid the slipperiness of which limited inerrancy positions are properly accused. I have not advocated the use of any sieve to remove difficult biblical assertions and ideas. I have only promoted the admittedly rigorous challenge—never perfectly mastered—of effective listening. If we are reminded again of the fact that this enterprise leaves us uncomfortably conscious of our own inadequacies, so be it; it is Christ alone who is our adequacy, even as we take up our posture before the Holy Scriptures he has offered for our instruction.

*   *   *

Concluding Remarks

The single most important thing to be said about Holy Scripture—in the final analysis the only thing that need be said—is that "in the sacred books the Father who is in heaven comes lovingly to meet his children, and talks with them."[8] Where this is known, all the exegetical toil, all the struggle against the urge to take control over Scripture, all the argumentation and elaboration of books like this one, are overwhelmed by the sound of the Word of God himself. Then and there all doubt about the complete trustworthiness of Scripture dissipates, and the very thought of such things is lost from view. Who will tell the Church that this portion or that is not worthy of such confidence, when the Lord of the Church is speaking? How dull we would be to listen to such a claim! Equally so, then, are we not desperately impoverished when in rejecting such claims we cannot shake loose from fussing and disputing about words, in order to regard rather the inexhaustible Truth to whom those words, in all their weakness, are constantly bearing true witness?

It is exactly in Scripture's service to Christ that we must find the keynote of every chord in our doctrine of Scripture. The Scriptures are *his* κανών, sceptered by *his* grace; he himself is their content and canonicity, and the proof of their canonicity. When we speak of inerrancy, which may be little more than a concession for the sake of unity with those who reject the present loose attitude toward Scripture—to disdain the scepter is, after all, to disdain the Crown—our eyes are certainly not fixed on the Bible as a collection of flawless data about God and the world. They are fixed on him who, in stooping to speak to his own as Man and through men, still speaks a word that never fails but always leads aright. It is only in this sense that inerrancy may come to stand for happier thoughts and assert itself as a "cause" worth embracing. For the recognition through Scripture of Christ himself and his will for mankind is the only real cause to which those of evangelical faith ultimately testify, and the Lordship of the living and active Word is their only reason for regarding the Scriptures as holy and confessing them as such.[9]

[8] Dogmatic Constitution on Divine Revelation, 21 (*Documents of Vatican II*, 762).

[9] Hans Küng (*Infallible? An Inquiry*, trans. Edward Quinn [Garden City, NY: Doubleday, 1971] 210), not without some justification, compares the confusion of Protestants over the Bible with the confusion of Catholics over Church and Pope: "Just as some Catholics believe less in God and his Christ than in the Church (confusing *credere in Deum* with *credere Ecclesiam*), so do many Protestants believe *in* the Bible." But the analogy is stretched to the breaking

This cause, I might add, which embraces every other pressing concern of our troubled times, clearly prospers in energetic *proclamation* of biblical truth, not in building opaque doctrinal walls around it; for "his word runs swiftly," as the psalmist says.[10] Certainly Scripture's truest defense is God's active judgment on those who do not *listen* to the word that is preached, on those whose listening is caught up in wrangling about words, and on those who substitute their own wisdom for that of the Spirit. "Woe to you experts in the law," said Jesus, "because you have taken away the key to knowledge."[11]

Finally, then, there is a question some have been posing to the evangelical community that will not go away: Are we free, as Packer phrases it, "to submit to biblical, historical, and theological analysis the 'inerrancy tradition' of the past one hundred years to see if it is really scriptural enough"? This freedom is of great importance, having both immediate and long-term ramifications. Some years ago Packer offered the following warning, based on his discussion of the exegetical circle in which the doctrine of Scripture is implicated:

> If, therefore, we allowed ourselves to treat a pre-packaged, deep-frozen formula labelled 'the evangelical doctrine of Scripture' as a kind of untouchable sacred cow, we should not only be showing ourselves more concerned about our own tradition than about

---

point when he tries to say that commitment to the infallibility of the Bible—rather than being corrected in functional, Christocentric terms—must go the way of commitment to the infallibility of the Pope. To say this is certainly to miss the significance of the Scripture principle of the Reformation and the Protestant understanding of canon. (Bloesch's brief critique of Küng's proposal that "indefectibility" replace "infallibility" in *Essentials of Evangelical Theology* 1. 68, 84, is apropos. "The problem with Küng," he suggests, "is that he creates the impression that the infallible truth of the Gospel can be conveyed through erroneous propositions." Truth, says Bloesch, may not inhere in the biblical proposition in and of itself, but does inhere in the proposition "in its relationship to Jesus Christ.")

[10] Ps 147:15.

[11] Luke 11:52. The Scriptures contain many such solemn warnings to all who dare to abuse the word of God; Jeremiah 23 is particularly powerful on a number of fronts, while Jer 8:8–9 concisely queries and condemns self-confident but deviant biblical scholarship. "To say it pointedly," writes Karl Barth (*God Here and Now*; trans. Paul M. van Buren [London: Routledge and Kegan Paul, 1964] 58), "when the Church lacks the authority of the biblical witness, it and its proclamation to the world can only dissolve into pious smoke and all sorts of religious and moralistic odors."

God's truth (and you do not need me to remind you how dangerous that would be); we should also be jeopardising our own prospects in the realm of biblical exposition.[12]

How can we protect our liberty for progress in these matters, which are so relevant to the health and vitality of the Church and its witness? By refocusing our doctrine of Scripture, our apologetics, and our hermeneutics on the dynamic spiritual reality of *God communicating* to us in Christ.[13] This focus will enable us to hold together the truths of Scripture and the living Truth of God, sacred texts and their canonical service, infallibility and hermeneutical effort—thus avoiding the damaging dichotomies in so much modern thinking about Scripture. Clinging firmly in all this to but one goal, namely, attention to the Lord himself, will keep us from wandering off on a spur track, where so much of the inerrancy debate ends up. Scripture itself demands precisely this, in order that the true end of its authority might be realized in us.

[12] "Hermeneutics and Biblical Authority," 9; the previous quotation is from "Encountering Present-Day Views of Scripture," in *The Foundation of Biblical Authority*, ed. James Montgomery Boice (Grand Rapids: Zondervan, 1978) 66.

[13] This indeed is Packer's own proposal with respect to hermeneutics at least, as I noted earlier. In the present work I have tried to carry the whole matter somewhat further.

Index of Authors

Index of Scripture References